Michel Foucault

Michel Foucault

Subversions of the subject

Philip Barker

HARVESTER
WHEATSHEAF

New York   London   Toronto   Sydney   Tokyo   Singapore

First published 1993 by
Harvester Wheatsheaf
Campus 400, Maylands Avenue
Hemel Hempstead
Hertfordshire, HP2 7EZ
A division of
Simon & Schuster International Group

Typeset in 10/12 pt Galliard
by Keyboard Services, Luton

Printed and bound in Great Britain by
BPCC Wheatons Ltd, Exeter

British Library Cataloguing in Publication Data

A catalogue record for this book is available from
the British Library

ISBN 0 7450 1397 X (hbk)
ISBN 0 7450 1398 8 (pbk)

1 2 3 4 5   97 96 95 94 93

To my mother and father

E. D. Barker (1918–1980)

F. C. Barker (1912–1983)

Contents

Acknowledgements

This work benefited from the input and encouragement of many people including: Jan Barker, Professor Paul Crittenden, Dr Stephen Gaukroger, Associate Professor Elizabeth Grosz, Professor Stephen Knight, Jim 'go for it' Morgan, Dr David Simpson, Christine Standish and the Foucault Reading Group. Special gratitude is due to Dr Jocelyn Dunphy and Dr John O. Ward who read a draft and offered helpful comments. My thanks go to my publisher Harvester for their foresight and in particular to Jackie Jones.

A full list of copyright permissions is given on p. 232.

Introduction

It is a commonplace that students in first year courses at university are given a sketch of the history of philosophy along the following lines. Philosophy began with the Greeks, first the Pre-Socratics and then Socrates, Plato and Aristotle, who collectively laid the foundations of future philosophy and established the fundamental divisions of the discipline: ethics, metaphysics, epistemology and logic. Then came the early Christian philosophers and patristic writers, the most notable being Augustine, followed by the Medieval period (which usually means scholasticism) and Aquinas, and finally the philosophical and epistemological revolution of Descartes in the seventeenth century, which laid the foundations for the scientific revolution and the birth of philosophy as 'science'. A second view, related to this but offering a different emphasis, suggests that late medieval Europe is marked by an increasing secularisation, eventually manifested in the Protestant revolution and the basis of knowledge in 'self'. This tendency finds its first expression in philosophy in the work of Descartes. In both these cases the role of Descartes as an innovator, or as a victor over the narrow-mindedness of medieval scholasticism is rarely challenged by holders of different theoretical persuasions, and becomes the pre-condition for the category of modernity and the 'modern age'.[1]

There are a number of historical and metaphysical issues involved. Is the prominence given to Descartes appropriate or well placed? What is highlighted and what is erased by the view that the *Cogito* is the basis or foundation of contemporary notions and experiences of the subject? How can these issues be analysed and discussed in an appropriate and effective way? One method that could be used to analyse these questions is the history of ideas, which, in its contemporary form, still commands respect and support from some of today's leading intellectuals. Foucault was not

1

one of those supporters. Indeed in a number of places in his work he is critical of the history of ideas and, not surprisingly, contemporary historians of ideas responded vigorously to this criticism: 'In the case of Foucault – the Foucault at least of *Les Mots et les choses* and *L'Archéologie du savoir* – his contempt for the traditional history of ideas cannot even in charity be said to be ill concealed.'[2] There is an element of truth in this; but is it just contempt for the history of ideas that Foucault manifests in his criticism, or is there more to it all than that? This inquiry is an assessment of Foucault's response to the history of ideas.

Clearly the division between the history of philosophy and historical studies can be a distinct one, but does not have to be so. Philosophers have often crossed the divide although not always successfully. Hegel's *Phenomenology of Spirit*, Hobbes' *Leviathan* and Rousseau's *Social Contract* all to some extent do the work of historians and it goes without saying that historians in the production of their work often do the work of philosophers. This is evident in Foucault's own work as he developed, explained and categorised his attitude to philosophy with his historical excursions, and his attitude to history with his philosophical excursions. After all, it was a significant insight of Foucault's that the construction of the divide between disciplines and even within disciplines has a historical and philosophical rationale that can be analysed.

My discussion of Foucault's interaction with the history of ideas will commence with a redefinition of the history of ideas beyond its more usual limits by the inclusion of the work of today's 'intellectual historians' and 'historians of philosophy'.[3] I then trace this contemporary work back to Lovejoy and Collingwood and add a more controversial contributor to this programme, Freud. Throughout the discussion and presentation of the history of ideas which follows in Chapter 1, I argue that in spite of apparently different foundations for their work today's intellectual historians and historians of philosophy share a number of significant features and assumptions with Lovejoy, Collingwood and Freud.

In Chapter 2 I will provide an account of Foucault's work and his specific criticisms of the history of ideas and the possible methodological alternatives for undertaking historical and philosophical work. Briefly, Foucault argues that the work of the historian is always ontological – what is at stake is always the *subject* as both subject and object of historical investigations.[4] The investigation of the subject (*subject*) and consciousness, a central part of ontology, is necessarily historical; the writing of history no less involves the investigation of the subject (*subject*) of consciousness, and is therefore an exercise in ontology. This is not a controversial point of view within philosophy as, in proposing it, Foucault is following Kant, Hegel and many others. We can surely agree that even if one reads the most naïve historical psychological pot-boiler, where historical personages act in a world entirely transparent to their wishes and desires, a subject is being posed and an ontology is being outlined. It is in this sense that history and historical studies produce something (*subjects*), and Foucault is anxious to analyse the conditions of this production, what is produced, what may be said about it, and what possibilities it draws out.

In this context, perhaps, Foucault does at times show not so much his contempt for the history of ideas but his frustration with what he sees as the erasing by the history of ideas of its role in the production and naturalising of a narrowly defined subject, the self-reflexive transparent *Cogito*. This leads me to take a positive view of Foucault's work and suggest that the critical tool of genealogy and his analysis of the power/knowledge network offers us a way of undertaking the work both of the historian and the philosopher simultaneously in a productive way. But where can this productivity be located? I argue that it can be found at the heart of the problem that Foucault is attempting to bring into focus. In general, most histories assume that the structure of the subject (*subject*) in historical actors is constant. A change may be allowed in its content but its structural integrity is maintained. Foucault quite explicitly repudiates this view. However, he wishes also to avoid a Hegelian alternative which suggests that, while the structure of consciousness changes throughout history, it changes according to a pattern that can be analysed, predicted and reduced to the consciousness of the individual subject (*subject*). So histories of the kind that Foucault undertook attempt to circumvent both constant structures and teleological ends for history. It is in this context that he returns to Nietzsche and examines the connection between the production and circulation of knowledge and the construction of the historical subject (*subject*). This allows him to re-introduce the body into history as the object of his research.

Chapter 3 documents some of the social and structural changes that occurred in north western Europe from the tenth to the twelfth centuries. Much of this work will not be new, particularly to the medievalist, but I hope to be able to use this information in a novel way. When Foucault suggests that the body is an important element in historical work he is not viewing the body simply as a consciousness enclosing vessel that makes acts possible, but as a diffuse materiality that eats, and engages in physical exercise and sexual practices of one kind or another. These material practices embodied in technologies of self, lead to the constitution of a subject (*subject*) in a process of reflexive subjection. Foucault examines these issues in the context of modern, Greek and early Christian culture and my inquiry uses the period from the tenth to the twelfth century as its archive.

In Chapter 4 I apply the information previously drawn out to explain the emergence of the modality of autobiography and its relationship with a particular philosophical perspective and its supporting subject (*subject*).

There are already two well-researched and documented approaches to the twelfth century: as the birth of humanism or as the foundation of a proto-capitalist economic structure.[5] But I will show that by applying Foucault's methodology to this epoch insights emerge that are not possible from other historical methodologies.

I will make use in Chapter 5 of the work already completed and draw this inquiry together with some general comments about intellectual history, the history of philosophy and the history of ideas.

But even at the inauguration of this work one is haunted by a fundamental question. Is it possible to cross the boundaries of history, philosophy, anthropology, economics and literature and still produce compelling work?[6] For above all else this is the task which Foucault bequeaths to his heirs:

> And now I understand better why I found it so difficult to begin just now. I know whose voice it was that I would have liked to precede me, to carry me, to invite me to speak, to lodge itself in my own discourse.[7]

·1·
Contemporary issues in the history of ideas

Intellectual history and the history of philosophy

Nowadays the history of ideas is an unfashionable term. People who might have been working in this field twenty or thirty years ago now usually prefer to be called intellectual historians or historians of philosophy. In the book *Philosophy in History* the construction of these two different though related modes of thought is developed and the impression is given that the theoretical field is divided up; people then seem to come down on one side or the other and in either case, the history of ideas disappears.[1] The index to the work includes the finest intellectual historians and historians of philosophy of the day, and yet the name of Lovejoy disappears while Collingwood makes only a fleeting appearance. What is it about the history of ideas that makes it unfashionable? Why do people not want to be associated with the history of ideas any more? That same index includes the names of Rorty, Hegel, Skinner, Kant, Moore, even Alfred Hitchcock makes an appearance as well as Bachelard and Foucault, while Lovejoy and Collingwood have all but vanished. Does this matter? There are reasons for thinking that it does.

First, the history of ideas in its day saw the production of some very fine work. Fine work is still occasionally produced under this name, unfashionable as it is: for example, *Omnipotence, Covenant and Order: An excursion into the history of ideas from Abelard to Leibniz* by Francis Oakley.[2] Nevertheless it is apparent that the history of ideas now appears to be under pressure and we should want to know why a once flourishing concern in its heyday is in danger of imminent demise. Secondly, and perhaps of more interest, there seems to be something about the name 'the history of ideas' that leads many people to wish not to be associated with it. In fact a good

5

deal of material currently being published today arguably belongs to the category of the history of ideas, but is not described in this way by its authors. Works of this kind would be Rorty's *Philosophy and the Mirror of Nature*,[3] Hayden White's *Metahistory*,[4] and Edward Said's *Orientalism*.[5] Then there is the influential journal *History and Theory: Studies in the philosophy of history*. Am I just being pedantic here? What would it matter if Rorty, Hayden White, Said and the whole editorial team of *History and Theory* did not want to call themselves historians of ideas?

But I want to suggest that the situation is more complex than this. I would argue that this refusal in part relates to the erasure of the place of Lovejoy and Collingwood in the history of intellectual history and/or the history of philosophy and has another rationale which cuts deeply into the programme itself. This is particularly apparent in the book *Philosophy in History* where there is an unresolved but constructive opposition between what might be broadly termed 'idealist/anti-realist' and 'realist' approaches to philosophy. It is unresolved because the assumptions of realism and idealism/anti-realism are not addressed. It is constructive in that it permits the work of practitioners of both approaches to attempt theoretical interchange without surrendering or having to defend their own theoretical integrity.

Philosophy in History begins (much as *Philosophy and the Mirror of Nature* ends) with a description of the ideal of intellectual history as conversations with dead philosophers. The ideal intellectual history would be one in which a resurrected philosopher of the past would find:

1. The description of their work intelligible and understand how certain questions of their day became transformed at a later date.
2. That the treatment of their work was sympathetically and accurately handled.
3. That philosophical debates are allowed to overlap and provide a sense of 'a collaborative inquiry on a subject of common interest'.

'We hope that intellectual history will weave a thick enough rope of overlapping desires so that we can read our way back through the centuries without ever having to ask "How could rational men and women have thought or done that?"'[6]

This work is then contrasted with the enquiry undertaken by historians of philosophy who are concerned with a different set of issues and arrive at them from different methodological practices. Historians of philosophy come to the historical project armed with definite problems and questions to be analysed that are determined by a special interest in philosophy. For example: 'He [the historian of philosophy] needs to see Spinoza's writings as organised around certain distinctively philosophical problems, and he needs to separate discussion of these problems from "the transient concerns of Spinoza's day".[7]

On the one hand, we have intellectual historians who report conversations real and imagined between the dead and the dead, the dead and the living and even one hopes, now and again, the living and the living. The emphasis here is that intellectual history is to be found by analysing ideas and so on that are ultimately derivable from the individual consciousness of a discrete subject. I would take this to be an anti-realist/idealist position and these intellectual historians to be descendants of Collingwood. On the other hand, we have historians of philosophy who trace the problems of philosophy in the past and attempt to answer the great philosophical questions and in so doing obtain the truth of the past in them and of them. These problems are ultimately accorded a universal status and are therefore essentially unchanging. The objective of the programme is to find the (T)rue answers to them. I would take this to be a realist position and these historians of philosophy are descendants of Lovejoy.

In *Philosophy in History* examples of the perspective of both intellectual historians and historians of philosophy are to be found and the effect of the undefined opposition between realism and idealism (historians of philosophy and intellectual historians respectively) facilitates and structures a debate on the nature of, as the subtitle to the work tells us, the 'historiography of philosophy'. This opposition is both necessary and essential to the production of the work:

> An opposition between intellectual historians and historians of philosophy seems to us as factitious as would an opposition between scientists and engineers, or librarians and scholars, or rough-hewers and shapers. It is an appearance created by the attempt to be sententious about 'the nature of history' or the 'nature of philosophy' or both, treating 'history' and 'philosophy' as names of natural kinds – disciplines whose subject and purpose are familiar and uncontroversial. Such attempts produce red-faced snortings about how a given book 'isn't what I call history' or doesn't count as 'philosophy'. They take for granted that there is a well-known part of the world – the past – which is the domain of history, and another well-known part, usually thought of as a set of 'timeless problems', which are the domain of philosophy.[8]

I would not disagree that the division between what is legitimate philosophy and what is not is to a degree an arbitrary one. But intellectual historians, according to the sentiments expressed in the Introduction of *Philosophy in History*, treat this division as benign rather than the malignant one that it often is when confronted in everyday practice in the Academy. In fact in *Philosophy in History* there is no substantial debate about the nature of the 'historiography of philosophy' in terms of realism and idealism/anti-realism. In this way the work escapes any analysis of the preconditions of its own existence even though it is the opposition between intellectual history and history of philosophy that allows a series of familiar metaphors to come into play – realism/idealism, he/she, hard/soft, science/art, truth/fiction and so on – which structure the work.

Philosophy in History, in functioning through the realist–anti-realist/idealist division is already following a pattern to be found in the work of two early contributors to the history of ideas programme, Lovejoy and Collingwood. It is by returning to their work that we find a clear expression of the role, consequences and implications of the realism and idealism division that remains for today's intellectual historians, historians of philosophy and historians of ideas.

The Great Chain of Being

Lovejoy suggests that the aim of his enterprise is to locate and in some sense interpret what he terms 'unit ideas', that is, ideas which have a structure analogous to that of the 'elements' in the theory of analytic chemistry. They are contrasted to 'compound ideas', a contrast that is derived from a parallel distinction in chemistry, and which suggests that 'unit ideas' are to be found behind compound ideas in ways which are not easily recognisable. As Lovejoy says: 'just as chemical compounds differ in their sensible qualities from the elements composing them, so the elements of philosophical doctrines, in differing logical combinations, are not always readily recognisable'.[9] The methodology of the history of ideas becomes the unfolding or revealing of unit ideas from behind compound ideas, and just as there are only a certain number of chemical elements, so there are only a certain number of unit ideas to be revealed.

Lovejoy offers us a number of ways to distinguish them from compound ideas. Unit ideas are variously referred to as elements, primary or primary persistent recurrent dynamic units,[10] and include: unconscious mental habits and assumptions, a disposition to think in terms of certain categories or imagery, endemic assumptions, nominalistic motives, the flower in the crannied wall motive, and metaphysical pathos, philosophical semantics,[11] and so on and a 'single specific proposition or "principle"', the latter being what Lovejoy claims he is attempting to analyse in *The Great Chain of Being*.

His strongly drawn analogy between unit ideas and chemical elements at the very beginning of the methodological chapter signals from the outset that in some general sense he is committed to methodological positivism and epistemological realism. The aim of the history of ideas is to break up compound ideas, which are by their very nature unstable, and refine them into their constitutive elements. This view has two implications. First, that unit ideas are fundamentally unchanging, that philosophers from Plato to Lovejoy are considering issues that are constituted by the same unit ideas. Secondly, that the way to arrive at these unchanging unit ideas is to break up their compound form into smaller and smaller units, until finally a unit is reached that can be divided no more, and this is then accorded the status of a unit idea or element.

Two points need to be immediately noted. First, that there is a debate within the philosophy of science about the appropriateness of the realist/positivist conjunction, and without detailing this here, it is important to keep in mind the fact that at the immediate level of the analogy that Lovejoy wants to make, a number of controversial methodological issues are involved.[12] Second and more significantly, in making this analogy Lovejoy does not argue for its appropriateness, but merely asserts it, so that even if we ignore the debate about positivism/realism within the philosophy of science, we are given no reason why a model that 'works' for science will also work for the history of ideas. This is particularly important because positivism, as it appears in its scientific form, namely empiricism, depends upon the ability to test its theorising against observable experimentation, a procedure which is not available to the historian of ideas.

It is true that Lovejoy is not attempting to write an epistemological manual in the style of Locke's *Essay Concerning Human Understanding*, but is trying to provide an account, both in theory and in the form of a case study, of the possibility of the history of ideas. Nevertheless this in itself implies a theory of history, a theory of the subject, a theory of meaning and an epistemology. This is particularly relevant when his theory of history, of the subject and meaning, all appear to be closely tied to the general methodological and epistemological considerations already outlined. Lovejoy argues that the world exists in a state of discontinuity and flux, and that the object of the history of ideas is to constitute a sense of stability, continuity and unity, but then a new problem emerges. The history of this discontinuous world would itself also exist in a state of discontinuity, unless the basic methodology of the history of ideas itself provides/produces unity, or continuity at the level of the study. This is to be the central feature of Lovejoy's approach which is evident throughout the text:

> In the whole series of creeds and movements going under the one name, and in each of them separately, it is needful to go behind the superficial appearance of the singleness and identity, to crack the shell which holds the mass together, if we are to see the real units, the effective working ideas, which in any given case are present.[13]

To the common logical or pseudo-logical or affective ingredients behind the surface-dissimilarities the historian of individual ideas will seek to penetrate.[14]

Lovejoy's argument is one that involves a double movement: first, the breaking down of what is seen as a coherent unity into a number of smaller units, and secondly, analysing these units into those elements that can then be designated 'unit ideas'. This also becomes the foundation of an interdisciplinary approach which again invokes the realist idea that there are only a finite number of ideas in the world and, whether they are to be found in the discipline of philosophy, anthropology or physics, they are fundamentally the same unit ideas:

It is inspired by the belief that there is a great deal more in common to more than one of these provinces than is usually recognised, that the same idea often appears, sometimes considerably disguised, in the most diverse regions of the intellectual world.[15]

It is concerned only with a certain group of factors in history, and with these only in so far as they can be seen at work in what are commonly considered separate divisions of the intellectual world; and it is especially interested in the processes by which influences pass over from one province to another. Even the partial realisation of such a program would do much, I cannot but think, to give a needed unifying background to many now unconnected and consequently, poorly understood facts.[16]

The effect of the intersection of these two approaches, namely, analysing into unit ideas, and covering the entire realm of theorisation, becomes a textual mirroring of Lovejoy's realism, as what emerges from applying his approach to the history of ideas is the pursuit of the unit idea from discontinuous texts, the pursuit itself unmasking differences and constituting continuities, and unities. Here we can see the beginnings of the theoretical loop that Lovejoy is adopting. Starting with a view of the fundamentally unchanging nature of unit ideas, and then utilising a methodological practice that constitutes continuity and unity as its central theoretical strategy, its original realist assumption is confirmed. So the demand for unity and coherence is predetermined by the epistemology itself and at the same time is the outcome of the methodological practice. Given the emphasis on perceptual experience and the belief that we live in a world of flux, decay, and change, the problem of epistemological foundations becomes crucial.

Lovejoy's response is to present the empirical world as objective, theoretically laden free, and capable of objective interpretation, and as a consequence of this assumes that there are fundamental universal problems that have always concerneed and still concern human existence and that are in the process of being solved, interpreted and finalised. The problem is not so much at the level of the assertion itself, which is arguable one way or the other, but that Lovejoy apparently fails to recognise that he is claiming a universal, objective, neutral status for his methodological approach and the subject that underpins it.

Lovejoy's theoretical loop and the interlocking of positivism and realism provides for him – indeed creates for him – a situation whereby interpretation precedes meaning, which then allows a supposedly objective interpretation to be made. This ultimately becomes a moment when unit ideas and irreducible universal meanings are the same. In this way a 'real other world', apparently theory free, enters this one and becomes both the guarantor and arbitrator of all meaning. This allows the truth of the real to become the truth of all things, history, meaning, life and so on.

If it is possible to see some difficulties at the deep epistemological level, some problems emerge closer to the surface of the methodology. One can see that in the realm of scientific research, positivism, where still adopted, can provide large quantities of data, as there are plenty of things to measure, weigh, describe and so on. However, Lovejoy is not dealing with objects like the chemical analyst. He is concerned with ideas, and the places they are to be found are in texts not in test tubes; so the status of his 'fact' is going to be different to those of the scientists.[17] This is a substantial difference because of the necessity to elaborate either implicitly or explicitly both a theory of interpretation and the subject (*subject*), and by implication a theory of language. In all these key areas Lovejoy finds himself in some difficulty as he traces ideas through texts into 'the workings of human thought'.[18] In spite of the fact that he describes one of his unit ideas as 'more or less unconscious mental habits',[19] he repeatedly wants, indeed needs to go beyond this to the pursuit of intentions by individual subjects.

If we follow Lovejoy's line of thinking we see him looking behind an -ism and tracing unities through to unit ideas. He then traces these unit ideas via texts to the individual subject (*subject*) as he ties the meaning of statements to the articulation of the unit idea. The effect of this is that ultimately he is required to explain the intention behind statements: 'The more significant factor in the matter may be, not the dogma which certain persons proclaim – be that single or manifold in its meaning – but the motives or reasons which have led them to it.'[20]

This involves a presupposition that the subject is transparent and interpretable and moreover that 'unconscious mental habits' are not over-determining. It is not so much that there is a sense of contradiction here but that when the implications of this view are followed through a number of problems become apparent. These arrive at an early stage when Lovejoy begins to discuss the work of Plato and proclaims:

I wish, so far as possible, in these lectures to avoid entering upon controverted questions of exegesis, or of the intellectual biography of individual writers....[21]

and also:

That Plato should, solely out of piety to his early teacher, have devoted a great part of his mature life as a writer to expounding, with apparent fervor and incomparable eloquence (which was certainly not that of Socrates himself), a doctrine which he did not desire to inculcate nor believe to be true, seems to me to be psychologically very improbable.[22]

Almost in the same breath we have a disavowal of biographical details, and the extensive adopting of them. Lovejoy's methodological approach places him in a position where he cannot avoid entering upon questions of psychological exegesis or intellectual biography, indeed they are central to his whole project and force him at times to defend a position of a naïve psychologistic interpretation of textual material:

Nevertheless so far as these limitations permit, we shall try to trace these ideas to their historic sources in the minds of certain philosophers; to observe their fusion....[23]

Now Aristotle was not a philosophically unintelligent person; he was for twenty years a pupil and associate of Plato's in the Academy; and when he wrote many other men were still living who could judge, from their own knowledge, of the general correctness of his interpretation.[24]

So it would seem that while it is not always visible at those moments when Lovejoy is at his most stimulating, underneath his work lies a less than sophisticated interpretative and reductive psychologism that re-emerges at the level of guaranteeing the interpretation he is offering as the correct one. As well as this two other things are implied that still need to be considered, a theory of the subject (*subject*) and a theory of language. Notwithstanding his comments about the unconscious thoughts of an age, Lovejoy is committed to a view of the subject as a *Cogito* unified, self-reflexive, structurally continuous and transparent.[25] This ensures for him that subjective intentionality becomes a permissible and defensible category, so that not only can he interpret intentions but the ideas that he, Plato and Aristotle are writing about are taken as essentially the same. So when Plato talks of 'otherworldliness' this can be translated and interpreted by Lovejoy through an essential resemblance, at the levels of meaning and interpretation, and, one also suspects, of structure. However, this also has rather unfortunate effects since it leads Lovejoy into drawing extensive and often indefensible parallels of the most generalised kind. So for example, he suggests Schiller was inadvertently commenting on a thought in the *Timaeus*, and that Dr Johnson was merely reiterating sentiments that were as old as those of Zeno of Elea.[26]

Although Lovejoy must be sure that for both him and Plato the language that constitutes their ideas is both epistemologically interchangeable and is describing an objective state of affairs, he seems not to take account of the effect that this has on his own work, whereby his criticism of other philosophers always amounts to noting that they are all talking about the same thing but that they have just got *it* wrong. This is not simply a question of a rather simplistic dogmatism on Lovejoy's part but connects with his realism, the *it* being a hypothesised 'real' world of existence comprised of universal ideas, which presents and has always presented certain problems for philosophy (which for Lovejoy is but a series of footnotes to Plato)[27] that attempts to and in some way is slowly 'getting things/it right' – this not being immediately possible as there is more to experience than meets the eye:

> Since man, for better or worse, is by nature, a reflective and interpretative animal, always seeking *rerum cognoscere causas*, to find in the bare data of experience more than meets the eye, the record of the reactions of his intellect upon the brute facts of his sensible existence constitutes, at the least, an essential part of the natural history of the species, or sub-species, which has somewhat too flatteringly named itself homo-sapiens; and I have never been able to see why what is distinctive in the natural history of that species should appear – especially to a member of it – a less respectable subject of study than the natural history of the *paramecium* or the white rat. No doubt man's quest of intelligibility in nature and in himself, and of the kinds of emotional satisfaction, which are conditioned by a sense of intelligibility, often, like the caged rat's quest of food, has found no end, in wandering mazes lost.[28]

Here Lovejoy argues that although there is more to experience than meets the eye this still can be revealed by the appropriate methodology as long as one adds the criterion of 'intelligibility'. Intelligibility is a process whereby a meaningless or unrelated experience is reinterpreted into a meaningful and intelligible framework. There are other aspects of this particular quotation that point to Lovejoy's commitment to positivism but perhaps more important than that, is that it appears at the end of the methodological chapter and is followed by:

> For though we have more empirical information at our disposal, we have not different or better minds; and it is, after all, the action of the mind upon facts that makes both philosophy and science – and, indeed, largely makes the 'facts'.[29]

The point that needs to be stressed here is that at various times in his methodological chapter Lovejoy indicates a commitment to positivism, and if one carefully examines his list of unit ideas what emerges is that they are all central aspects of that particular epistemology, either as tenets of the theory or as criticisms of it from within that overall tradition or perspective. Lovejoy's programme is one which conducts the search for knowledge in a terminology that is consistent with the approach of positivism. So he supports the idea that knowledge is obtained by immediately grasping it from a detailed and close analysis through which knowledge is divided up into smaller and smaller bits that are more immediate and therefore more likely to be 'true'. Secondary or larger pieces of knowledge are not considered as significant. Furthermore there is an emphasis here on simplicity with all its Cartesian implications.

These principles function in the following ways, first by giving the history of ideas a long diachronic sameness, from Plato to Lovejoy and second by ensuring that at any given time everybody is referring to the *same* thing. It is here that the criterion of intelligibility becomes even more important as the process of making intelligible reduces all other possible interpretations to the same one as Lovejoy's. The question then is not so much 'Is Lovejoy's interpretation the correct one?', but rather 'Why is it necessary that there should be a correct one?' To answer this we must look again at Lovejoy's two central categories, continuity and plenitude. What emerges is that these categories, apparently abstracted from the 'great chain of being', are actually part of Lovejoy's initial methodological assumptions. The world must be 'full' and 'continuous' in order that it be open to the kind of interpretation required by the methodology. Having followed Lovejoy into adopting these categories we find ourselves committed to an epistemological framework which precludes at the outset that certain questions be asked. Why is it necessary to conceive of the world in the terms of continuity and stability? Why must the subject be represented as transparent? Why must things be intelligible? Why must chance be rejected as a mechanism of history? What role does the return of the same and recurrence play? How is meaning produced?

Lovejoy would probably answer along the following lines. The world must be conceived of as continuous and stable or it could not be discussed at all, as it would not be the same *thing* from moment to moment. The subject must be like a *Cogito* and transparent so that it is possible to know what ideas are in people's heads, allowing them to be spoken of with some confidence. Meaning is produced by getting things right or true, in so far as they correspond to or resemble objective reality. Rationality must have a *telos* because we know that the Greeks and ourselves are basically talking about the same world and yet we have a more complete view of it than they did. This means we have progressed towards a more complete or truthful understanding of the world through a cumulative, teleological and progressive rationality. Chance must be rejected because it would undermine the rational unfolding of both the world and history and would make interpretation impossible. The universality of the concept guarantees diachronic history, the possibility of meaning, and intelligibility. It is here that the third aspect of Lovejoy's realism comes into play as an epistemological realism suddenly becomes an historical one. It is this that allows the generalisations from Plato to Schelling to be made, which is reinforced by Lovejoy's tendency to write within a realist historicist framework in spite of claiming and indeed presenting his work initially as if he were offering just one interpretation among many possible ones.

Furthermore his realism demands the categories of continuity and plenitude be utilised, as without their validation realism itself collapses. A further effect of this is the need to sustain a view of the subject that is fundamentally transparent and unified, and which in turn both demands and frequently utilises an interpretative intentionality thesis. Of course both realism and the thesis of the transparent subject can be defended; that is not what is at issue here, but rather their exclusiveness, and the fact that in this context they exclude all other possibilities and represent this moment of erasure as politically, historically and epistemologically neutral.

On the one hand we have the intuitive appeal of the chosen model of the 'great chain of being', while on the other hand, we must consider the methodological and epistemological implications of the chosen method. This can lead us to the greatest danger, that of adopting Lovejoy's method uncritically, where what is presented as a disguised positivist/realist epistemology can become a positivist/realist history of philosophy. References to Whitehead both open and close the case study, and Lovejoy leaves us in no doubt as to why idealism, evolutionism, and teleological rationality are all rejected by him in the last chapter, as *The Great Chain of Being* emerges in the last analysis as the history of those philosophies that were attempting to grapple with the consequences of not adopting realism as the basis of both their methodology and epistemology.

The Idea of History

On the other side of this debate in contemporary terms are the intellectual historians whom I have characterised as idealist/anti-realist. Their position has many similarities with that of Collingwood, another early contributor to the history of ideas programme whose work I shall now examine. My central argument is that Collingwood is working within the same methodological and epistemological framework as Lovejoy, although he stands within this tradition as a critic of many of its presuppositions and assumptions.[30] But some careful distinctions need to be made since Collingwood uses a number of concepts in a way specific to the time in which he was writing. This applies particularly to the key terms in this account, 'realism' and 'idealism'.

By realism Collingwood means two things. First the more general view that there are ongoing issues in philosophy that one must simply attempt to 'get correct'. 'Getting things correct' means looking at all the answers given to the enduring questions of philosophy in the correct temporal sequence in which they are given:

> the 'history' of philosophy is the study by which people ascertain what answers have been given to these questions, in what order and at what dates. In that sense, the question, 'what was Aristotle's theory of duty?' would be an 'historical' question. And it would be wholly separate from the philosophical question, 'was it true?'[31]

This interpretation is close to the view of realism that I have been attributing to Lovejoy. Collingwood also uses the term 'realism' in a second, much more specific way to describe a version of realism being taught at Oxford by Cook Wilson and others at the time that he was there. This largely involved the presentation of logic as the only reality for philosophy to engage with, and became, according to Collingwood, a degenerating and destructive form of philosophy in the hands of all but a few.[32] Interestingly enough, one of these few exceptions, Whitehead, provides a direct link between even this specific type of realism and Lovejoy, for Lovejoy begins *The Great Chain of Being* with a quotation from Whitehead and concludes it with a reference to him. In general, unless stated otherwise, I will only be using the word 'realism' in the first, more general, sense, although it can be said that ultimately Collingwood's two kinds of realism merge and become difficult to disengage from each other.

In an attempt to specify his own position in the realist/idealist debate in the context of Oxford between the wars, Collingwood makes it clear that he does not consider himself to be an idealist, and in that specific context he is probably quite right. However, in general a rather loose definition of idealism can legitimately be applied to aspects of his work, and this will allow a clear distinction to be made between the approaches of Lovejoy and Collingwood to the history of ideas on the basis of realism/idealism, and will draw my comments back to my opening account of the current debate within 'intellectual history'.

Collingwood makes a detailed and extensive attack on realism in both his autobiography and in *The Idea of History* . He argues that ultimately the realists propose a view that is based on universals. This means that if you take two texts on political theory, the connection between them is that their sameness is a universal and their difference is the difference between two instances of a universal. This sameness is also to be found in the fact that both texts are claimed to be discussing the *same* problem, and from this it follows that conceptions expressed in different languages at different epochs are immediately translatable from one to the other. Therefore the Greek word for State expresses the same universal as the Hobbesian word State.[33] Furthermore there is an implication that the truth of things is being approached, and that the history of philosophy reflects conceptual progress, as the real nature of the universe is being slowly and more completely understood. This presentation of realism does incorporate a number of those views that were previously suggested to be central to Lovejoy's work.[34]

Collingwood argues against this view on a number of theoretical and practical grounds, suggesting that realism engenders dogmatism for a number of reasons. As there are only a certain number of issues to be addressed, any philosophical discussion is either reduced to these defined issues or is not considered philosophical. There was a tendency for the realists at Collingwood's Oxford to simply gloss on the 'great' philosophical problems through the texts under study. According to Collingwood this glossing prompted a move away from reading the primary sources themselves, in favour of a total dependence on the glosses of secondary sources. This led to a reinforcing of the already manifest tendency of realism towards dogmatism. Collingwood further suggests that the implications of realism were a self-depreciating ethics. While the realists were well aware that different people at different times acted and behaved in different ways, this difference was measured from the perspective of how one 'ought to behave', whereby the 'ought' in fact referred to a meaning that was 'unchanging and eternal'. Collingwood rejects this out of hand, arguing that 'convictions about the eternity of problems and conceptions' are baseless and at the very best fail to acknowledge the history of the struggle of philosophical doctrines from obscurity to popular belief. Collingwood incorporates this argument into his more general criticism of the realist conception of history, and finally argues against realism on what he considers to be strong logical grounds. He maintains that realism is dependent on a distinction between two questions. First, the historical question: what was X's theory of such and such? Secondly, the philosophical question: were they right? The possibility of making this distinction presupposes the permanence of the philosophical problems one is referring to, and this Collingwood maintains is impossible. He suggests that to claim that a number of philosophers are really talking about the same problem P, is to mask that P is really a number of transitory problems, P 1, P 2, P 3, whose distinctions are covered over by the realists' lack of historical understanding.[35] Furthermore, if we allow that Leibniz is dealing with problem P 14, then we have to make the judgement whether he was right or wrong and this becomes impossible to determine meaningfully. If Leibniz was confused enough not to solve his problem, it is not clear that the reader will be in a position to be able to say what the problem was in the first place:

> For one and the same passage states his solution and serves as evidence of what the problem was. The fact that we can identify his problem is proof that he has solved it; for we only know what the problem was by arguing back from the solution.[36]

Collingwood's overall approach to the history of ideas was constituted out of his response to realism and his arguments need some evaluation. The charge of dogmatism that Collingwood addresses to realism does have some force. It is true that dogmatism can emerge from any theoretical programme, be it Marxism, Rationalism or anything else. However, it is apparent as I showed earlier, that when one is supporting a position with a fundamental dependence on universals (which Collingwood correctly attributes to the realism of his day), there is a strong tendency that the view will become dogmatic. Also, while Collingwood's comments about the realist movement away from primary texts cannot be solely applied to realism there is something in Collingwood's complaint. Without a doubt there is a propensity for the realist practice of glossing on primary sources to overtake those same sources and consume them from within the overall framework. Textual specificities and differences become simply 'apparent' discrepancies concerning the elaboration of the same fundamental problems. The ethical implication of realism's self-depreciating ethics might be well placed and would tie in with the general realist attitude to history; however, this would only apply to a fairly specific interpretation of realism. It is much more difficult to maintain such a charge against Lovejoy, who manages to incorporate a dynamic of change within his overall framework and does take into account the specific relation of an epoch to a universal theoretical paradigm. Finally, Collingwood has identified one of the major difficulties of realism that was discussed previously in relation to Lovejoy: that is the commitment of realism to a history of long continuities that overrides specific historical problems and incorporates them into a universal pattern. Collingwood's views on realism were undoubtedly applicable to the version of realism which he was acquainted with. However, some of his other criticisms must still be taken into account, in so far as they have a more general effect on the formulation of his own approach to the history of ideas.

For Collingwood, history is a process of raising questions and solving problems, not in an attempt to get them true, but to get them right, which for Collingwood has a very specific meaning: 'By "right" I do not mean "true". The "right" answer to a question is the answer which enabled us to get ahead with the process of questioning and answering.'[37] Collingwood's view here is that to claim 'truth' for an historical account is to claim far too much. His approach is far more pragmatic, whereby the object of historical work is to present a convincing account of the past that will be the most right account possible at any particular time. Historical work becomes a process which is fundamentally open-ended as both the questions raised and the problems solved are continually renewed. While this does not involve either a progression towards a more complete account of the world, or even a process of increasing rationalisation, this often amounts to overcoming previous dogmatism with a kind of theoretical warfare:

> It was an 'open' subject, an inexhaustible fountain of problems, old problems re-opened and new problems formulated that had not been formulated until now. Above all, it was a constant warfare against the dogmas, often positively erroneous, and always vicious in so far as they were dogmatic, of that putrefying corpse of historical thought, the 'information' to be found in text-books.[38]

If problems are not to be found in textbooks they emerge from the philosophical part of the history of philosophy: 'Philosophy is reflective. The philosophizing mind never simply thinks about an object, it always, while thinking about any object, thinks also about its own thought about that object. Philosophy may thus be called thought of the second degree, thought about thought.'[39]

History then, according to Collingwood, takes on a philosophical dimension and becomes thought about thought. This thought at either the primary or secondary level is not arbitrary or unmotivated, because as disciplines both history and philosophy are forms of knowledge and the characteristic of knowledge is that it proceeds, 'not "from the known to the unknown", but from the "unknown to the known." '[40] This amounts to the complete reversal of the realist paradigm, whereby knowledge is amassed not progressively but cumulatively, its object being not the establishment of universal knowledge but self-knowledge:[41] 'Knowing yourself means knowing, first, what it is to be a man; secondly knowing what it is to be the kind of man you are; and thirdly knowing what it is to be the man *you* are and nobody else is.'[42]

But if knowledge is fundamentally self-knowledge, then Collingwood is beginning to take us back to the self-reflexive transparent subject, the subject that begins to know itself through its philosophical and historical work and is becoming a *Cogito*. If this process occurs at this second level of thought about thought, then it is not clear how this second order level can be distinguished from the primary level. While Collingwood has a lot less invested epistemologically in this distinction than Lovejoy, it is still appropriate to note that this distinction is not clearly argued.

If we reconstruct Collingwood's method in much the same way as we did with Lovejoy, we begin with traces, which are any kind of material remains that exist in the world: ruins, monuments, documents and so on: 'In order that a past event should have left in the present world a 'trace' of itself which to the historian is evidence for it, this trace must be more than any material body, or state of a material body.'[43] A trace or an event becomes evidence when it is thought about by a historian and is contemplated in terms of solving the problems that it raises.[44] In this way it becomes thought and is part of the progression of knowledge, the essential characteristic of both history and philosophy. Having followed Collingwood from material traces to evidence we now find ourselves having to evaluate that evidence in order to make it 'rightly' historical, since it is clear from Collingwood's point of view that one cannot just say anything about anything. This is largely because history does not automatically present itself to the historian for judgement. The acts of history are long gone, so the historian must bring them back to a place from where they can be accessed:

> The events of history do not 'pass in review' before the historian. They have finished happening before he begins thinking about them. He has to re-create them inside in his own mind, re-enacting for himself so much of the experience of the men who took part in them as he wishes to understand.[45]

So in order to make an event the object of historical contemplation it must be re-enacted by historians in their own mind and 'understood'. The possibility for this understanding emerges out of the nature of a historical event which has two sides, the inside and the outside:

> The historian is never concerned with either of these to the exclusion of the other. He is investigating not mere events (where by a mere event I mean one which has only an outside and no inside) but actions and an action is the unity of the outside and inside of an event . . . . his main task is to think himself into this action, to discern the thought of its agent.[46]

The traces or outside events become historical–philosophical when the historian-philosopher re-enacts them by thinking about them. Collingwood's argument here raises issues about the nature of historical objects and history itself, which fall under the two central issues of presentism and the mind of the Other.

Presentism is a view that suggests that all historical writing to some extent or other involves examining the antecedents of contemporary issues. This may be accomplished as part of a search for an accurate description of the origins of a particular problem but also could be undertaken simply to provide a rationale for a continuing study. So, for example one might take as a project the history of capitalism. This could involve two approaches:

1. The study of forms of capitalist organisation in earlier societies where one then might trace a history of the development of 'embryonic' capitalist structure in Greek and Roman society through to the advanced capitalism of eighteenth- and nineteenth-century England.
2. If one had an interest in 'crisis' theory within capitalism, one might look at the nineteenth-century economic crisis. Not to find the origin of a later crisis in an earlier one but simply to make the point that states of crisis and capitalism go together and so the continuing study of the mechanics of economic crisis should always be undertaken by economic historians.

The antithesis of this presentist view could be described as an extreme form of positivism and would claim that in order to write 'good' history one must consciously avoid allowing present-day thought to intervene in the process of writing objective history. Or to re-express it, that 'good' history is written from an objective standpoint, so contemporary issues and categories should not be allowed to overwrite the production of 'objective' history. There are many issues here that could be discussed in some detail such as: what does the term 'good' history mean, what are the epistemological foundations of 'objective' history, and so on, and these issues will be taken up later. But for the moment it can be seen that at least in an extreme form the 'objectivist' view becomes absurd. It is impossible to imagine how every present day concern could be expurgated in the process of writing history, unless one was totally committed to an extreme and naïve realist historicism. I have already criticised this approach, which would in all probability prevent any research that could be called history or historicist from being undertaken.[47] However, aspects of the problem of presentism when addressed to Collingwood still remain:

> The historian (and for that matter the philosopher) is not God, looking at the world from above and outside. He is a man, and a man of his own time and place. He looks at the past from the point of view of the present: he looks at other countries and civilizations from the point of view of his own.[48]

That would seem to be reasonable enough as Collingwood is attempting to avoid a delicate problem. If he argues that history is in the past and that all the historian is doing is reformulating new answers to old questions, filling in the blanks with new historical research and techniques, he is committed once again to the 'objectivist/realism' of the Lovejoyian kind, which he is anxious to avoid. If, on the other hand, he argues that history is always the history of the present, there is a danger of disconnecting history from the past altogether and falling into a rather naïve presentism, scepticism or relativism, to which he is equally opposed.

He attempts to get around this difficulty with his own definition of history, which for him, as has already been suggested, includes the re-enactment of the thought of historical agents. This then takes him outside the fundamental realist criteria of history as dealing with universal problems and is also a rejection of historical presentism, scepticism or relativism. Thus for Collingwood history is neither the overlaying of today's concerns on the past, nor is it updating age old issues of the realist kind, nor is it producing a scientific history of the facts along strict positivist lines, nor is it just claiming anything about anything and being unable to evaluate the claims.[49] It is an act of conscious cognition by entering the mind of prior existing historical agents, considering the problems they faced, answering them according to the evidence, and by this process making of them simultaneously historical/philosophical knowledge and self-knowledge. It would seem, therefore, that charges of presentism, at least as usually conceived, and scepticism or relativism are not appropriate for Collingwood; conversely there are still problems with his view at the level of its epistemological implications.

Collingwood develops his view from the idea that it is not enough to simply read a historical text in order to find out why a particular action was taken at a particular time, for the historian must know/understand what the problem was that the author of a particular text was addressing:

> I began by observing that you cannot find out what a man means by simply studying his spoken or written statement, even though he has spoken or written with perfect command of language and perfectly truthful intention. In order to find out his meaning you must also know what the question was (a question in his own mind, and presumed by him to be in yours) to which the thing he has said or written was meant as an answer.[50]

Texts are material objects that represent and resemble thoughts, and thoughts can be rethought at any time: 'By that I mean not that their writings and so forth are still in existence as material objects, but that their ways of thinking are still in existence as ways in which people still think. The survival need not be continuous.'[51] For Collingwood history can only be written after an engagement with the process of re-enacting the acts of historical agents and, by this re-enactment, simultaneously criticising them and making any judgement on them that the evidence compels one to make:

> The cause of an event, for him, means the thought in the mind of the person by whose agency the event came about: and this is not something other than the event, it is the inside of the event itself.[52]

The historian not only re-enacts past thought, he re-enacts it in the context of his own knowledge and therefore, in re-enacting it criticizes it, forms his own judgement of its value, corrects whatever errors he can discern in it.[53]

Almost immediately problems begin to emerge, as the consequence of this is that one is committed to entering the mind of the historical agent one is attempting to historicise: 'I plunge beneath the surface of mind, and there live a life in which I not merely think about Nelson, but am Nelson, and thus in thinking about Nelson think about myself.'[54]

Collingwood's definition of the history of ideas and the method that he adopts has a number of consequences, the first one being the problem of intentionality. It is crucial for his theory that not only the problem behind the action be understood but that the intentions behind the action are open to interpretation, a point to be examined later. Furthermore it is essential for his project to succeed even in its own terms, that thoughts bear a relation of resemblance to each other and that they are in fact translatable from one mind to another. This leads him to a contradiction. At one level he has clearly rejected any universal or essentialist theory of language and is committed to the view that language is organic and subject to process and context. At another level, given the importance of direct translatability of thought from one epoch to another, there is an implication that in fact language does not substantially change. Exactly how could one plunge into Nelson's mind? If one did what would be the relationship between one's own response to a particular situation and Nelson's? At the very least Collingwood's view requires that thoughts (if not language) can jump the translatability gap from epoch to epoch. This implies that the structure of the subject and the nature of thought is fundamentally the same from the Greeks to the present day, which would seem to contradict his anti-realist views. While, according to Collingwood, historical knowledge adds to our understanding at the level of 'know thyself', the contribution of the history of ideas becomes a subjective one and it is not clear exactly how this process can be effectively evaluated. This issue will be taken up later in the context of Foucault.

The further one investigates Collingwood's methodology and, in particular, some of the apparent difficulties, the clearer it becomes that in the work of Collingwood and Lovejoy we have two different method-ologies, that are bound by the same epistemological borders. Each responds within the terms of theoretical considerations appropriate to this general epistemological field that covers, on the one hand, realism/positivism, and on the other, idealism/anti-realism. Both Collingwood and Lovejoy are concerned to get at the truth, which for Lovejoy amounts finally to saying all that there is to be said about the subject in question, and for Collingwood means saying what must be said by the compelling nature of the evidence. However, the criterion of truth is never argued for in its own terms. In

Collingwood's case this is disappointing as he appears to come close to suggesting that historical truth is a strategic/polemical construct and yet for him ultimately (T)ruth is accepted as the objective of historical work at the level of 'what really happened': 'The novelist has a single task only: to construct a coherent picture, one that makes sense. The historian has a double task: he has both to do this, and to construct a picture of things as they really happened.'[55]

Here, in returning to how things really happen, Collingwood is giving up many of the gains he has made over realism, and it is hard to meaningfully distinguish the underlying assumptions of their respective positions. They both have a commitment to a similar notion of the subject as neutral, ahistorical and transparent to itself. Lovejoy is dependent on the transparent subject, as he moves behind the -ism that he is analysing, to the intention underlying the statements of individual subjects. Collingwood arrives at much the same position, since he must be sure that by his process of overlaying the thoughts of the present onto the problems of the past he is in fact gaining access to a transparent subject, a *Cogito*. If this was not the case he could not claim that his approach had any bearing on the *past* at all. Furthermore, as we have already seen, when pressed on the issue of the 'real' of history Collingwood is prepared to acknowledge that this does indeed exist at the level of 'what really happened' in the transparent consciousness of past historical agents.

Some of the points directed specifically towards Lovejoy at the end of the previous section can be reiterated here in a wider context. Both Lovejoy and Collingwood as representatives of two different traditions within the history of ideas can be seen to be part of the same theoretical terrain and, because of this, share some similar difficulties. They are dependent on some general conception of the self-reflexive transparent subject that is accorded universal status, which neither argues for. It is not clear why this subject should be accepted as the model of the universal subject for the history of ideas. Rather it could be argued that such a subject is a specific sociocultural event within the history of ideas, or alternatively that this is not the only descriptively acceptable model of the subject. Other models could be Freud's theory of the unconscious, Kant's transcendental subject, Merleau-Ponty's phenomenological subject, Sartre's existentialist one, and so on. Of course, this is not to suggest that the transparent subject is not a defensible category, but it can be said that for both Collingwood and Lovejoy the notion of the transparent subject is essential to their theoretical practice – which assumes the universality of this kind of subjectivity in such a way that the question of the relation of this specific subject to the method of the history of ideas cannot be raised.

I want to suggest, therefore, that Lovejoy and Collingwood both offer important contributions to the history of ideas, but that they do so from within a theoretical terrain where some theoretical issues and conceptual problems are precluded from the start by an already functioning historical, philosophical and epistemological debate. It is to Collingwood's great credit that he recognised many of the difficulties of this debate and tried to overcome them, and in doing so came very close to stepping outside it altogether.

He stands at the verge of bringing a number of new and important considerations into the history of ideas, considerations such as the nature of truth, the effect of certain conceptions of the subject, the nature of the inter-discursive domain as one of warfare, and the whole question of the function of history, autobiography, and the relation between writing and death. While it is true that he does not follow through these considerations as much as I might want him to, within the limits of his theoretical paradigm he goes a long way towards opening up a practice of the history of ideas, which can be summed up under the conception of problematising, one of the categories to be developed later in this inquiry.

In Collingwood and Lovejoy we have two different methodologies, which are bound by the same epistemological borders. Each responds within the terms of theoretical considerations appropriate to this general epistemological field that covers both realism/positivism and idealism/anti-realism. Both methodologies are concerned to get at the truth, which for Lovejoy amounts to finally saying all that there is to be said about the subject in question, and for Collingwood means saying what must be said by the compelling nature of the evidence. Each depends on a self-reflexive transparent subject that exists as a disembodied observing consciousness over-determining the world in which it finds itself: The classic *Cogito*. They may have some disagreement about the extent to which consciousness is passive or active in the acquisition of knowledge, but for both the world is rational and coherent and the mind has the ability by intuitive reflection and reasoned experience to understand it.

I would argue that today's historians of philosophy, as they define themselves within current debates in 'intellectual history', adopt a position that at a fundamental level has a great deal in common with that of Lovejoy. Part 2 of *Philosophy in History* is devoted to historians of philosophy and the most immediate thing one notices is that of the seven essays presented by historians of philosophy only one raises any methodological questions relevant to the theoretical interchange fore-shadowed in the Introduction. All but one of these historians of philosophy have ignored the very *raison d'être* of the book as presented by its editors and a defence of their methodology appears unimportant to them even in a volume that is constructed around the problematic of methodo-logical interchange. For the most part, their position is well expressed by Burnyeat:

For I believe that, at least in some central areas of philosophical discussion, the sense of a difference between philosophical and ordinary questions lies deep in most of us: much deeper than any particular articulation of it that you might meet yesterday or today in Harvard, Oxford or California.[56]

The appeal here to the intuition of the subject stands in place of having to make an attempt at a methodological interaction with the intellectual historians. When the methodological defence does come from Peter Hylton it is presented in the following terms:

The claim that I am making is a claim about what it is to understand Russell's concern with the nature of the proposition. Understanding here demands that we recapture Russell's presuppositions and motives, that we see what general views he takes for granted, or wishes to advance, or wishes to oppose; and that we see how he interpreted these views and how he connected them with one another and with other views. To identify the problems at stake, and the arguments being put forward, we have to articulate the framework within which the problems arise and the arguments operate.[57]

Here the question of realism and the difficulties I have been outlining in the context of Lovejoy return, displaced from Plato and Aristotle, to Russell. We can see how the preoccupation with presuppositions and motives directs us back to the subject and the *Cogito* and the point at which Lovejoy and Collingwood overlap. But if historians of philosophy are not committed to participating in a methodological interchange with the intellectual historians, the latter appear to have a great concern with promoting this interchange.

Typically in *Philosophy in History* intellectual historians introduce their papers with a methodological discussion that continues to promote the division between intellectual history and the history of philosophy set down in the Introduction to the work and which I outlined early in this chapter . Charles Taylor opens Part 1 of the book with a critique of analytic philosophy (read history of philosophy):

Past authors may be read, but they are treated as if they were contemporaries. They earn a right to enter the dialogue because they happen to offer good formulations of one or another position which is worthy of a hearing. They are not explored as origins, but as atemporal resources.[58]

After perpetuating the division between the exploration of origin and atemporal problem solving and opening up the fault line between intellectual history and the history of philosophy, he opts for the recovery, or search for origins model of history so much criticised by Foucault:

It is very important to my thesis that even in this negative case, where you want to break loose, you need to uncover the past in order to liberate yourself. But liberation is not the only possible motive. We may also find ourselves driven to earlier formulations in order to restore a picture, or the practices it is meant to inform.[59]

Just as historians of philosophy sometimes find themselves crossing the divide to seek subjective intentions behind previous formulations of a problem, so intellectual historians cross the line to seek a stability for language and previous articulations on pragmatic grounds in the hope that they can adopt aspects of the realist programme while still being quarantined from its epistemological implications:

> The issue is whether we can give a less distorted account of the rise and continuation of these practices abandoning this presumption of exclusivity. The issue arises within a culture and history; within a set of practices, as between rival formulations of these practices.[60]

The debate between intellectual history and the history of philosophy is reintroduced at the beginning of the essays by both Macintyre and Rorty and through Rorty the conversational aspect of intellectual history is firmly fixed by intellectual historians as an essential aspect of their programme, which moves from a general metaphysics of presence to blinding self-awareness:

> As Skinner (1969: 52–3) rightly says, 'the indispensable value of studying the history of ideas' is to learn 'the distinction between what is necessary and what is the product merely of our own contingent arrangements'. The latter is indeed, as he goes on to say, 'the key to self-awareness itself'.[61]

> What does matter is making clear that grasping the meaning of an assertion is a matter of placing that assertion in a context – not of digging a little nugget of sense out of the mind of the assertor. Whether we privilege the context which consists of what the assertor was thinking about around the time he or she made the assertion depends upon what we want to get out of thinking about the assertion. If we want, as Skinner says, 'self awareness', then we need to avoid anachronism as much as possible. If we want self-justification through conversation with the dead thinkers about our current problems, then we are free to indulge in as much of it as we like, as long as we realise that we are doing so.[62]

Interestingly, the same sentiment was noted in relation to Collingwood and Lovejoy and concludes the *Philosophy in History* volume in Peter Hylton's paper, in the persona of a historian of philosophy:

My subject in this paper has been an issue in the history of philosophy, but my ulterior aim has been philosophical self-knowledge. What I hope I have conveyed in these concluding remarks is the idea that philosophical self-knowledge and an understanding of our own philosophical history are intimately connected.[63]

In drawing us back to 'self awareness' both sides of the fault line between intellectual historians and historians of philosophy have again implicated us in the *Cogito* that I suggested earlier was underlying both Collingwood and Lovejoy.

My reading of *Philosophy in History* suggests that the ontological and epistemological terrain of intellectual history and history of philosophy clings to the adoption of a theoretical paradigm that includes both realism and idealism. The point at which the two come together is the same one at which Lovejoy and Collingwood coincide, the pre-eminence of the self-reflexive subject, the *Cogito*.

It may be of interest to ask whether it is just a convenience that Lovejoy and Collingwood (whose realism and idealism are quite explicit) are not generally brought into the picture? Perhaps it is more useful for today's intellectual historians and historians of philosophy to maintain a certain fuzziness about exactly what is meant by realism and idealism/anti-realism in the context of their contemporary work? In fact, one suspects it cannot be spelt out too clearly, as the kind of 'conversation' that occurs in *Philosophy in History* would be rather more difficult unless the final point of agreement is that, in spite of all possible differences, undertaking intellectual history or history of philosophy is ultimately reducible to the interchange of ideas, conversation, work, writing and so on in a rational way between fundamentally rationally determined beings. This allows the fundamental assumptions of both realism and idealism/anti-realism to remain unchallenged and outside the debate while the 'work' continues.

This takes us back to the subject (*subject*) of the history of philosophy itself, and conjures up a specific history from Socrates to Descartes, Kant and beyond. It is not an escape from the traditional history of ideas or its problems which might allow a new kind of history to be written that might satisfy both intellectual historians and historians of philosophy. On the contrary, it is the assuming and taking on of a very specific story within the history of philosophy; for if intellectual history is just to be a conversation, it is one between specific subjects (*subjects*) about familiar subjects (*subjects*) with their own particular and specific histories.

In presenting this analysis of Collingwood and Lovejoy and the work of the composers of *Philosophy in History*, undoubtedly I have been over simplistic and unsympathetic to the particular subtleties of their analyses. However, I do not intend these brief comments to be seen as a definitive commentary on the body of work existing under the nomenclature history of ideas, intellectual history or history of philosophy, but rather I wish to uncover a moment of silence. A moment of silence that allows the *Cogito* and its derivatives to exist under erasure. A moment of silence that inhibits the developing of a series of questions which would explore the *Cogito* at the level of a problematic inquiry. This is not a question of attempting to follow Rorty's advice and reopen a conversation with Descartes, or of reformulating the question of the *Cogito* within the problems of the history of philosophy. It is rather a question of bringing back on the scene the thought: why is it that it is so difficult to write: *A Cogito?* (A shrugging of the shoulders must be imagined at the moment the ? is typed). This question and its opening mark arises from an awareness that the necessary existence of the *Cogito* is so difficult to qualify because it is inimical not only to what it is to undertake intellectual work today but also to our relation with *ourselves*. In light of the work of Foucault we can now understood the *Cogito* as a technology of self *par excellence*.

Of course, there are those that might suggest that the question of the problematic of the *Cogito* and the self-reflexive subject (*subject*) has been raised and severely dealt with in the field of psychoanalysis.[64]

Totem and Taboo

It is therefore necessary briefly to place Freud and discuss his work within the general theoretical terrain I have just been outlining. In keeping with the approach adopted so far *my* Freud is evaluated in relation to the field of the history of ideas as the historian of the Oedipus complex. As such his work incorporates intellectual history, history of philosophy, and an historical methodology that suggests a theory of the unconscious that would appear to be a possible critique of the *Cogito*.

Freud presents psychoanalysis as both a science of the mind and the art of interpreting the mind in relation to the history of culture. As the historian of the Oedipus complex Freud is the classic historian of ideas, but, more than this, in the context of the conversation elaborated in *Philosophy in History* between intellectual historians and historians of philosophy Freud has a foot in both camps. He stands astride the fault line I have been outlining. In so far as he is the historian of the idea of the Oedipus complex he is the classic idealist; at the same time, as the discoverer of the 'maybe' science of psychoanalysis he is the classic realist. Indeed the opposition between realism and anti-realism/idealism that I have suggested is endemic to the history of ideas, and contemporary intellectual history constitutes the very possibility of psychoanalysis. There are three issues that can be drawn out of Freud's anthropological and historical texts: first, his attitude to history in general; second, the kind of epistemological status he wants to attribute to the history of psychoanalytic theory; and third, the kind of subject his position presumes.

In *Leonardo Da Vinci*, Freud gives an account of how the writing of history came about, and divides history into two kinds, the age of heroes and the age of history. He suggests that while nations lived in a primitive state they gave no thought to the writing of history, but rather were more concerned with maintaining their physical existence, defending themselves against the incursions of their neighbours and where possible gaining new territory at their expense. Then came the age of history when men started to reflect on their existence and wanted to know where they had come from and how they had developed. What began as the history of the present became the accumulation of the past:

> Historical writing, which had begun to keep a continuous record of the present, now also cast a glance back to the past, gathered traditions and legends, interpreted the traces of antiquity that survived in customs and usages, and in this way created a history of the past.[65]

Freud argues that these early attempts to write history suffered from their location in the present, and as the details of the past were distorted to fit in with the polemics of the age in which they were written their history could not be objective: 'Moreover people's motive for writing history was not objective but a desire to influence their contemporaries, to encourage and inspire them, or to hold a mirror up before them.'[66]

He then draws a comparison between the operation of consciousness/ unconsciousness and the writing of history, claiming that adult conscious memory parallels the first kind of historical writing, a polemical chronicling of current events, while childhood memories are like a nation's earliest history, which was 'compiled later for tendentious reasons'. So we have in Freud a theory of history in which it unfolds from the unsophisticated non-historical chronicling of heroes to a history of the present, to the elementary polemical looking back to the past, and finally to objective/scientific history. In detailing how this heroic/mythical age operates on us today, however, Freud also includes it within a more general conception of the 'historical', and posits a more hermeneutical rereading of meaning:

> Yet in underrating this story one would be committing just as great an injustice as if one were carelessly to reject the body of legends, traditions and interpretations found in a nation's early history. In spite of all the distortions and misunderstandings, they still represent the reality of the past: they are what a people form out of the experience of its early days and under the dominance of motives that were once powerful and still operate to-day; and if it were only possible, by a knowledge of all the forces at work, to undo these

distortions, there would be no difficulty in disclosing the historical truth lying behind the legendary material.[67]

Two points emerge clearly from this. First, for Freud, the historian is fundamentally committed to the representation of an objective reality. Where there is a deviation from this, as in the case of myth, it is because we are not yet able to discover the key to unlocking the historical truth behind the myth. Secondly, the single feature of all experience in any age is that human beings act under the influence of the 'dominance of motives' that are still at work, and cause the distortion of historical truth into myth. This view is quite close to the one that I attributed earlier to realism and involves an apparent contradiction: historical understanding is evolving towards the status of a science, but the conditions under which this operates are fundamentally unchanging, mere repetitions that are always liable to distort historical reality. It is only possible to reconcile these positions by acknowledging that the advancement of history into science allows the historian retrospectively to rediscover the objective truth lying behind myth. Because of the circularity of this argument it never manages to escape the original contradiction and tension that it creates. Either the repetition of the 'dominance of motives' ensures a state of historical stasis that always distorts the historical truth, or the nature of the motives is that they themselves ought to develop with the advance of history and slowly come to correspond to historical truth. In either case, what is at stake here is a retrospectively constructed teleology.[68]

Freud's most historical text is *Moses and Monotheism*, in which he attempts to reconstruct the historical activities of Moses, and in doing so adds more detail to his theory of history.[69] His general method is to accept the approach of the positivist historian Breasted, but he begins his research by adopting Sellin's hypothesis about Moses and its epistemological requirement of producing authentic/true history:

> We will borrow from Sellin his hypothesis that the Egyptian Moses was murdered by the Jews and the religion he had introduced abandoned. This allows us to spin our threads further without contradicting the authentic findings of historical research. But apart from this we shall venture to maintain independence of the authorities and to 'proceed along our own track'.[70]

The reference to the authentic findings of historical research and its presupposed opposition to the unauthentic, becomes the basis for the asserting of the historical truth: 'We must uncover other similar tendentious purposes. If we find means of recognizing the distortions produced by those purposes, we shall bring to light fresh fragments of the true state of things lying behind them.'[71]

Once again in Freud there is a suggestion of a hermeneutical approach, as the site of truth is behind the fragments, beyond the 'tracks', under the distortions.[72] This is very reminiscent of Lovejoy's tracing of unit ideas from behind compound ideas. Amid references to Herodotus as the father of history Freud offers his account of history in much the same terms as previously outlined but with two important additions: that historical work must be pledged to 'unswerving truthfulness', and that it developed from a practice of shaping itself according to the needs of the moment. As though 'it had not yet recognised the concept of falsification', enabling a discrepancy to exist between the written record and the oral transmission of the same material, which Freud designates as tradition. To resolve this discrepancy, Freud argues that one must look to tradition, as it is less liable to suffer from the distortions of the early non-scientific histories, and yet by its nature it is liable to be less stable and definite than written history and is always exposed to changes as it is passed down from generation to generation. This ultimately exposed tradition to a number of possibilities, including that it would simply be crushed by the written record, or it would itself become the written record by a process of historical incorporation.[73]

It appears that the original development thesis of history now falls into two stages: non-scientific history, which also includes heroic histories and tradition, and objective/scientific history which promises the possibility of decoding and incorporating tradition, and heroic and non-scientific history, into it. In this way it is made objective, true and a 'real' representation of the past. What links all this together is the unfolding progressive nature of history, and if the individual steps have become less than clear, it has ultimately led to scientific, objective history. This development thesis becomes crucial to Freud's account of the history of Western civilisation, and is detailed in *Civilisation and Its Discontents* in which Freud attempts to maintain a double thesis: first that 'civilisation' is progressive, and secondly, that in the process of this progression certain archaic traces remain.[74]

Freud begins *Civilisation and Its Discontents* by alluding to the development of animal species and notes that despite the existence of animals that at first sight seem to bring this notion of development into question, this is only an apparent anomaly because the lower species existing today are not the 'true' ancestors of the more highly developed species. Thus, even allowing for this apparent difficulty, all the intermediate species can be made known to us by the process of reconstruction. However, in matters of the mind, this kind of reconstruction is not necessary as the 'primitive' exists alongside the transformed version: 'In the realm of the mind, on the other hand, what is primitive is so commonly preserved alongside of the transformed version which has arisen from it that it is unnecessary to give instances as evidence.'[75]

Here we are given two kinds of procedures: that of the analysing of the development of species by careful reconstruction, and that of the immediate recognition of the 'primitive' in the human mind. Freud gives an account of the development of the State from a situation of 'brute' force to the establishment of a community, and when this is added to that already presented in *Leonardo Da Vinci*, something of a Hobbesian history emerges, from the primitive attempts of unorganised groups struggling to survive to the founding of the State and the overcoming of the impact of the 'brute' force of the individual. The use of the concept 'brute' here is crucial as it re-emphasises the connection between the animal species and the human species. What appears to differentiate the two, is that animal species progress and develop along biological and physiological lines, while mankind develops along social and material lines within the context of civilisation. Given Freud's claim that primitive forces exist side by side in the human mind with transformed/civilised ones, mankind appears to be locked in a historical contradiction that makes him 'discontented'. The dynamic of this 'discontent' is that while social and material life progress, the structure of the mind and its essential contents do not, but remain a universal constant. What exactly this constant is comprised of is not explained at this time, but we know that it has something to do with 'specific historical events'. Freud then suggests that the process of civilisation is analogous to the maturing of the individual and argues that civilisation is built up on a renunciation of instincts, which entails non-satisfaction of instincts, and which also applies to the maturing of the individual. This leads Freud to ask an important question:

> But if we want to know what value can be attributed to our view that the development of civilization is a special process, comparable to the normal maturation of the individual, we must clearly attack another problem. We must ask ourselves to what influences the development of civilization owes its origin, how it arose, and by what its course has been determined.[76]

Armed now with an outline of Freud's approach to history, and compelled to seek the 'origin' of the intersection between the impetus for the progressive development of civilisation and that of the maturation of the individual, we can now reconstruct the 'chain' of events back into the archaic past of mankind and follow Freud's account of this through *Totem and Taboo*.[77] This is a particularly interesting Freudian text for my purposes, and one to which Freud reaffirmed his commitment to at the end of his career.[78]

In *Totem and Taboo* Freud presents us with a technique of historical reconstruction, the object being to get as close to reality as possible while at the same time developing an account of two conflicting processes, the static state of taboo and the continual transformation of totem. After discussing the general operation of totemic systems in 'primitive societies' Freud begins to look for specific underlying events behind the systems of totem and taboo, providing both a historical and psychological account of how totem developed so as to systematise the prevention of incest. In order to achieve this, he uses a method of historical reconstruction that operates backwards from his account of the Oedipus complex. The analogy of Oedipus is then overlaid on to totemism:

> If the totem animal is the father, then the two main commandments of totemism, the two taboo rules which constitute its nucleus – not to kill the totem animal and not to use a woman belonging to the same totem for sexual purposes – agree in content with the two crimes of Oedipus, who slew his father and took his mother to wife, and also with the child's two primal wishes whose insufficient repression or whose reawakening forms the nucleus of perhaps all neuroses. If this similarity is more than a deceptive play of accident it would perforce make it possible for us to shed light upon the origin of totemism in pre-historic times. In other words, we should succeed in making it probable that the totemic system resulted from the conditions underlying the Oedipus complex, just as the animal phobia of "little John" and the poultry perversion of "little Arpád" resulted from it. In order to trace this possibility we shall in what follows study a peculiarity of the totemic system or, as we may say, of the totemic religion, which until now could hardly be brought into the discussion.[79]

This is the beginning of a subtle shift in the epistemological status of the Oedipus complex from a literary event to a singular Greek historical event, to the precondition of all human existence. There has been a folding back of the effects of civilisation, namely neurosis, to an explanation of the possibility of civilisation and culture. A specific historical subject is accorded a universal status, consistent with the circularity that was pointed out in relation to Freud's general comments on history (and is reminiscent of the technique underlying Lovejoy's realist loop), and the original rather unclear overlapping, of what is subject to change and what is subject to stasis, remains. This becomes particularly evident when Freud finally recounts the basis of totemism, and what underlies the Oedipus complex and confers on it universal status:

> One day the expelled joined forces, slew and ate the father, and thus put an end to the father horde. Together they dared and accomplished what would have remained impossible for them singly. Perhaps some advance in culture, like the use of a new weapon, had given them the feeling of superiority. Of course these cannibalistic savages ate their victim. This violent primal father had surely been the envied and feared model for each of the brothers. Now they accomplished their identification with him by devouring him and each

acquired a part of his strength. The totem feast, which is perhaps mankind's first celebration, would be the repetition and commemoration of this memorable, criminal act with which so many things began, social organisation, moral restriction and religion.[80]

They undid their deed by declaring that the killing of the father substitute, the totem, was not allowed, and renounced the fruits of their deed by denying themselves the liberated women. Thus they created two fundamental taboos of totemism out of the sense of guilt of the son, and for this very reason these had to correspond with the two repressed wishes of the Oedipus complex. Whoever disobeyed became guilty of the only two crimes which troubled primitive society.[81]

Invoking Darwin as the authority for the primal horde Freud makes it clear that this is a *real* historical event that took place over and over again: 'The story is told in an enormously condensed form, as though it had happened on a single occasion, while in fact it covered thousands of years and was repeated countless times during that period.'[82] Here we have an expression of the resolution of the tension produced between the contradictory themes of progress and stasis. By claiming universal status for the events of the primal horde, according it scientific objectivity and allowing that traces of this moment of cultural origin to remain transformed throughout the social and material progress of civilisation (via Oedipus to the contemporary neurotic), the circular movement of Freud's argument about history and the pre-conditions of social life is broken. However, in order to achieve this Freud has had to take on the methodological terminology criticised earlier. He is forced to deal with large chronological unities, huge continuous temporal spans, even larger than those of Lovejoy and Collingwood, and to pose an exclusive theory of universal subjectivity that in many ways is more all embracing than that of Lovejoy and Collingwood. It would appear that if one wants to use Freudian theory as a basis for a critical account of the transparent subject, one is forced to engage with exactly the same theoretical apparatus on which that subject (*subject*) is founded. So the function of Freud's history and its complicity in the production of an exclusive theory of the subject applies as much to Freud as it does to Lovejoy and Collingwood.

Even though the retention of the universal content and structure of human subjectivity forces Freud into providing an account of how this is transmitted through the progression of culture – an account that commits him to a less than satisfactory phylogenetics – he is aware that to abandon this would lead him back into irreconcilable difficulties. So alongside the positing of universal trans-cultural subjectivity emerges a principle of the phylogenetic transmission of psychical mechanisms.[83]

In many ways Freud's position is more rigid than even Lovejoy's. A consequence of his view of phylogenetics is that not only is the structure of consciousness universal, as might be a traditional realist view, but that the content of consciousness is also universal. The notion of a universal subject with a consciousness that is specific would not seem to be much of an advance on the notion of the *Cogito* and self-reflexive subject presented previously. But one could still argue that Freud is offering an alternative view of the structure of this universal transcultural subject which is critical of the transparent subject that I have been attributing to the other intellectual historians and historians of philosophy I have discussed to date. But is he?

There are two issues to be considered here. First, as Freud argues that the development or maturation of the individual is analogous to that of culture itself, the representation of consciousness is also caught up in the same dynamic of stasis and progress, transformations and archaic traces, which all operate simultaneously. Secondly, in *Civilisation and its Discontents*, Freud re-triangulates the Oedipal subject, not only around that of father, mother, child, but also within the dimensions of Death, Desire and Law. This double triangulation creates a field of interpretation that unfolds from its archaic traces on to the present day. The resolution of the original tension of progress and stasis was ultimately resolved by collapsing the specificity of a particular Oedipal subject to that of the primal horde, a universal category. With the application of a retrospective teleological reconstruction, the double-triangulated subject collapses into itself along with the unconscious into consciousness, at the hands of the analyst. Indeed the two processes are intimately related and involve and presuppose the mental reconstruction of the 'origin', the site of the original act of violence, through which the truth of the subject (*subject*) can be made known to them. This truth is their participation in the murder of the father, and their engagement in the interplay of Desire, Death and Law. And as Freud suggests, the question of a real murder here is now no longer at issue, for through phylogenesis and our place in our civilisation and culture we are all bearers of the transmitted and inherited original act:

> Whether one has killed one's father or has abstained from doing it is not the decisive thing. One is bound to feel guilty in either case, for the sense of guilt is an expression of the conflict due to ambivalence, of the eternal struggle of Eros and the instinct of destruction or death. The conflict is set going as soon as men are faced with the task of living together. So long as the community assumes no other form than that of the family, the conflict is bound to express itself in the Oedipus complex, to establish the conscience and create the first sense of guilt.[84]

It is here that psychoanalysis promises to return to the subject the transparency that it initially denies. Through its promise of decoding the transformations of the present into the origin, psychoanalysis offers the subject *(subject)* the possibility of a total knowledge of itself, the return to that moment of metaphysics where there was no distinction to be made between the act and the event, between Self and Other, between Word and the Object:

> And the law-language (at once word and system) that psychoanalysis takes such pains to make speak, is it not that in which all signification assumes an origin more distant than itself, but also that whose return is promised in the very act of analysis? It is indeed true that this Death, and this Desire, and this Law can never meet within the knowledge that traverses in its positivity the empirical domain of man, but the reason for this is that they designate the conditions of possibility of all knowledge about man.[85]

As Foucault suggested it should be noted that Freud's induction of the whole of civilisation into the dynamic of incest, ensures that for all time sexuality is demarcated by the rule of law.[86]

Once having established that we are all existing under the sway of this universal transcultural law that splits the subject, psychoanalytic practice restores transparency to that same subject by returning it through discourse to the site of the origin from where all later transformations of the original event can now be made intelligible:

> But the major benefit, of course, is that it conceals the crisis in which we have been involved for so long, and which is constantly growing more serious: a crisis that concerns that transcendental reflexion with which philosophy since Kant has identified itself; which concerns that theme of the origin, that promise of the return, by which we avoid the difference of our present; which concerns an anthropological thought that orders all these questions around the question of man's being, and allows us to avoid an analysis of practice; which concerns all humanist ideologies; which, above all, concerns the status of the subject. It is this discussion that you would like to suppress, and from which you hope, I think, to divert attention, by pursuing the pleasant games of genesis and system, synchrony and development, relation and cause, structure and history. Are you sure you are not practising theoretical metathesis?[87]

Far from psychoanalysis helping us to escape from the realism/idealism structure and its supporting *Cogito*, it further naturalises it and *subjects* us at a severe cost – the difficulty we have within modern philosophy of putting the *Cogito* into question. In Descartes the potentially damaging effect of the evil demon is deferred by the re-introduction of God as the basis on which true knowledge can be guaranteed. But within the Freudian model it is man's own self-knowledge that is guarantor of the true knowledge of the universal conditions and the limits of man's existence.

If, therefore, we analyse the work of historians of ideas, intellectual historians, or historians of philosophy, there are some fundamental problems that consistently emerge. These can be arranged in relation to three reference points: realism, idealism/anti-realism, and what we might call a cultural or ethnological approach. The first two views have a long history in contemporary representations of the history of philosophy. The last, the Kantian double, is a late comer that has become an integral part of the development of the social sciences. Each of these views has fundamental and specific problems but they share a similar dependence on the concept of the self-reflexive transparent subject, the *Cogito*.

It would seem that we are faced with a complicated and densely structured impasse. We must be for or against realism, we must be for or against idealism, we must be for or against intellectual history, we must be for or against history of philosophy, we must be for or against our mothers and fathers, we must be for or against the *Cogito*, we must be for Descartes or against Freud, we must be for or against *ourselves*, and so it goes on ... we have become a thoroughly adversarial culture.

In *What is Enlightenment?* Foucault cautions against being blackmailed and drawn into the for and against existence.[88] The issue is rather to take up the question I posed some time ago with more patience than I previously gave it. Why is it so difficult to write a *Cogito*? And further to that, under what theoretical conditions can this difficulty be overcome?

A series of sub-questions now spills easily on to the page. Is it just that if one wants to produce historical work, one must accept this notion of the subject in order to undertake it? What kind of historical work could be undertaken without accepting as a pre-supposition the existence of a universal subject – a *Cogito*? Is it the case that all historical inquiries must accept in some way or other a universal subject in order to be accomplished? If that is so then how could one ever historicise the development of that same subject?

It seems that either we have to surrender the possibility of presenting a history of the emergence of the *Cogito* in history or we must define an alternative approach to our work. If the latter can be achieved then perhaps it will be possible to examine further why it was so difficult to raise the question of the subject (*subject*) from within intellectual history, the history of philosophy and the history of ideas in the first place? This draws me directly to the work of Foucault.

·2·

History and systems of thought

Towards an archaeology

Foucault's work is in many ways difficult to appraise according to the usual methods of philosophers – difficult because not only did Foucault change his mind about his work and its general direction many times during his career, which is not so unusual, but also he seemed to delight in these changes and the apparent contradictions and anxiety they created. On occasions he constructed colourful metaphors to describe the way in which he worked, referring to it as a slalom and his general attitude as that of a whale diving deep and occasionally coming to the surface to blow. These kinds of description, endearing as they are, do not help the would-be Foucauldian come to terms with his corpus. But then neither do his theoretical pronouncements on the general function of commentary, the creation of the author and the *œuvre*.

Three questions come to mind. How might one find a way of entering his work and directing it toward the issues at hand? How can one avoid the difficulties of commentary and exegesis that Foucault has alerted us to? What are the most convenient entry and exits from Foucault's work for the project I have before me? Provisionally I suggest three conceptual strategies that address these questions:

1. *History and systems of thought* This emerges directly out of misreading the title of Foucault's Chair at the Collège de France.[1] This phrase signals that I will be using my interpretation of Foucault's work to focus on my interest in intellectual history, the history of philosophy and the history of ideas. As I suggested in the Introduction to this inquiry the history of philosophy, where it is still practised, is often presented as the history

of systems of thought. Typically institutions teaching it would offer a programme, for example from Plato to the modern day and now perhaps even to Foucault himself. So what then is significant about the change I am suggesting from the history *of* systems of thought to history *and* systems of thought?

The point is to change the balance between the two concepts. In the first case the function of the 'of' is to create an active/passive tension between the history and the systems of thought that apparently were, and still are, according to this view, the arbitrary product, of that history. Systems of thought are passive, objective elements existing in a historical past lying in wait for a historical methodology to recover or dig them out. However, in the second case, history and systems of thought are given even weighting, they are co-joined. The system of thought and the historical methodology that describe it, are equally dependent on each other. They are intimately interwoven; neither can exist in any particular form without the other.[2] The use of the conjunction 'and' constructs a line of interchange, of interplay between history and systems of thought. This interplay becomes one of mutual dependence, systems of thought are no longer the passive objects of a historical methodology but an active element in the process of historiography; each is constitutive of the other. To acknowledge this in one's historical work demands a recasting of the terminology and a subtle although not insignificant shift in the approach of both the practitioner and the status of their practice.

2. *Drawing a diagram* A rich and dense series of metaphors emerge out of the drawing of diagrams if we allow for the intersection of the English word 'to draw' and Deleuze's concept of the diagram:

> The diagram or abstract machine is the map of relations between forces, a map of destiny, or intensity, which proceeds by primary non-localizable relations and at every moment passes through every point, 'or rather in every relation from one point to another'. Of course, this has nothing to do either with a transcendent idea or with an ideological superstructure, or even with an economic infrastructure, which is already qualified by its substance and defined by its form and use.[3]

The verb 'to draw' and its various uses cover many pages in the Oxford English Dictionary, but what I want to note is both its use as the process by which a diagram is produced and also its reference to drawing out. Foucault is, at least for those of us that never met him, nothing more than a diagram of a future opportunity.[4] A figure ahead of his time that draws us along behind him, presents us with a sketch of our culture and draws off its poisonous limitations as he unmercifully poultices us. A draughtsman who produces both diagrams and draughts – an untimely ill wind.[5]

3. *Philosophy with a tuning fork* This is a variation of philosophy with a hammer as described by Nietzsche in the *Twilight of the Idols*:

> This little essay is a great declaration of war; and regarding the sounding out of idols, this time they are not just idols of the age, but eternal idols, which are here touched with a hammer as with a tuning fork: there are altogether no older, no more convinced, no more puffed up idols – and none more hollow. That does not prevent them from being those in which people have the most faith; nor does one ever say 'idol,' especially not in the most distinguished instance.
>
> *Turin, September 30, 1888*
>
> *on the day when the first book of the* Revaluation
>
> of All Values *was completed.*
>
> Friedrich Nietzsche[6]

Musical metaphors are particularly appropriate when the work of Foucault is under consideration. If we pause over the image of striking the idols of our age with a hammer *as with a tuning fork* we can understand Foucault's enterpise as a thoroughly productive one – if we choose to hear. But we must be especially careful to listen for the partials, the overtones and the harmonics. What we must observe and bring to light are the different entrances and exits, the multiplicity of tunes, the dischords – and harmonies.

The analysis of Foucault's work which follows allows me to multiply the possibilities of the inquiry that I can undertake. Its aim is not to reduce Foucault's work to a mutual dialogue so that we can politely correct each others deficiencies;[7] it is to use Foucault's work (and some of the critical responses to it) as a point of departure in much the same way as Foucault described his relation to the work of Nietzsche:

> The only valid tribute to thought such as Nietzsche's is precisely to use it, to deform it, to make it groan and protest. And if commentators then say that I am being faithful or unfaithful to Nietzsche, that is of absolutely no interest.[8]

Of course, this is a task not without its risks. At its best it can produce astounding work such as Deleuze's book on Foucault, which, by its very intensity and sensitivity, tells us much about the role that Foucault has played in the development of Deleuze's work. At its worst it produces work that degenerates into a self-congratulatory mode, invoking the name of the Other to justify its own excesses. One hopes it is possible to achieve a modicum of the former and an absence of the latter. But these problems are not confined to a Foucauldian or Nietzschean, they equally apply to the work of intellectual historians and historians of philosophy. In this respect we can recall both the indispensable collection of thoughtful criticism of Foucault's work gathered together by David Couzens Hoy, and the embarrassing diatribe of Merquior.[9]

But if the risk of failure or producing embarrassing inadequate work underlies one's intellectual activity this masks another possibility – the risk of changing oneself through this activity. This is the moment at which one's work becomes a technology of self, a rewriting and a movement towards the possibility of thinking differently – of being other. After all, what is a corpus but the relation of one's body to one's body of work?

Aspects of this moment were discussed by Foucault when he distinguished his concept of '*histoire*' from the practice of the '*historien*':

> The studies that follow, like the others I have done previously, are studies of 'history' by reason of the domain they deal with and the references they appeal to; but they are not the work of a 'historian.' Which does not mean that they summarize or synthesize work done by others. Considered from the point of view of their 'pragmatics,' they are the record of a long and tentative exercise that needed to be revised and corrected again and again. It was a philosophical enterprise. The object was to learn to what extent the effort to think one's own history can free thought from what it silently thinks, and so enable it to think differently.[10]

Here Foucault is suggesting that his project is fundamentally a philosophical one. Certainly it has a historical dimension, but this historical dimension is subservient to its philosophical object which takes on an added ethical dimension: 'This last is what might be called a history of "ethics" and "ascetics," understood as a history of the forms of moral subjectivisation and of the practices of self that are meant to ensure it.'[11]

Thus according to Foucault the project that he is engaged in, at least at the end of his career, is one of history that is not of the kind practised by the *historien*, and to confuse the issue further by forcing a re-evaluation of his earlier work Foucault says: 'My objective, instead, has been to create a history of the different modes by which, in our culture, human beings are made into subjects.'[12] How can this claim be reconciled both with Foucault's early work and, at a more general level, the history of ideas? In terms of the distribution of similarities and differences it would seem that this project is not so far from that of Lovejoy and Collingwood, but this similarity soon disappears because Foucault is allowing a certain ambiguity that exists in French in relation to the word '*histoire*'. As Foucault maintains throughout his work, the questions to be addressed are: How is it that the distinction between history and story/fiction comes about? What is the function of this division when it is made? And what is the effect of this on subjects (*subjects*) that experience it?

If we recall my earlier comments on Collingwood's practice, it is evident that for him it is crucial that history be clearly demarcated from fiction. In Collingwood's case this is undertaken simply by referring to a real historical past which precludes the kinds of questions that Foucault enjoins us to ask. For Foucault they can only be analysed in terms of the politics of discourse, not in the facticity of history because the facticity of history is something that can be neither logically nor empirically known.[13] There is something Kantian about this; history as events in the past occurs and these events function as an a priori for our own existence, but they can never be apprehended directly. They become no more than the conditions of possibility for our own discourses without having any overdetermining action on their specific content.[14] As a result of this it can be seen that what concerns Foucault is the effect that discourses – and clearly this includes discourses embedded in history – have on the production of the modes of our subjectivity and our experience of ourselves as a subject (*subject*):

> There is no specific moral action that does not refer to a unified moral conduct; no moral conduct that does not call for the forming of oneself as an ethical subject; and no forming of the moral subject without 'modes of subjectivisation' and an 'ascetics' or 'practices of the self' that support them. Moral action is indissociable from these forms of self-activity, and they do not differ any less from one morality to another than do the systems of values, rules and interdictions.[15]

This has been a consistent theme throughout Foucault's work, but one which has been repeatedly modified and honed in the overcoming of the many theoretical difficulties it has revealed. Perhaps this takes us back to the question of the history of ideas or more appropriately the very issue that the conjunction of history and ideas raises. It is a question that causes a fundamental problem for all those with a tendency towards historical realism. How is it that a universal subject can claim to present an objective history when the history of the category of the universal subject itself is historically specific? This must lead either to a rejection of history altogether in favour of a realist stasis or the facing of an inevitable contradiction, which, as Cousins and Hussain suggest, is particularly apparent in the social sciences:

> Psychology, sociology and the study of myths and literature all use historical materials. But it is usually the case that a certain price must be paid for this. They suffer from a form of contamination. In psychology, categories such as consciousness, memory, perception tend to become destabilized by contact

with historical problems. The appropriateness of categories becomes problematized. A second form of contamination occurs because the social sciences are forced to admit that they too have a history. This opens up a whole area within the social sciences which is concerned to describe itself as a form of historical self-consciousness which attempts to locate itself within history. In this way history bears an ambiguous relation to the social sciences. On the one hand it provides a favourable milieu for the attempts by the social sciences to situate themselves and their object of knowledge. On the other hand it introduces an instability by questioning the universality of their assumptions through historical relativization.[16]

It is an examination of this problematic that inaugurates Foucault's work with the publication of *Mental Illness and Psychology*, although it did not reach a detailed expression until the publication of *Madness and Civilisation*, which examines how subjects were constituted as mad, and then attempts to analyse the effects this has had on Western culture. But if the object of Foucault's work is to theorise the relation between history and systems of thought, it is because for him history acts in Western culture as the founding instance of the subject (*subject*) – that momentary point of cohesive identity that allows a certain kind of theorising, particularly historical theorising, to take place, be legitimated and experienced. Foucault directs his theoretical interventions towards undermining this circularity and as each text modifies his own theoretical apparatus the precise point of the intervention will change. So the traditional chronological approach to the *œuvre* that represents the unfolding of a continuous chronological theorisation is not useful in attempting to come to terms with Foucault's work. As an alternative it might be better simply to divide his work into the archaeological and the genealogical texts, still an arbitrary division but one that is more in keeping with Foucault's own claims about his enterprise. But another question interrogates us.

At what point does Foucault's work intervene in the problems raised by intellectual history, the history of philosophy and the history of ideas as I have already delineated them? This goes to the very heart of the series of issues that have been previously raised and which I will restate here.

1. There are a number of difficulties that emerge from the notion of the self-reflexive transparent *Cogito vis à vis* intentionality, universality and historical continuity.
2. At a general level there is a commitment to a realist conception of history that depends on a recovery of the real past.
3. There is a commitment to speaking the truth, where to speak in this way is to say everything there is to say about an historical epoch or to follow the compelling nature of the 'evidence', but in neither case is the conceptualisation and construction of truth brought into question.

4. There is a necessary rejection of discontinuity, chance, accident and contingency as elements in the production of knowledge.
5. From within their shared theoretical and methodological assumptions intellectual historians, historians of philosophy and historians of ideas are unable to put the subject (*subject*) and all the associated categories that sustain it in question.

With my three analytic categories in mind – history and systems of thought, drawing a diagram and philosophy with a tuning fork – and with the above thoughts on Foucault's intervention into intellectual history, the history of philosophy and the history of ideas in focus, I shall begin a sketch of Foucault's work. This does not stand in the place of the many works that directly deal with Foucault's work in great detail. However, my purpose is to undertake an inquiry in which I have an interest and which was formulated as I worked with my ever-changing diagram of Foucault, an inquiry that could not have been initiated or modified but for the already said of Foucault.

Within my crude classifying of Foucault's work into archaeological and genealogical, three texts immediately seem to escape. They are *Mental Illness and Psychology*, *Madness and Civilisation*, and the *Birth of the Clinic*.[17] In so far as *Mental Illness and Psychology* was published initially in 1954 but not translated into English until 1976, there is some doubt as to how useful a discussion of it is for a re-evaluation of Foucault's work – beyond making observations about the influence of phenomenology. This impression is enhanced by Foucault's own attempts to prevent the publication of this work in English after such a long interval. But more significantly, it seems that in *Madness and Civilisation* some of the issues raised in *Mental Illness and Psychology* are developed and examined in a more sophisticated way and promote a level of discussion that is more conducive to a thoughtful examination of Foucault's early work.

Madness and Civilisation begins characteristically with a discussion of the method that it will adopt:

> We must try to return in history, to that zero point in the course of madness at which madness is an undifferentiated experience, a not yet divided experience of division itself. We must describe, from the start of its trajectory, that 'other form' which regulates Reason and Madness to one side or the other of its action as things henceforth external, deaf to all exchange, and as though dead to one another.[18]

There are two important themes that Foucault develops here: first, that his method is to recapture an experience; second, that he wants to return to an origin, to a zero point of history from which the history of madness unfolds.

Both these techniques will be reformulated, but in *Madness and Civilisation* they mark the beginnings of a temporary theoretical trajectory:

> What, then, is this confrontation beneath the language of reason? Where can an interrogation lead us which does not follow reason in its horizontal course, but seeks to retrace in time that constant verticality which confronts European culture with what it is not, establishes its range by its own derangement? What realm do we enter which is neither the history of knowledge, nor history itself; which is controlled by neither the teleology of truth nor the rational sequence of causes, since causes have value and meaning only beyond the division? A realm no doubt, where what is in question is the limits rather than the identity of a culture.[19]

Here Foucault raises two different issues: how to write the history of the experience of madness without entering history, the teleology of truth or the rational sequence of causes, while still putting into question the limits of culture; and how to rearticulate the hitherto silent experience of madness.[20] If we bring these considerations together, the methodological questions that emerge may be reiterated in the following way. How can one write a history without entering history, the teleology of truth, or cause and effect? How can one put into question the limits of our culture, while still bringing into discourse the silent speech of the mad? But before assessing where attempting to answer these questions leads Foucault, it is important to specify the object of Foucault's intervention into the history of madness:

> I believe I wrote *Madness and Civilisation* to some extent within the horizon of these questions. For me, it was a matter of saying this: if, concerning a science like theoretical physics or organic chemistry, one poses the problem of its relations with the political and economic structures of society, isn't one posing an excessively complicated question? Doesn't this set the threshold of possible explanations impossibly high? But on the other hand, if one takes a form of knowledge (*savoir*) like psychiatry, won't the question be much easier to resolve, since the epistemological profile of psychiatric practice is linked with a whole range of institutions, economic requirements and political issues of social regulation? Couldn't the interweaving of effects of power and knowledge be grasped with greater certainty in the case of a science as 'dubious' as psychiatry.[21]

Foucault suggests that there are two kinds of intervention that he is trying to make into psychiatry. First, at the specific level of the history of psychiatry, a history which sees the emergence of psychiatry from out of the ignorance and superstition of the Middle Ages as a moment of 'blinding' rationalism. On the one hand, this liberated humanity from the barbarous practices of the Middle Ages; on the other, it began the process of coming towards a scientific understanding of the operation of the human mind.

Secondly, at a more general level this raises questions about the histo
the science as it is articulated in the history of those sciences tha
presented in a 'clearer light', namely physics and chemistry. So one
important aspect of Foucault's technique, to which he maintains a
commitment throughout his career, is to destabilise the historico-
epistemological foundations of the sciences in which he is interested. If this
is to become more overt in Foucault's later works, it is not so for *Madness
and Civilisation*, which remains highly problematic in many ways as he takes
on the methodological prescriptions outlined at the beginning of the text by
adopting a methodology that emerges out of the conjunction between
phenomenology and a structural analysis. (This general argument, which is
convincingly developed by Dreyfus and Rabinow, received some support
from Foucault himself.)[22] It is phenomenological to the extent that
Foucault's aim is to reconstruct the 'experience' of the mad, in some sense or
other as lived experience, a phenomenological emphasis that re-emerges
transformed in Foucault's later work in relation to his analysis of the body.
It is structural in so far as Foucault uses oppositions with which he
orientates his work, and in particular the opposition reason/unreason.[23]
Whilst accepting the Dreyfus/Rabinow view at a general level, some
attempt must be made to distinguish Foucault's project even at this early
stage from what might be called classical structuralism as developed by Lévi-
Strauss. For Foucault the concept of structure is used to delineate not a
resolution of the ambiguity of discourse, but rather a functional grid
determining its possibility:

> As a matter of fact, beneath these reversible meanings, a structure is forming
> which does not resolve the ambiguity but determines it. It is this structure
> which accounts for the transition from the medieval and humanist experience
> of madness to our own experience, which confines insanity within mental
> illness.[24]

In a classical application of structuralism such as Lévi-Strauss's *The Raw
and the Cooked*, structures are taken to exist at a deep level and are then
drawn out so that structural oppositions can be used to resolve the
ambiguities of the social system.[25] However, for Foucault discursive
structures stand in surface relations to each other, and the application of his
structural method neither attempts to resolve their ambiguities, nor accepts
any interchange between a deep and surface level, but only allows the
surface phenomena to reveal their content without any attempt at
methodological reduction. At this point Foucault's methodological practice
becomes at times laboured, unclear and problematic. If he is only reordering
the surface phenomena of discourse it can be said that his practice becomes
simply the proliferation of meanings and the expansion of the possibilities

of discourse. It is not necessarily evident that the process of proliferation in itself is worthwhile, although Foucault could still argue that such a practice would still be viable as a critique of holism and the universal claims of structuralism which tends to become an exclusive theoretical model. In this sense Foucault's work is still effective as working at the level of the proliferation of discourse, it retains the fundamental value of being anti-holist, and it prevents attempts at theoretical and interpretive closure. It is therefore directly opposed to a structure of immobile forms or universalising constants:

> But from one of these experiences to the other, the shift has been made by a world without images, without positive character, in a kind of silent transparency which reveals – as mute institution, act without commentary, immediate knowledge – a great motionless structure; this structure is one of neither drama nor knowledge; it is the point where history is immobilised in the tragic category which both establishes and impugns it.[26]

This amounts to a reversal of the structuralism of Lévi-Strauss, Piaget, or Lacan, as Foucault is suggesting that both structures and their meaning are already located in their historical specificity. Therefore they cannot be accorded universal or transhistorical status but must be placed within the historical framework appropriate to them and which we can analyse:

> a meaning has taken shape that hangs over us, leading us forward in our blindness, but awaiting in the darkness for us to attain awareness before emerging into the light of day and speaking. We are doomed historically to history, to the patient construction of discourses about discourses, and to the task of hearing what has already been said.[27]

This specific history must be articulated as part of a lost and silent speech; it must be re-experienced, reattained, not by resorting to commentary (with its implied metaphysics of the excess, of the remainder that lies in wait for a later articulation), but by 'specifying' its appearance from amid the conditions of possibility in which it is implicated. One statement would then be differentiated from another not by intentionality, or by commentary, but by its difference from other statements within the discursive field that surrounds it.

It is these considerations that allow Foucault to attempt to differentiate his project from the history of ideas:

> Until recently, the history of ideas was only aware of two methods: the first, aesthetic method involved analogy, with diffusion charted in time (geneses, filiations, kinships, influences) or on the surface of a given historical space (the spirit of a period, its *Weltanschauung*, its fundamental categories, the

organisation of its sociocultural world). The second, which was a psychological method, involved a denial of contents (this or that century was not as rationalistic, or irrationalistic as was said or believed), from which there has since developed a sort of 'psychoanalysis' of thought, the results of which can quite legitimately be reversed – the nucleus of the nucleus being always its opposite.[28]

But are the methodological procedures Foucault has outlined in *Madness and Civilisation* and the *Birth of the Clinic* capable of meeting the aims he has set for himself? Can he engage with structural theory (not structuralism) and phenomenology while still meeting the demands he has set for himself – neither to seek the truth nor use intentionality as an underlying category? Will he be able to avoid theorising in terms of cause and effect or universality, while still putting into question the epistemological limits of the discourses he is criticising?

Perhaps there is something of an implicit contradiction in Foucault's work at this stage between its phenomenological and structural strains, a contradiction between the lived experience of madness in the classical age which Foucault is redescribing, and the reduction of this to the conditions of possibility of discourse. At any event with the publication of the *Order of Things* Foucault's phenomenological work took on less significance, and for a short time structural analysis became predominant. The *Order of Things* has a specific point of intervention in the discourse of the sciences of Man, namely economics, theories of language, anthropology, ethnology and psychoanalysis, and indeed all those disciplines that take Man as their object of investigation. The analysis of this is highly specific, as it attempts to re-orientate the history of the sciences of Man as those disciplines themselves articulate it. It is here that one can appreciate the ironic force of Foucault's claim that the birth of the Sciences of Man is paralleled by the disappearance of Man from Western culture. This is precisely because in the discourses of man, man is both the subject (*subject*) and the object of his own theoretical knowledge. It is an impossible double.

Foucault describes his task as a study of comparative discourse, from the seventeenth century to the nineteenth century, not to construct the *Weltanschauung* of this period, but to analyse the conditions of possibility for certain statements, that will culminate with the foundation of the sciences of Man:

> This book must be read as a comparative, and not a symptomato-logical study. It was not my intention, on the basis of a particular type of knowledge or body of ideas, to draw up a picture of a period, or to reconstitute the spirit of a century. What I wished to do was to present, side by side, a definite number of elements: the knowledge of living beings, the knowledge of the laws of language, and the knowledge of economic facts, and to relate them to

the philosophical discourse that was contemporary with them during a period extending from the seventeenth to the nineteenth century.[29]

He then attempts to reassess his earlier work in the introduction to *The Order of Things*, by distinguishing it from the work of contemporary structuralists and phenomenologists:

> If there is one approach I do reject, however, it is that (one might call it, broadly speaking, the phenomenological approach) which gives absolute priority to the observing subject, which attributes a constituent role to an act, which places its own point of view at the origin of all historicity – which, in short, leads to a transcendental consciousness. It seems to me that the historical analysis of scientific discourse should, in the last resort, be subject, not to a theory of the knowing subject, but rather to a theory of discursive practice.[30]

> In France certain half-witted 'commentators' persist in labelling me a 'structuralist'. I have been unable to get into their tiny minds that I have used none of the methods, concepts, or key terms that characterize structural analysis.[31]

One suspects that the care and at times the vehemence with which Foucault attempts to distinguish his work from both phenomenology and structuralism, suggests the ease with which his work was being systematically mischaracterised. In response to this misrecognition and mischaracterisation Foucault makes a number of important points. First, he is right in acknowledging that his terminology has little in common with the practising structuralists of his day. Secondly, as I have already indicated, he reaffirms his attempts to resist the universalising claims of structuralism[32]. Thirdly, he argues against the Kantian implication of phenomenology by suggesting that the conditions of the possibility of discourse precede the phenomenological subject. This means that any theory of the knowing subject must be preceded by a theory of discursive practice. In his attempts to distinguish his work from structuralism and phenomenology, Foucault takes on the obligation to develop an alternative kind of analysis:

> Quite obviously, such an analysis does not belong to the history of ideas or of science: it is rather an inquiry whose aim is to rediscover on what basis knowledge and theory became possible; within what space of order knowledge was constituted; ... what I am attempting to bring to light is the epistemological field, the *episteme* in which knowledge, envisaged apart from all criteria having reference to its rational value or to its objective forms, grounds its positivity and thereby manifests a history which is not that of its growing perfection, but rather that of its conditions of possibility; in this account, what should appear are those configurations within the *space* of

knowledge which have given rise to the diverse forms of empirical science. Such an enterprise is not so much a history, in the traditional meaning of that word, as an 'archaeology'.[33]

We find here the introduction of some of the terminology that will occupy Foucault's work for some time, most notably the conceptions of the *episteme* and archaeology, and to this must be added the use of the much criticised theme of discontinuity. As I have already shown the theme of discontinuity emerged at the very inception of the history of ideas and both Lovejoy and Collingwood attempted to come to terms with it in somewhat different ways. But Foucault suggests an alternative approach; rather than trying to either overcome or ignore the problem of discontinuity he prefers to acknowledge the effect of both the overcoming and the constitution of discontinuities:

> Establishing discontinuities is not an easy task even for history in general. And it is certainly even less so for the history of thought. We may wish to draw a dividing-line; but any limit we set may perhaps be no more than an arbitrary division made in a constantly mobile whole. We may wish to mark off a period; but have we the right to establish symmetrical breaks at two points in time in order to give an appearance of continuity and unity to the system we place between them? Where, in that case, would the cause of its existence lie? Or that of its subsequent disappearance and fall? What rule could it be obeying by both its existence and its disappearance? If it contains a principle of coherence within itself, whence could come the foreign element capable of rebutting it? How can a thought melt away before anything other than itself? Generally speaking what does it mean, no longer being able to think a certain thought? Or to introduce a new thought?[34]

Foucault's account of discontinuity has been a major point of contention among his interpreters. As is well known, he resisted the label of the 'philosophy of discontinuity' being applied to his work. What concerns him about the discontinuities, continuities and periodisations that appear in historical work is the unconscious way they are adopted. It is as if to apply a term such as the Victorian age, from year x to year y, blocks out the overlapping periods at the beginning and the end of this particular epoch. But more than this there is a tendency that once the characteristics of a particular period of continuity have been defined, things that do not quite look to have these particular characteristics are often excluded from it. This was precisely the same point that I made previously when I was discussing the work of Lovejoy. In fairness to many historians, they are acutely aware that this overlapping occurs and of its impact on their work.

But this is not the only point that Foucault is making here. The analogy is something like this: suppose one has hundreds of articles to file away, one could divide up each filing cabinet drawer to cover the letters of the alphabet and file them all away alphabetically by author's name. Of course, some problems such as a hyphenated name will be easy to overcome. This is the level at which our historian who is aware of some of the difficulties of continuities is working. But the point that Foucault is making is rather more like this. What if an article were in Japanese, how would we file that? Would we have the author's name translated into English? How would our use of the Western alphabet and the author's name effect what we considered to be a collectable article? Suppose that there were no author? Would our response be that this does not fit our system so we must exclude it? Or would we invent an author so that we could file it somewhere? In other words the continuities, epochs and periodisations that we use have direct effects on the kind of analysis that we permit ourselves to undertake. When I began to describe this in the previous paragraph I used the word 'unconscious' and I meant this to be taken with some of its technical force. Foucault's objective is to try to make this process of the construction of epochs and historical continuities operate at a conscious level, so that there is an awareness of the necessary exclusions that will emerge from any periodisation, discontinuity, continuity or historical epoch. The thesis of discontinuity is posed to bring this about, to argue that the world, life, the subject, history is fundamentally discontinuous.

However, subjects (*subjects*) constitute continuous categories, systems of thought and so on to decode a discontinuous universe in order to make it meaningful. But we must understand that this is something that we do as human beings existing at a particular epoch. Continuity, order and so on do not exist in the universe where we just happen to discover them. They are our creation and like every creation have their own effects, some of which are productive and some of which are not. In a discontinuous world we must do two things: create the local continuities which will allow us to undertake the kind of analysis that we choose; and undermine the great universal continuities that impede our work and lead to it becoming reified. Maurice Blanchot describes it this way:

> Now Foucault, when concerning himself with discourse, does not reject history but distinguishes within it discontinuities, discrete – local rather than universal – divisions, which do not presuppose subsisting beneath them a vast, silent narrative, a continuous, immense, and unlimited murmur which would need to be suppressed (or repressed), in the manner of something enigmatically unspoken or unthought that would not only await its revenge, but would obscurely gnaw at thought, rendering it forever dubious.[35]

For Foucault discontinuity is not the end of history, it is a pre-condition for historical work to be undertaken. It is the point at which one marks out a horizon and a terrain and undertakes a project as a subject. This in turn introduces the question of the status of the subject (*subject*) directly into the project and leads Foucault to a genealogical revaluation of his own work. So the archaeological Foucault opens up the kinds of questions and issues that I suggested could not be raised from within the epistemological and methodological framework of Lovejoy, Collingwood and Freud and that persists with today's intellectual historians and historians of philosophy. Yet even at the very first pronouncement of archaeology, we are advised that 'The problems of method raised by such an "archaeology" will be examined in a later work'. This foreshadowing of *The Archaeology of Knowledge*, in *The Order of Things*, entered the debate that was engendered by the publication of *The Order of Things*, which, far from serving to distinguish Foucault's work from other structuralists, only complicated the issue further. One suspects that by the time *The Order of Things* was published it had already reached the limits of the kind of analysis that it heralded. So much so that with the arrival of the methodological explanatory text, *The Archaeology of Knowledge*, the central conceptual construction of the *episteme* was already being abandoned by Foucault. If at one level this marks a continuing reassessment of his work by Foucault it is also clear that whatever the productive and polemical value of *The Order of Things*, it was restricted by its slide into universalising the *episteme*: 'In any given culture and at any given moment, there is always only one *episteme* that defines the conditions of possibility of all knowledge, whether expressed in a theory or silently invested in a practice.'[36]

   This definition of the *episteme* surrendered most of the gains that Foucault had made over both structuralism and the more general practice of the history of ideas. Worse than this, however, it was precisely the kind of terminological definition needed by those who wanted to read Foucault as a crypto-structuralist. In spite of these difficulties and to the extent that for Foucault archaeology represented a kind of history not practised in the traditional history of ideas, *The Order of Things* continued his interest in the way that history as a general discipline functions in our culture:

> History, as we know, is certainly the most erudite, the most aware, the most conscious, and possibly the most cluttered area of our memory; but it is equally the depths from which all beings emerge into their precarious, glittering existence. Since it is the mode of being of all that is given us in experience, History has become the unavoidable element in our thought: in this respect, it is probably not so very different from Classical Order.[37]

It is here we can see that despite the apparent failure of Foucault's structural analysis, the contradiction that it brings out leads him back to the question of the function of history for Western culture:

It is no longer origin that gives rise to historicity; it is historicity that, in its very fabric, makes possible the necessity of an origin which must be both internal and foreign to it: like the virtual tip of a cone in which all differences, all dispersions, all discontinuities would be knitted together so as to form no more than a single point of identity, the impalpable figure of the Same, yet possessing the power, nevertheless, to burst open upon itself and become Other.[38]

The more History attempts to transcend its own rootedness in historicity, and the greater the effort it makes to attain, beyond the historical relativity of its origin and its choices, the sphere of universality, the more clearly it bears the marks of its historical birth, and the more evidently there appears through it the history of which it is itself a part (and this, again, is to be found in Spengler and all the philosophers of history); inversely, the more it accepts its relativity, and the more deeply it sinks into the movement it shares with what it is recounting, then the more it tends to the slenderness of the narrative, and all the positive content it obtained for itself through the human sciences is dissipated.[39]

History then, according to Foucault, creates an origin, a place of birth, where what emerges is both a specific subject (*subject*) and the historical methodology that articulates and inaugurates it. In that the aim of *The Order of Things* is to raise the problems of history and historicising at the very heart of the sciences of Man, it is appropriate that Foucault concludes *The Order of Things* with the intersection of psychoanalysis and ethnology, and raises the impossibility of solving the paradox of the birth of the objective sciences of Man from the subjective historical anthropology of the nineteenth century.

If in these specific terms it can be argued that *The Order of Things* was a success, it was one that was to be revalued in *The Archaeology of Knowledge* where the question of history and the articulation of a methodology that would not be implicated in its founding function of stabilising a particular mode of the subject, the self-reflexive Cartesian *Cogito*, is further developed. It is consistent with these interests that Foucault begins *The Archaeology of Knowledge* with an analysis of the history of philosophy and the history of ideas, and enjoins us to suspend the old questions and their methods and develop alternative methodological techniques and different questions that will not allow history to become the founding principle of our own subjectivity:

The old questions of the traditional analysis (What link should be made between disparate events? How can a causal succession be established between them? What continuity or overall significance do they possess? Is it possible to define a totality, or must one be content with reconstituting connexions?) are now being replaced with questions of another type: which strata should be isolated from others? What types of series should be established? What criteria of periodization should be adopted for each of them? What systems of relations (hierarchy, dominance, stratification, univocal determination, circular causality) may be established between them? And in what large-scale chronological table may distinct series of events be determined?[40]

Referring directly to Bachelard, Foucault introduces into his analysis a critical terminology developed from Bachelard's programme.[41] He urges the consideration of a number of themes that indicate a changing awareness of his own theoretical practice and acknowledges the relevance of contemporary epistemology (as derived from the work of Bachelard and Canguilhem). This leads him to abandon any attempt to return to origins, a theme implicitly operating in his earlier work, and to turn instead to developing his thesis of discursive discontinuity. While this was one of the organising principles of *The Order of Things* it became absolutely central to *The Archaeology of Knowledge*: 'attention has been turned, on the contrary, away from vast unities like "periods" or "centuries" to the phenomena of rupture, of discontinuity ... one is now trying to detect the incidence of interruptions. Interruptions whose status and nature vary considerably.'[42]

Foucault sees this general pattern at work in both literary criticism and the history of philosophy, but notes the failure of these considerations to be taken up at the level of historical research,[43] and argues that whether it is a question of discontinuity or unity, the problem can be located around the same field that is demarcated by the document:[44]

> But each of these questions, and all this critical concern, pointed to one and the same end: the reconstitution, on the basis of what documents say, and sometimes merely hint at, of the past from which they emanate and which has now disappeared far behind them; the document was always treated as the language of a voice since reduced to silence, its fragile, but possibly decipherable trace.[45]

> The document, then, is no longer for history an inert material through which it tries to reconstitute what men have done or said, the events of which only the trace remains; history is now trying to define within the documentary material itself, unities, totalities, series, relations.[46]

Foucault then clarifies what had underpinned his early work and makes explicit the role of history itself, offering perhaps one of the clearest articulations of the aim of archaeology, which will become the foundation of the later genealogical studies:

> If the history of thought could remain the locus of uninterrupted continuities, if it could endlessly forge connexions that no analysis could undo without abstraction, if it could weave, around everything that men say and do, obscure synthesis that anticipate for him, prepare him, and lead him endlessly towards his future, it would provide a privileged shelter for the sovereignty of consciousness. Continuous history is the indispensable correlative of the founding function of the subject: the guarantee that everything that has eluded him may be restored to him; the certainty that time will disperse nothing without restoring it in a reconstituted unity; the promise that one day the subject – in the form of historical consciousness – will once again be able to appropriate, to bring back under his sway, all those things that are kept at a distance by difference, and find in them what might be called his abode. Making historical analysis the discourse of the continuous and making human consciousness the original subject of all historical development and all action are the two sides of the same system of thought. In this system, time is conceived in terms of totalization and revolutions are never more than movements of consciousness.[47]

This is precisely the point at which I suggested Lovejoy, Collingwood, Freud and today's intellectual historians and philosophers of history have a blind spot. It encapsulates Foucault's view of the function of history from Descartes to Hegel, where the sovereignty of the subject is located in the correct methodological application of the *Cogito*, which guarantees that the subject (*subject*) is the apparently objective and arbitrary outcome of the unfolding of history itself. The illusion of the free sovereign consciousness is only possible because of the use of categories that lead back towards the origin. This origin is a home, a place from which one is now separated but which can be recaptured in all its metaphysical glory through history. Foucault argues that the category of the origin must be abandoned, and with it the parallel categories of transparency, unfolding temporality, large-scale continuities and unities. This becomes the basis of Foucault's critical account of Western metaphysics, and in particular the history of metaphysics as represented by the history of philosophy, a history that has managed to divert the two major critiques of Western metaphysics that have recently emerged. These critiques offered by Nietzsche and Marx threatened major decenterings of the subject. On the one hand, this radical potential in Marx has been captured and reorientated by Marxist anthropology and the history of totalities which gives rise to Marxist humanism. On the other, Nietzsche is interpreted as a transcendental philosopher and his radical genealogy transformed into the search for the origin:

But the historians had long ago deserted the old fortress and gone to work else-where; it was realised that neither Marx nor Nietzsche were carrying out the guard duties that had been entrusted to them. They could not be depended on to preserve privilege; nor to affirm once and for all – and God knows it is needed in the distress of today – that history, at least, is living and continuous, that it is, for the subject in question, a place of rest, certainty, reconciliation, a place of traquillized sleep.[48]

The place of the 'tranquillized sleep' is the armchair of Descartes as he meditates in front of his fire. Archaeology and the now embryonic genealogy must act in order to awaken this sleep, to unsettle the slumbering *Cogito*, and to offer the subject no security, no home and no sleepy certainty from which to speak.[49] This is the most controversial aspect of Foucault's theoretical practice and is to be developed and argued for in greater detail in the genealogical texts. At first glance it appears that Foucault's view of the importance of the *Cogito* entails an uncritical adoption of the traditional divisions made in the history of philosophy. The periodisations that he utilises such as the Classical Age, Greek philosophy and so on, which emerge even more strongly in his latest texts, are those of the traditional presentation of the history of philosophy. It can also be argued that his objection to the force of the Cartesian *Cogito* is based too much on an acceptance of the familiar periodisations of the history of philosophy, and it is not immediately clear that it is enough merely to assume that the *Cogito* must be accorded a certain historical prominence which then can simply be responded to without any critical historical analysis of this pre-eminence. There is a certain ironic force in this, that one of the most profound critics of the founding role of history in Western culture adopts the portrayal of that history as it is presented in the traditional history of philosophy, and this is a point that I will return to later in this work. This observation is made not to suggest that Foucault's comments on the function of history and its relation to the subject (*subject*) are not to be taken seriously or are not defensible, but it also needs to be said that in Foucault's early work it is not always clear why the self-reflexive transparent subject is so objectionable that it needs to be undermined and destabilised.

Foucault's attempt to argue that *The Archaeology of Knowledge* is not a structuralist book is theoretically and polemically much stronger once the problems of historicity have been specified and he has shown us that the fundamental aim of his project is to unsettle totalities:

In short, this book, like those that preceded it, does not belong – at least directly, or in the first instance – to the debate on structure (as opposed to genesis, history, development); it belongs to that field in which the questions of the human being, consciousness, origin, and the subject emerge, intersect,

mingle and separate off. But it would probably not be incorrect to say that the
problem of structure arose there too.⁵⁰

At the beginning of *The Archaeology of Knowledge*, Foucault relocates his
work largely in a negative way around the problem of history and its
founding function, and makes explicit a renewed consideration of the
problem of the relation between the subject and history. This necessarily
leads him directly back into the history of ideas, and to the requirement to
spell out the archaeological method in detail in a positive way and to offer an
analysis of its benefits and difficulties, and this is to occupy the rest of the
book.

The Archaeology of Knowledge begins with a list of themes to be avoided in
the history of ideas, suggesting that one must first destabilise and unsettle
the hold of the following concepts: tradition; influence; development and
evolution; spirit; pregiven unities and links; familiar divisions and group-
ings; the *œuvre*; and two linked but opposite themes, the origin and the
already said.⁵¹ He then details his suspension of these categories, noting
that their point of intersection is that they all serve to overlay onto the
history of ideas, continuities and unities. Nowhere is this more apparent
than in the one example that Foucault uses in an exemplary way on a
number of occasions, 'the *œuvre*', where the history of the *œuvre* becomes
both the unity of the intentionality of the author thus validating the subject,
(*subject*) and the chronological basis that allows that same unified history to
be written. In adopting the category of the *œuvre*:

> One is admitting that there must be a level (as deep as it is necessary to imagine
> it) at which the *œuvre* emerges, in all its fragments, even the smallest, most
> inessential ones, as the expression of the thought, the experience, the
> imagination, or the unconscious of the author, or, indeed, of the historical
> determinations that operated upon him. But it is at once apparent that such a
> unity, far from being given immediately, is the result of an operation; that this
> operation is interpretive (since it deciphers, in the text, the transcription of
> something that it both conceals and manifests); and that the operation that
> determines the *opus*, in its unity, and consequently the *œuvre* itself, will not be
> the same in the case of *Le Théâtre et son Double* (Artaud) and the author of the
> *Tractatus* (Wittgenstein), and therefore when one speaks of an *œuvre* in each
> case one is using the word in a different sense.⁵²

This theme is enlarged and developed in the article 'What is an Author?',
but in *The Archaeology of Knowledge* Foucault uses the concept of the *œuvre*
to indicate both the force and the function of the unities and continuities
utilised by the history of ideas.⁵³ His methodological approach is tactically
to suspend these unities, expressly not to reject them out of hand as never
being of any use, but strategically to suspend their use:

These pre-existing forms of continuity, all these syntheses that are accepted without question, must remain in suspense. They must not be rejected definitively of course, but the tranquillity with which they are accepted must be disturbed; we must show that they do not come about of themselves, but are always the result of a construction the rules of which must be known, and the justifications of which must be scrutinized: we must define in what conditions and in view of which analyses certain of them are legitimate; and we must indicate which of them can never be accepted in any circumstances.[54]

An important distinction that is being made here must be emphasised, as it is one that has caused some confusion among interpreters of Foucault. Archaeology does not entail the abandoning of the categories of unity and continuity but rather the temporary suspension of their operation, specifically so that the security and slumber which they engender can be unsettled. Furthermore Foucault is suggesting that the categories in question are themselves products of the construction of discourses and as such they have their own history and a specificity that makes them relevant or irrelevant in certain circumstances, but they can never be allowed to claim an arbitrary or objective status. Foucault then draws a contrast between his project as the 'pure description of discursive events', and the concerns of the traditional history of ideas:

> It is also clear that this description of discourses is in opposition to the history of thought. There too a system of thought can be reconstituted only on the basis of a definite discursive totality. But this totality is treated in such a way that one tries to rediscover beyond the statements themselves the intention of the speaking subject, his conscious activity, what he meant, or, again, the unconscious activity that took place, despite himself, in what he said or in the almost imperceptible fracture of his actual words; in any case we must constitute another discourse, rediscover the silent murmuring, the inexhaustible speech that animates from within the voice that one hears, re-establish the tiny, invisible text that runs between and sometimes collides with them. The analysis of thought is always *allegorical* in relation to the discourse that it employs.[55]

Here in *The Archaeology of Knowledge* we see one of the theoretical contradictions that underpins the text. Foucault, in reactivating the phenomenological terminology of *Madness and Civilisation* and re-emphasising the metaphor of the incitement to discourse that it proposes, and then combining this with the metaphors of archaeology and allegory, raises a theoretical paradox. He demands the suspension of categories previously listed and the commitment to a surface discursive analysis, but the metaphors of archaeology and allegory themselves hint that deeper analysis be undertaken. Foucault himself is acutely aware of this possible phenomenological/hermeneutical reading and attempts to discount it:

> We do not seek below what is manifest the half silent murmur of another discourse; we must show why it could not be other than it was, in what respect it is exclusive of any other, how it assumes, in the midst of others and in relation to them, a place that no other could occupy. The question proper to such an analysis might be formulated in this way: what is this specific existence that emerges from what is said and nowhere else?[56]

This leads Foucault to distinguish between events/statements and facts on the basis that the latter are based on the theory of the transparent subject (*subject*) or some other principle of unity while the former meets the demand of maintaining the level of analysis on the surface, and the event emerges as a central category of archaeology.[57] It is the success or failure of this distinction that allows the above contradiction to be dealt with, and there is some room for doubt about this attempt to distinguish his work from structuralism and hermeneutics.

But if the question of the level of analysis is to unsettle some of the preconditions for the self-reflexive *Cogito*, it is not to be assumed that the subject is therefore banished from Foucault's work altogether. This is not the unequivocal end of the subject, nor the return to a wholly determined subject of discourse; it is rather that the pre-conditions of the subject are changed to become the pre-conditions of subjectivities, which returns us to the concerns that Foucault elucidated at the end of his career:

> The positions of the subject are also defined by the situation that it is possible for him to occupy in relation to the various domains or groups of objects: according to a certain grid of explicit interrogations, information, he is the listening subject, and, according to a table of characteristic features, he is the seeing subject, and, according to a descriptive type, the observing subject; he is situated at an optimal perceptual distance whose boundaries delimit the weight of relevant information; he uses instrumental intermediaries that modify the scale of the information, shift the subject in relation to the average or immediate perceptual level, ensure his movement from a superficial to a deep level, make him circulate in the interior space of the body – from manifest symptoms to the organs, from the organs to the tissues, and finally from the tissues to the cells. To these perceptual situations should be added the positions that the subject can occupy in the information networks (in theoretical teaching or in hospital training; in the system of oral communication or of written document: as emitter and receiver of observations, case-histories, statistical data, general theoretical propositions, projects, and decisions).[58]

Can this concern with the proliferation of subjectivities be reconciled with the analysis of the surface of discourse, while still avoiding the difficulties of other theories of linguistic analysis? Foucault thinks that it can provided that the methodology for the analysis is specified and that the programme takes into account the relation of the statement/event to the wider base of the analysis in discursive practice:

> Lastly, what we have called 'discursive practice' can now be defined more precisely. It must not be confused with the expressive operation by which an individual formulates an idea, a desire, an image; nor with the rational activity that may operate in a system of inference; nor with the 'competence' of a speaking subject when he constructs grammatical sentences; it is a body of anonymous, historical rules, always determined in the time and space that have defined a given period, and for a given social, economic, geographical, or linguistic area, the conditions of operation of the enunciative function.[59]

Whether Foucault is describing and theorising discursive practice, the statement, or even the archive which functions as a rather Kantian a priori,[60] the precise nature of the intervention that he is making always returns back to the status and history of the subject (*subject*) as it is represented in the theorising of the theoretical enterprises with which he is concerned.

In Part IV Chapter 1 of *The Archaeology of Knowledge*, he brings together some of the points he has been taking up specifically in relation to the history of ideas by contrasting the theoretical approach of archaeology with the traditional concerns of the history of ideas. In referring to archaeology as a machine,[61] and invoking the possibility of failure in a way not entirely unlike Lovejoy, Foucault attempts to spell out his objections to the traditional approach to the history of ideas and his alternative archaeological approach, arguing that there is a fundamental opposition built into the history of ideas. Either it is a discipline that draws its methodology from here, there and everywhere, never describing the history of a science but always the history of those disciplines that have never quite made it – alchemy rather than chemistry, phrenology rather than physiology. Or it deals with 'those shady philosophies that haunt literature, art, the sciences, law, ethics, and even man's daily life'. It becomes almost impossible to fix its limits, its boundaries, and as a discipline lacks any 'stability' or 'rigour'. Conversely, in attempting to describe disciplines from the outside, and dealing with knowledge through the medium of the system or the *œuvre*, it shows how bodies of knowledge are composed and decomposed, how they come and go, or are reconstituted in a new way.

The history of ideas, then, according to Foucault, is the discipline of 'beginnings' and 'ends', the description of 'obscure continuities and returns', 'the reconstitution of developments in the linear form of history'. It can therefore never serve to show the diffusion of knowledges, as it attempts to bring to life various parts of discourses that will be briefly constituted into a concretised whole. The issue for Foucault is that these two roles are overlaid on each other and coalesce to produce the history of the great continuities, of the permanent unfolding that is presupposed beneath the births and deaths which operate underneath the transitions from non-scientificity to sciences, from non-literature to the *œuvre*:

> Genesis, continuity, totalization: these are the great themes of the history of ideas, and that by which it is attached to a certain, now traditional form of historical analysis. In these conditions, it is normal that anyone who still practises history, its methods, its requirements and possibilities – this now rather shop-soiled idea – cannot conceive that a discipline like the history of ideas should be abandoned; or rather, considers that any other form of analysing discourses is a betrayal of history itself.[62]

Foucault attempts to distinguish major differences between archaeology and the history of ideas:

1. It does not treat documents, or thoughts, or representations, or themes as signs of something else. It is therefore neither interpretive nor allegorical, but is only concerned with how discourse obeys rules, and takes discourse as a monument.
2. It does not deal in continuities but rather takes up the analysis of specificity and differences.
3. Archaeology expressly does not deal with the conception of the *œuvre*. It can define the rules of discourse that run through a number of different works but 'the authority of the creative subject, as the raison d'être of an oeuvre and the principle of its unity is completely alien to it'.
4. Archaeology does not attempt to restore thoughts, wishes, experiences, nor capture the point at which the author and the *œuvre* exchange identities in an unaltered expression of the same before the deploying into discourse. 'It is not a return to the innermost secret of the origin; it is the systematic description of a discourse-object.'

Here in this definition of archaeology an embryonic genealogy takes shape as Foucault takes up one more issue from the history of ideas, the distinction between the original and the regular which emerges from a reconsideration of the question of continuity, and the identity of the author. Foucault suggests that the history of ideas has two attitudes to the question of discourse. It has to be either considered as old or new, traditional or original, normal or deviant. This implicitly involves two kinds of evaluation: that things are most highly valued or rare when they appear for the first time (which in itself implies the metaphysics of the origin); and that those discourses are just the repetition of the already said. The first view leads in the history of ideas to the histories of transformation, a slow progression from error to truth, of the waking of consciousness to the awareness of things as we know them today, which is typified by *The Great Chain of Being* and today's historians of philosophy. The second view leads to a history of ideas that treats discourse in the terms of commonality or regularity, where uniqueness is covered over, as well as temporal specificity, as they are measured, tracked, and made to become the measure of the thought of men, that can then be used to define an overall pattern; and this is the major technique of *The Idea of History* and today's intellectual historians:

> In the first case, the history of ideas describes a succession of events in thought; in the second, there are uninterrupted expanses of effects; in the first, one reconstitutes the emergence of truths or forms; in the second, one re-establishes forgotten solidities, and refers discourses to their relativity... It is true that, between these two authorities, the history of ideas is continuously determining relations; neither analysis is ever found in its pure state: it describes conflicts between the old and the new, the resistance of the acquired, the repression that it exercises over what has so far never been said, the coverings by which it masks it, the oblivion to which it sometimes succeeds in confining it.[63]

The Freudian technique emerges as a combination of the two. By the end of *The Archaeology of Knowledge* Foucault has provided us with a powerful critique of intellectual history, the history of philosophy and traditional historiography and yet this does not amount to a rejection of historical work. Indeed he has already begun to develop some of the embryonic features of genealogy. After *The Archaeology of Knowledge* his own work takes on a more historical aspect than ever, and to enable this to be undertaken Foucault develops the historical methodology of genealogy that he derives and refines from the work of Nietzsche.

I have been arguing that throughout Foucault's archaeological investigations, whether he was theorising in a mode similar to that of a phenomenologist or a structuralist, what distinguished his work from both was that he was preoccupied with the relationship between history and systems of thought, and the metaphysics that underpins it. This led him to the conclusion that the subject as *Cogito* occupies a pivotal place in this relationship. In response to this insight he began to develop genealogy as a historical practice which allowed him to deconstruct this complex relationship, its Cartesian pivot and accompanying metaphysics. This led him through his analyses of power/knowledge, the institutional regime, the body, and the ethics of self which both clarified his earlier endeavours and constituted a change in the direction of his work, a change that began with the *Discourse on Language*.

The *Discourse on Language* begins with Foucault's analysis of how the non-discursive regime functions in society and culminates with the inclusion of genealogy into his methodological programme. This parallels the introduction of a reformulated conception of power and the re-orientation of his work from what had become an almost exclusive interest in discourse, to a renewed assessment of the importance of the institutional regime within the history of Western culture.[64] If it seems that this repeats the work of *Madness and Civilisation* and the *Birth of the Clinic*, it is a repetition that corresponds to a theoretical transformation of his earlier work without correcting it, defending it, or attempting to modify it.

In the *Discourse on Language* Foucault continues his pre-occupation with discursive analysis but adds to this non-discursive elements. They are described not in terms of an opposition to the 'discursive' but are placed within a wider cultural field which produces a network of discursive and non-discursive practices that manifest themselves with different intensities. These include pedagogy, the book system, publishing, libraries, learned societies, and the way that knowledge itself is, 'exploited, divided and in some way attributed'.[65]

This process brings together elements in what will become a characteristically Foucauldian relationship: desire, power, the will to truth, knowledge, exclusion, and the role of institutional support. They are seen as threads which run through the discursive and non-discursive web and which combine to produce truth effects where the illusion of truth is sustained precisely by abstracting it from the network where its effects are produced. This serves to conceal what is invested in its production: 'True discourse, liberated by the nature of its form from desire and power, is incapable of recognizing the will to truth which pervades it; and the will to truth, having imposed itself upon us for so long, is such that the truth it seeks to reveal cannot fail to mask it.'[66]

For Foucault the configuration of truth and power/knowledge is a network prefixed by the 'will to', and is determined by the discursive and non-discursive struggle it constitutes, a struggle that in the *Discourse on Language*, is one in which the basic strategies are in the negative: exclusions, blockages, forbidding, prohibitions, and so on. Nowhere does this operate with greater intensity than in the areas of politics and sexuality. It is the negative aspect of the strategies of truth and power/knowledge that is reassessed by Foucault in his later work, in a series of hypotheses centring on the repressive hypothesis, which in turn relates to a concept of power that is revised to that developed in the *Discourse on Language* and becomes the beginnings of the genealogical method.

Towards a genealogy

Foucault's genealogical method is more easily described in terms of a negative characterisation; it has no recourse to metaphysics, it is not teleological, it does not search for origins, it is not based on continuity, and it does not seek either to establish singular historical meaning, nor to recover the essential truth and unity of history:

> Genealogy does not oppose itself to history as the lofty and profound gaze of the philosopher might compare to the molelike perspective of the scholar; on the contrary, it rejects the meta-historical deployment of ideal significations and indefinite teleologies. It opposes itself to the search for 'origins'.[67]

In the first instance genealogy must refuse to engage in the pursuit of the origin as this presupposes an idyllic time in the past which the present is now separated from and is attempting to recapture. The point of origin is supported by an 'Eden bound' metaphysics that imposes itself on the history of philosophy. Rather than attempting to engage with the metaphysics of the return, the genealogical method aims to make it visible, not by simply revealing what was previously hidden which would amount to a kind of hermeneutics, but by throwing light on strategic connections that have themselves become invisible with the passing of history. This is not simply a movement away from an archaeology of the discursive to a genealogy of the non-discursive, but a tactic adapted to rendering visible disparate concepts and events embedded by mis-history into a historico-ontological meta-physical unity that necessitates a change in the level of historical analysis. In the very process of inducing visibility, new connections are made, new tactics are revealed and opened up, and new objects are placed in relation to each other throughout the entire discursive and non-discursive domain. Without invoking methodological limits to genealogy Foucault indicates some of its central features:

> Genealogy is gray, meticulous, and patently documentary. It operates on a field of entangled and confused parchments, on documents that have been scratched over and recopied many times.[68]

> it must record the singularity of events outside of any monotonous finality; it must seek them in the most unpromising places, in what we tend to feel is without history – in sentiments, love, conscience, instincts; it must be sensitive to their recurrence, not in order to trace a gradual curve of their evolution, but to isolate the different scenes where they engaged in different roles. Finally, genealogy must define even those instances where they are absent, the moment when they remained unrealized.[69]

Genealogy is a method for analysing a history without a plan, without a teleology and with no essential continuity or unity – a history which functions to produce and induce an effect of any or all of these things from events, accidents, and coincidences that are placed in relation to each other. It is the inherent multi-perspectivism of the genealogical method that makes this function of history visible. Foucault argues that this is a function of history that has hitherto been concealed and with it the realisation that history is a struggle for domination.

A particularly dense point in this struggle is to be found at the site where the subject anchors itself in relation to the power/knowledge network. Genealogy reveals this through the principle of multi-perspectivism which refuses to proclaim the singular truth, resists absolutes, and shows us that the 'past' is an effect of a specific historico-philosophical method, and a metaphysics that is ultimately fragile and when shattered, shatters the subject (*subject*).

It is this shattering of the subject that brings the methods of genealogy and archaeology into a close tactical proximity. If it is archaeology that allows Foucault to specify the effect of 'history' in its construction of the subject (*subject*), then it is genealogy that allows the production of a 'history' that will shatter the unity of this subject (*subject*). In order to accomplish this Foucault attempts to reinscribe historical methodology with a set of criteria that emerge out of the play of tactics, strategy and domination, where knowledge itself becomes a particular tactic in the play of dominations that flow in and around the socio-cultural web of relations. This constitutes a war that may be fought out in terms of meaning, unity, interpretation, and truth but precisely what these categories mask is the combatants' stake and investment in power and desire:

> The history which bears and determines us has the form of a war rather than that of a language: relations of power, not relations of meaning. History has no 'meaning', though this is not to say that it is absurd or incoherent. On the contrary, it is intelligible and should be susceptible of analysis down to the smallest detail – but this is in accordance with the intelligibility of struggles of strategies and tactics.[70]

Genealogy uses the principles of strategy and tactics to expose the fact that all history, indeed all knowledge, proceeds through participation in a struggle of competing methods that produces coherence, unity, continuity and meaning out of countless accidents, coincidences, and chance events. The effect of this is at particular moments to authorise certain discourses, and certain speakers to articulate the 'truth' and conceal their own investment in the power/knowledge network. Genealogy reveals that the question of 'knowledge' has never been one of the search for the 'truth', but one of authorised discourse – of who could speak in a particular way, of where one was located on the power/knowledge network, of how one's status could be guaranteed as theologian, as philosopher, as an academic, as a radical, as a professional speaker and so on, which amounts to the recognition of one's place as a specific rather than a universal subject.[71] It is in fact not a question of 'K'nowledge at all, but rather a quest for knowledge that is played out on a terrain where what is masked, what is concealed – the self-reflexive subject – is fragile and is always at risk. By utilising the genealogical method, history can be forced to crack, split and fragment and with it the *Cogito* on which it depends. Established unities are dissolved, continuities broken, and the past multiplied *ad infinitum*, which fragments the historicity of being, leading to the dissolution of the subject (*subject*), and shatters the mono-perspectivism of history, knowledge and truth: 'It is no longer a question of judging the past in the name of truth that only we can possess in the present; but risking the destruction of the subject who seeks knowledge in the endless deployment of the will to knowledge.'[72]

This applies to Foucault's own work, that it is not to be taken as an *œuvre*, as the basis for discovering the real unified biographical Foucault, the Foucault that develops along an expanded or progressive theoretical trajectory. Rather each text should be considered a tactic that engages with a specific object such as medicine, criminology, psychoanalysis, prison, sex, the functioning of institutions and so on. Each text produces different effects, and reveals not a uniform theoretical vantage point, but, on the contrary, diversity, fragmentation and multiplicity. As the fragility of knowledge and truth is revealed it exposes a series of micro-relations within the cultural grid in which the power/knowledge network is deeply embedded. It is no longer a question of producing history from outside power/knowledge but of revealing what is at stake in such an attempt. A revelation which indicates that knowledge is not a struggle for Truth but for power.

So Foucault's change in the analysis of power from the repressive/ discursive conception to that of non-repressive/institutional mechanisms is a tactical one that allows a number of specific projects to be undertaken. He explicitly does not deny that repressive power remains or that discursive power does not still operate. His point is rather that if power is only conceived of as 'repressive' or 'non-institutional' this will have a number of specific effects on the kind of analysis that will be possible using these categories. This is an insight that for Foucault emerged from his previous work where earlier deficiencies are for the most part not modified, but are considered to have problematised a number of categories or method-ological difficulties that demand later consideration. So for Foucault what sometimes appears in his work as an inexplicable change of direction is the ·

result of the way a previous work has 'problematised' some alternative issue for him. It is this aspect of Foucault's work that poses a danger for would-be Foucauldians and is also the basis of an objection to his work. In response to a reading of Foucault that fails to come to terms either with the question of 'problematising' or Foucault's account of the operation of the *œuvre*, some defenders of Foucault have on the basis of the last book (whatever it might have been) presented a unified account of his work. This is an approach that discusses Foucault's work as if he is a phenomenologist or a structuralist or an 'inconsistent theorist of totalities'. There then develops an argument between these positions that allows a sidestepping of the fundamental intervention that Foucault claims he is attempting to make, which is to undermine the conception of totality, *œuvre*, author, subject and so on. It is by recognising Foucault's use of 'problematising' that one is able to read his inconsistencies more productively. Foucault's own account of this is illuminating:

> There are times in life when the question of knowing if one can think differently than one thinks, and perceive differently than one sees, is absolutely necessary if one is to go on looking and reflecting at all. People will say, perhaps, that these games with oneself would better be left backstage; or, at best, that they might properly form part of those preliminary exercises that are forgotten once they have served their purpose. But, then, what is philosophy today – philosophical activity, I mean – if it is not the critical work that thought brings to bear on itself? In what does it consist, if not in the endeavour to know how and to what extent it might be possible to think differently, instead of legitimating what is already known?[73]

Here Foucault is describing what he sees as the relationship between his intellectual and theoretical endeavours. Moreover there is a close connection drawn here between the Nietzschean project of genealogical history as an anti-mnemonics (counter-memory) with its effect of producing an anti-mnemonics of self which Foucault rearticulates as counter-memory. In the initial elaboration of genealogy he attempts to draw a very fine line between a critical historical practice – that is, expressly not a critique – and historical nihilism. On the one hand while giving up any epistemological claims to historical realism, it is quite clear from his case studies that Foucault does not give up positivist-based research. Indeed he is very much involved in obtaining a history of cohesive and coherently based events. The problem with both realism and conventional positivist history is at the level of epistemology where they are dependent on the metaphysics of exclusiveness in so far as they claim a direct relation to a presupposed absolute Truth, and a particular notion of the subject (*subject*). However unless the intervention of genealogy into conventional historiography is placed in a critical relation to the principle of exclusiveness and its epistemological consequences of realism and the *Cogito*, then genealogy itself becomes a foundational methodology that simply promises to become a universal method for writing the history of everything about anything. This would be an empty, politically useless meta-method, which would be inconsistent with Foucault's aims. Keeping this in mind and reminding ourselves again of the status of ethics in Foucault's project I will now combine my previous concerns and examine how genealogy as a historical methodology intersects with the destabilising of the subject at the point of the origin.

In the article 'Nietzsche, Genealogy, and History',[74] Foucault details his analysis of the 'pursuit of the origin'. He argues that in the Preface to the *Genealogy of Morals*, Nietzsche makes a distinction between *Herkunft* and *Ursprung*.[75] Foucault interprets *Ursprung* as the search for origins, embodying the earlier Nietzschean terms of Antiquarian, Monumental and Objective History, and *Herkunft* as Critical History which he will recast, and transform as 'genealogy'.[76] He then argues that there are three problems with the search for origins:

1. It is an attempt to capture the essence of things, their purest moments, which implies that at the end of it all lies some pure immobile form underlying a world of chance or coincidental effects. It appeals to some primordial truth, some original true identity under a series of masks.
2. The moment of origin is a metaphysical concept derived from the idea that things are 'most' precious and essential at the moment of their birth. That 'once upon a time', things were perfectly clear, good, and everything was known. Then came the fall – time, space and history.
3. A combination of (1) and (2) is that 'the postulate of the origin' is ultimately the site of truth. The origin becomes the place of loss, where the truth of 'things' corresponds to the truthful discourse – the sight of 'a fleeting articulation that discourse has obscured and finally lost'.

And to this might be added a fourth point derived from Foucault's other writings:

4. The construction of history as a unity, marked by an unfolding temporality, becomes the founding instance of transparent subjectivity within Western culture. Whether this subject (*subject*) is Rationalist, Dialectical, Positivist and so on, it is parasitic on specific notions of continuity, temporality, truth and transparency, and so on.

As a response to this search or return to the origin and its necessary engagement with metaphysics, Foucault offers the strategic alternative of genealogy. Genealogy becomes a history of descent, a history of articulating the differences and disunities that underlie the disassociation of self. 'Descent' does not go back in time in an attempt to retrace an unbroken continuity up to the present, but rather disperses history.[77] He then develops the concept of 'emergence', as an instance of arising. Not a continuous arising but a momentary instance, not the end of historical development but a transition between points that emerge momentarily from within the play of dominations and subjections. Genealogy and the history of descent do not seek origins nor offer ultimate meanings or continuities but only trace the play of dominations as genealogy 'seeks to re-establish the various systems of subjection: not the anticipatory power of meaning, but the hazardous play of dominations'.[78]

Foucault attempts to bring together the various elements of genealogy under the sign of 'effective' history, history that is without any reference to metaphysics, universals or constants, and from which not even the body or the subject escape:

> History becomes 'effective' to the degree that it introduces discontinuity into our very being – as it divides our emotions, dramatizes our instincts, multiplies our body and sets it against itself. 'Effective' history deprives the self of the reassuring stability of life and nature, and it will not permit itself to be transported by a voiceless obstinacy towards its millenial ending. It will uproot its traditional foundations and relentlessly disrupt its pretended continuity. This is because knowledge is not made for understanding; it is made for cutting.[79]

'Effective history' is the history of dispersal, of events, disruptions, and discontinuity and is a methodology that presupposes a history of chance, random events, and the analysis of the microcosm, the body and the nervous system – but above all it revels in its multi-perspectivism. It is a methodology that implicitly acknowledges the perspectivism of the historian's own path of descent and shatters the reflections of self as an objective, universal, neutral subject.

Foucault's attempt to criticise the use of the origin in the history of philosophy and its fundamental metaphysics appears to be well placed. It acknowledges the weight of that 'history' for contemporary culture, but it refuses to allow this to operate as a closure which would force the acceptance of this metaphysics as the inevitable condition of possibility for contemporary subjectivity. This marks a fundamental difference between the genealogical Foucault and the Derrida of *Of Grammatology*. Any attempt to synthesise these entirely different positions and the resulting tactics of genealogy and deconstruction into a unified conception of post-structuralist theory would be unconvincing and in many ways highly suspect. For Foucault the origin is a question of history, not an ontological necessity over-determined by metaphysics, which is itself but the result of a specific history from among many possibilities.

However, the overall project of effective history might appear at first sight to be opposed to ineffective 'bad' histories that sustain the *Cogito* and its relation to the origin. But this rather naïve characterisation of genealogy would be an oversimplification suggesting that genealogy be opposed to other histories. This oppositional strategy, which requires that historical methods be dichotomised into good/bad and so on, is not part of the conceptual approach of the genealogist. The point is rather that theories of history depend on, constitute and are constituted in relation to modes of the subject (*subject*). These modes can be specified and their effects reflected on, which enables alternative histories to be developed that in themselves affect subjects. Intellectuals both as the subject and object of the history which they constitute and compose, necessarily engage in their own ethics of self, which is the point where genealogy forces the intersection between history and the body. This becomes in effect the Nietzschean response to the problems of the kind of phenomenological analysis of *Madness and Civilisation*. At the one time, genealogy ensures an analysis of the materiality of experience without abolishing the question of the possibility of 'subjectivities', as genealogists specify their own lines of descent, which in turn become the very condition of genealogy.

Finally, genealogy does not entail either the abolishing of archaeology or even its strategic suspension. Just as archaeology allows a synchronous approach complete with the bracketing of certain questions, genealogy allows a long diachronous sweep and the problematising of the issues to be analysed.[80]

It is now appropriate to consider another aspect of genealogy. If Foucault's analysis of power introduced the materiality of the body into his methodology and at one level committed him to a thoroughgoing materialism, the most persistent theme throughout his work which I have referred to a number of times is his analysis of the subject. It is this analysis and the problematising of the subject that leads him to a continual revaluation of his own work, a revaluation that is incorporated into the principle of genealogy itself and has some resonances with Nietzsche's transvaluation of all values.

The transformation of the proposed history of sexuality into a genealogy of the subject continues this process and incorporates an approach to intellectual life that is the opposite of a dogmatic persistence in one's position, but it should not be confused with a subordination to intellectual fashion. It is rather a consequence of the concern to always address present problems; and it requires 'a studious, slow and arduous modification, governed by a constant concern for the truth'.[81]

At the heart of this is Foucault's critical assessment of the relation between history and systems of thought, the problematic formulation of the subject and the attending temporalities, continuities and unities that are constituted by historical research. This introduces his attack on humanism, for its refusal to acknowledge the possibilities of subjectivities other than those which it recognises as itself. Here Foucault raises the question of the will to truth and the complicity of the subject, the *Cogito*, in covering its operation, and he offers a clear proposition of the kind of political engagement he is attempting to make:

> In short, humanism is everything in Western civilisation that restricts *the desire for power*: it prohibits the desire for power and excludes the possibility of power being seized. The theory of the subject (in the double sense of the word) is at the heart of humanism and this is why our culture has tenaciously rejected anything that could weaken its hold upon us. But it can be attacked in two ways: either by a 'desubjectification' of the will to power (that is, through political-struggle in the context of class warfare) or by the destruction of the subject as a pseudo sovereign (that is, through an attack on 'culture': the suppression of taboos and the limitations and divisions imposed on the sexes; the setting up of communes; the loosening of the inhibitions with regard to drugs; the breaking of all the prohibitions that form and guide the development of a normal individual). I am referring to all those experiences which have been rejected by our civilisation or which it accepts only within literature.[82]

This attack on the subject (*subject*) becomes a double one through the application of genealogy, which is a destabilising form of theorisation that serves also to proliferate subjectivities in the course of its application. This it achieves by engaging openly with the power/knowledge network and manifesting both one's will to power and one's personal investment in generating the play of the will to truth. It is the failure to do this that for Foucault is the index of the failure of alternative approaches to 'history':

> It has been a tradition for humanism to assume that once someone gains power he ceases to know. Power makes men mad, and those who govern are blind; only those who keep their distance from power, who are in no way implicated in tyranny, shut up in their Cartesian *poêle*, their room, their meditations, only they can discover the truth.[83]

This is why Foucault is careful not to claim that he is writing outside truth, or, to use his terminology, truth effects/games of truth (*jeux de verité*). He is acutely aware that to make such a claim would undermine his entire theoretical practice. For Foucault there is no position outside the general distribution of truth and power/knowledge within society. Lines of distribution circulate power, truth and knowledge and validate certain discourses, certain bodies, desires and gestures, which then fold back on to the subject (*subject*) and make manifest the self as experienced. This process of distribution can be analysed, but only from the inside out, not the outside in.

At the end of Foucault's career he reassessed the question of the effect of power on subjects by problematising the subject itself. Problematising stresses both that genealogies can only emerge from questions raised out of the present context and that it necessarily involves the revaluation of one's own theoretical practice:

> Problematisation does not mean the representation of a pre-existing object, nor the creation by discourse of an object which does not exist. It is the whole set of discursive and non-discursive practices which causes something to enter the game of truth and falsity, and constitutes it as an object of thought (whether this be in the form of moral reflection, scientific knowledge, political analysis, etc). . . . In the first case it was on the whole a question of knowing how one 'governed' the mad; now it is how one 'governs' oneself.[84]

This governing of oneself becomes also the basis of a personal intellectual ethics. An ethics that commits one to a continual re-evaluation of one's own work, and an ongoing engagement with 'games of truth' which become the horizon of possible subjectivising:

> Writing a book is a certain way of abolishing the preceding one. Finally one perceives – to one's comfort and dismay – that what one has done is fairly close to what one has already written. . . . To be both an academic and an intellectual is to attempt to bring into play a kind of knowledge and analysis which is taught and accepted in the university, in such a way as to modify not only the thought of others but also one's own. This work of modifying one's own thought and that of others seems to me the *raison d'être* of intellectuals.[85]

One last point needs to be established, the difference between genealogy, presentism and relativism. Presentism appears in two familiar versions in the philosophy of history. First, in an extreme form where one takes a contemporary issue and then locates its origins in a past historical epoch and traces its unfolding on to the present day. This is not the practice of genealogy, which both refuses the origin and the unfolding of long temporal sequences and involves quite a different practice altogether. Secondly, presentism can be presented as a theory for providing the basis for a specific kind of historical enquiry. This does not suppose the origin of the present in the past, but rather is simply concerned with discussing how contemporary issues have been shaped, and how previous cultures have dealt with problems that appear to be similar to our own. It is possible that this second kind of presentism is close to genealogical practice and that

Discipline and Punish falls into this category. However, such an argument must be accepted with some caution in view of the emphasis that genealogy places on its critical intervention into epistemology. If this weaker form of presentism still relies on the 'real' recoverable past and has a *Cogito* as its theoretical underpinning, it would still not fall into the category of genealogy but would be rather more like those cyclical histories of Toynbee. While they entail no obvious attempt to capture the origin of the present in the past they are structured by theoretical realism and the transparent subject.

The question of relativism also emerges out of this same problem. It is sometimes argued that because genealogy gives up a claim to Truth with a capital 'T', or even some sort of weak historical realism, in the end all histories are equally viable and it becomes impossible to distinguish the value of one from another. This view makes two errors. Far from being unable to choose between histories, genealogists are forced to acknowledge the politics of all historical interpretations and assess a response to them on this basis. Rather than all histories being accepted as of equal value, each will be analysed by the genealogist in terms of its relation to both its politics and the function it has within ongoing struggles of domination. This demands an ethical perspective that will not allow no choice to be made but insists on a continuing engagement with political practices that emerge at the local level of tactics and strategy. The second error being made with the relativist charge against genealogy is in confusing methodological scepticism with relativism. Methodological scepticism demands only the suspension of belief in the categories that one is analysing at a particular time, but not necessarily a permanent and ongoing refusal of them.

Foucault does not argue that theoretical categories should be rejected out of hand; rather he utilises methodological scepticism to enable 'problematising' to be undertaken which can then be used to transform the original theme under analysis. In the *History of Sexuality, vol. 1*, he does not suggest that repression does not operate in our culture or that power does not emanate from the State, but that these interpretations block out other possible ones that would unmask the dominating effect of those with which we are familiar. Methodological scepticism allows the revelation of other possibilities and with them the end of the hegemonic effects of already established interpretations. Furthermore the suspension of truth as an absolute category does not entail its total rejection: 'What I try to write is the history of the relations between thought and truth, the history of thought insofar as it is thought of truth. Only the simple minded can say that for me truth does not exist.'[86]

Of course there are problems with genealogy, not the least of which is that Foucault's repeated retheorising and honing of it ceased with his untimely death. Often at the level of metaphor there are signs of Foucault's entrapment within theoretical perspectives that were the object of his genealogies. The metaphor of the tool box, the reference to knowledge as not being 'made for understanding but for cutting', and the place of the sovereign subject in Foucault's work, all contain resonances to psychoanalytic theory. Whether this is a function of genealogy itself or just its first faltering steps remains to be seen, but at the present time it is fair to say that genealogy is still seeking appropriate metaphors for describing itself.

But difficulties with genealogy go beyond the level of metaphor.

1. On occasions it might be difficult to meet the demand of genealogy to draw a fine line between critical historical practice and historico-nihilism.

2. More significantly, there is always a danger that genealogy and archaeology become foundational methodologies that begin to take on the form of universal categories. As such they would merely repeat the structures of the methodologies that they are criticising.

3. If it is forgotten by genealogists that the object of their genealogy is not the 'real' of history but the representation that a theory/methodology has of its own history, the 'events' based positivism of genealogy simply repeats the 'facts' based positivism of the realist and enters into the trap of realism and metaphysics. This would only serve to reinforce the universal subject and the genealogical study would be accepted or rejected solely on the basis of its historical accuracy. This problem was made clear by Foucault himself in *Discipline and Punish*, a text where perhaps he failed to stipulate clearly that the object of that particular genealogical intervention was not the 'real' history of prisons in the nineteenth century, but the history of internment and criminology as it is represented within penology.

4. Foucault's main argument against realism and the self-reflexive subject is that their exclusiveness is restrictive. This can be seen to imply that proliferation of theoretical perspectives is a 'good' thing in itself. Although I have some sympathy with this view, it allows Foucault at times to fail to engage with actual realist/*Cogito* arguments but to depend on creating a more general feeling that exclusiveness is somehow fundamentally bad. While one must take into account his view that not only is he opposed to the exclusiveness of the self-reflexive *Cogito* but also its inability to critically assess its own epistemological and methodological history, it must also be noted that other intellectual historians and historians of philosophy such as Collingwood are more successful than Foucault in a direct engagement with realism.

5. Some doubts remain about Foucault's ready acceptance of certain

periodisations – for example the Classical Age and the role of Descartes – that are apparently adopted uncritically from the traditional history of philosophy.

Whilst these cautions and problems must be kept in mind they do not sound the death-knell of genealogy. This is largely because there is no reason why these uncertainties cannot be incorporated into the genealogical method itself and used to destabilise and problematise its own foundations. This would then ensure that genealogy is not allowed to adopt that certainty, smugness and complacency that it is anxious to disturb and unsettle in those theoretical practices to which it applies its critical methodology.

In the context of Foucault's genealogical work it is important to make one last point. The adoption of genealogy in the first instance does not require the abandonment of the work of other intellectual historians, historians of philosophy and historians of ideas but only a temporary suspension of some of the categories that they utilise and an awareness of the limitations of their epistemology and methodological practices. This will be enough to allow the genealogical method to be engaged.

Power/knowledge

When Foucault was reflecting on his work towards the end of his career he described it in the following way:

> What I have studied are the three traditional problems: (1) What are the relations we have to truth through scientific knowledge, to those 'truth games' which are so important in civilization and in which we are both the subject and the object: (2) What are the relationships we have to others through those strange strategies and power relationships: And (3) what are the relationships between truth, power and self. I would like to finish with this question: What could be more classic than these questions and systematic than the evolution through questions one, two, and three and back to the first? I am just at this point.[87]

In this way, Foucault situated his work around three relations: to truth games; to others; and to self. Each represents a drawing of the subject: the subject of science, the subject of power and the subject of techniques of self. Collectively they constitute a diagram – a diagram of the contemporary experience of oneself as a subject. So the subject as experienced does not exist in a substantive space that would allow it to claim priority over the knowledge it has of itself. On the contrary the subject is nothing but a mode of the experience of itself as drawn out, a diagram produced by the interplay of the power/knowledge network. The subject is simultaneously both the subject and object of the power/knowledge relation:

> There are two meanings of the word *subject*: subject to someone else by control and dependence, and tied to his own identity by a conscience or self-knowledge. Both meanings suggest a form of power which subjugates and makes subject to. Generally, it can be said that there are three types of struggles: either against forms of domination (ethnic, social, and religious); against forms of exploitation which separate individuals from what they produce; or against that which ties the individual to himself and submits him to others in this way (struggles against subjection, against forms of subjectivity and submission).[88]

The subject is an effect of the interplay of tactics and strategies on the power/knowledge network which produces self-knowledge from the multiplicity of possible subjections. It is a component in the power/knowledge relation and a point of transfer, of interchange and conduction. This drawing of the subject by Foucault is a result of his analysis of the power/knowledge dynamic. It emerges out of a concern that major contemporary theories of society provided by both the Right and the Left share at a general level some fundamental assumptions about power. The Right see power as part of the Constitution and the role of the Sovereign – that is in juridical terms, the terms of the Law, sentencing, judging and so on. The Left view power as being primarily embodied in the State apparatus, the police, the army, the bureaucracy and so on. Both positions conceive of power as a pyramid, whereby power is most intense and dense at the top of pyramid and filters down from the apex to lower levels. In these terms power is conceived of as an object that can be obtained and then used to oppress or liberate.

Foucault offers a number of working hypotheses on power that are elaborated in order to allow power to be conceived of in a different way to the previous model:

1. Power is co-extensive with the social domain. There is no realm outside power nor are there any spaces in its network where some 'primal liberty' or 'freedom' exists.
2. Relations of power are interwoven with other kinds of relations, such as production, kinship, family, sexuality and so on.
3. These relations do not act simply on the model of repression, prohibition and punishment but are also productive and are multiple in their form.
4. The interconnections of power relations mark out general conditions of domination and this domination is organised into a certain coherence

and unitary form. In this sense power is local in its application but global in its effects. There is no binary division between the dominators and the dominated, or the master and the mastered – rather power circulates between them creating specific strategies, tactics and forms of resistance which are in themselves partial and yet able to be integrated into overall strategies.

5. Power relations serve, not because they are at the behest of certain economic or political interests, but because they can be utilised in strategies.

6. There are no relations of power without resistances, and these resistances are formed precisely where power is being exercised. Resistance to power needs not be theorised from elsewhere according to global strategies or universal political models – it emerges from the site power is applied, the body, sexuality and so on. Resistance occupies the same geography as power and emerges at multiple local and individual levels that can be integrated with global strategies.[89]

Power is not an object. It is not a thing that can be held on to and used for political purposes. Rather, power is a force acting upon the body, through a series of relations, relays, modes of connection. It is transmitted, it cannot be possessed because it is constantly in play, acting on individuals who are its conduits, its subjects (*subjects*). Individuals are the effects of power relations – as it circulates, is exercised and constitutes and composes.[90] 'We have in the first place the assertion that power is neither given, nor exchanged, nor recovered, but rather exercised, and that it only exists in action.'[91] 'Power is everywhere not because it embraces everything but because it comes from everywhere', it is in effect an interplay of relations that are intentional but non-subjective.[92]

One consequence of Foucault's account of power is that Truth cannot be separated from its production within power/knowledge relations. Truth is no more than the result of the rules in operation at the time and in the place that it emerges. It has no essential or universal component. This does not mean for Foucault that truth does not exist, only that truth is the effect of material processes. This is what Foucault draws attention to when he refers to games of truth, as he writes:

> Not a history that would be concerned with what might be true in the fields of learning, but an analysis of the 'games of truth', the games of truth and error through which being is historically constituted as experience; that is, as something that can and must be thought. What are the games of truth by which man proposes to think his own nature when he perceives himself to be mad; when he conceives of himself as a living, speaking, laboring being; when he judges and punishes himself as a criminal?[93]

The reference to games is not to suggest that truth is trivial or unimportant but rather that even the most fundamental claims about the truth of being, are produced according to rules, strategies and tactics that can be defined and analysed. This aspect of Foucault's analysis of power empties both truth and the subject (*subject*) of any metaphysics and makes them entirely 'things of this world.'

> Modern humanism is therefore mistaken in drawing this line between knowledge and power. Knowledge and power are integrated with one another, and there is no point in dreaming of a time when knowledge will cease to depend on power; this is just a way of reviving humanism in a utopian guise. It is not possible for power to be exercised without knowledge, it is impossible for knowledge not to engender power.[94]

A consequence of this for Foucault is the impossibility of undertaking productive political or theoretical action on the basis of the truth/ideology distinction, which eliminates both a liberal humanist politics and a Marxist politics of historical materialism.

Therefore, from the early pages of the Introduction to this work, where I argued that intellectual history, history of philosophy and the history of ideas were unable to critically raise the question of the history of the subject (*subject*) from within their shared paradigm, Foucault has created an opening whereby this work can be undertaken by analysing the ways in which people constitute themselves as subjects (*subjects*) against the background of the distribution of power/knowledge through the social domain.[95] This task can only be undertaken by participating in a rigorous methodological nominalism from which nothing is initially allowed to escape. Foucault referred to his nominalism on a number of occasions and many of his exegetes have noted this.[96] But at the same time he is careful to distinguish his nominalism from the extreme nominalism where discourse is just 'wind':

> Well, it is the interest I have in modes of discourse, that is to say, not so much in the linguistic structure which makes such a series of utterances possible, but rather the fact that we live in a world in which things have been said. These spoken words in reality are not, as people tend to think, a wind that passes without leaving a trace, but in fact, diverse as are the traces, they do remain. We live in a world completely marked by, all laced with, discourse, that is to say, utterances which have been spoken, of things said, of affirmations, interrogations, of discourses which have already occurred. To that extent, the historical world in which we live cannot be dissociated from all the elements of discourse which have inhabited this world and continue to live in it as the economic process, the demographic, etcetera, etcetera. Thus spoken language, as a language that is already present, in one way or another

determines what can be said afterward either independent of or within the general framework of language.[97]

Foucault's nominalism allows him to present himself as a draughtsman and serves primarily as a critique of metaphysics, essentialism and quasi-transcendental categories, but it is underpinned by a radical materialism.[98] Foucault can and does claim that power and truth are just words, yet he does not suggest that they should be ignored.

This returns us to the question of the subject (*subject*). There is no doubt that for Foucault there is no essential core of being or universal category, the subject that is referred to in his diagram.[99] In response to this it has been argued that Foucault's account of power relations and the subject (*subject*) rather than opening up new kinds of analysis leads to pessimism and irrationalism.[100] In this case an argument is developed that in Foucault's analysis the omnipresence of power means that human beings are victimised by the power/knowledge network and being unable to escape from it are doomed to remake themselves in a futile struggle. This presentation of power as omnipresent, however, can only be developed at the expense of misreading Foucault's account. We must recall once more Foucault's nominalism and that he presents us with different modalities of power: disciplinary power, pastoral power. Power has no *in itself*; it is an aggregation of different tactics and strategies, and individuals experience themselves in relation to these tactics and strategies. This is not a pessimistic view – but it is a profoundly non-essentialist, non-transcendental and non-metaphysical view. In fact it is clear that Foucault's schema does allow – if not expect – that change is possible:

> There's an optimism that consists in saying that things couldn't be better. My optimism would consist rather in saying that so many things can be changed, fragile as they are, bound up more with circumstances than necessities, more arbitrary than self-evident, more a matter of complex, but temporary, historical circumstances than with inevitable anthropological constants.... You know, to say that we are much more recent than we think isn't a way of taking the whole weight of history on our shoulders. It's rather to place at the disposal of the work that we can do on ourselves the greatest possible share of what is presented to us as inaccessible.[101]

But if we simultaneously dispense with essentialism, transcendentalism and metaphysics, then will this not just lead to an irrational world where all values are relativised and politics is left to the domain of the strong, where argument is replaced by domination and violence? This would remove from us the foundation of humanitarian politics as they are practised in the liberal state today.[102] A number of issues are conflated here that need to be extricated from each other.

First, Foucault is unequivocal in his denunciation of violence. He argues that in situations of extreme violence or torture, there is no power relation – precisely because there is no possibility of resistance. By definition, for Foucault a power relation involves a certain symmetry of action upon the action of others. In contrast to this, violence acts directly upon the body or on things – it closes or minimises the possibility of resistance and is directed toward producing passivity:

> a power relationship can only be articulated on the basis of two elements which are each indispensable if it is really to be a power relationship: that 'the other' (the one over whom power is exercised) be thoroughly recognized and maintained to the very end as a person who acts; and that, faced with a relationship of power, a whole field of responses, reactions, results, and possible inventions may open up.[103]

While extreme violence is always a possibility as an instrument or technology of power, a power relation by definition is a relation of action upon the action of another and does not incorporate this violence as part of its nature (whatever that might mean):

> In itself the exercise of power is not violence; nor is it a consent which, implicitly, is renewable. It is a total structure of actions brought to bear upon possible actions; it incites, it seduces, it makes easier or more difficult; in the extreme it constrains or forbids absolutely; it is nevertheless always a way of acting upon an acting subject or acting subjects by virtue of their acting or being capable of action. A set of actions upon other actions.[104]

Violence is to be opposed not as a result of an appeal to universal or transcendental moralities but because it is self-defeating and limiting. It limits the possibility of the self-creation for both self and other as it endlessly repeats the cycle of oppressor and victim and erases the proliferation of possible resistances that would enable one to make the choice to constitute themselves – as Other.

Power necessarily involves the possibility of freely made choices and therefore violence is not supported within the Foucauldian ethical paradigm. But if we grant him this, then is not moral relativism and irrationalism still implicit in his account? This would be an appropriate reading only if one elides Foucault's nominalist and diagrammatic perspective. Foucault does not suggest it is bad to live a rational life: only that it is dangerous to treat discourse as if it had an essential foundation. It is not therefore a question of choosing rationality or irrationality, which is posed as a false choice – as if one must take the side of one or the other. It is a question of how one lives one's life. What are the actual choices made? In what way is one's discourse caught up in the power/knowledge network?

I think that the central issue of philosophy and critical thought since the eighteenth century has always been, still is, and will, I hope, remain the questions *What* is this reason that we use? What are its historical effects? What are its limits, and what are its dangers? How can we exist as rational beings, fortunately committed to practicing a rationality that is unfortunately crisscrossed by intrinsic dangers? One should remain as close to this question as possible, keeping in mind that it is both central and extremely difficult to resolve. In addition, if it is extremely dangerous to say that Reason is the enemy that should be eliminated, it is just as dangerous to say that any critical questioning of this rationality risks sending us into irrationality. One should not forget – and I'm not saying this in order to criticize rationality, but in order to show how ambiguous things are – it was on the basis of the flamboyant rationality of social Darwinianism that racism was formulated, becoming one of the most enduring and powerful ingredients of Nazism. This was, of course, an irrationality, but an irrationality that was at the same time, after all, a certain form of rationality.[105]

Foucault illustrates this even more succinctly elsewhere:

My point is not that everything is bad, but that everything is dangerous, which is not exactly the same as bad. If everything is dangerous, then we always have something to do. So my position leads not to apathy but to a hyper- and pessimistic activism.[106]

But on what basis can action be incited within Foucault's schema? Only on the basis of self-knowledge. That is, in making oneself the object of one's work, one's *corpus*.[107] This means nothing less than an ethics of self by drawing out our differences and similarities with other epochs and then making of them a diagram with which to think ourselves differently in the present. This task can only be undertaken within the already said, within the existing relations of power/knowledge that open up their own tactics and strategies. As there is no normative or universal code we can refer to by way of some shorthand but instantly understood language, we are compelled to undertake the never ending task of re-formulating and reconstituting ourselves as a subject (*subject*). It is true that the wins and losses will be at the capillary level, and that their relation to the more diffuse practices that are embodied in power/knowledge may be unpredictable or even unintended, but it is also true that the disasters will perhaps also be small and experienced at a local and capillary level and will act to diffuse the globalising schemas of intellectuals of totality.

Furthermore if there is no essential, transcendental or metaphysical subject, and if subjects (*subjects*) are constituted in terms of the relations they have to themselves, which are in turn produced out of a range of knowledges/power, tactics and strategies, then a valid object of research for a historian of the present is precisely to give consideration to the possible ways in which human beings constitute themselves as subjects through modes of subjectivisation:

> I tried to locate three major types of problems: the problem of truth, the problem of power, and the problem of individual conduct. These three domains of experience can only be understood in relation to each, not independently. What bothered me about the previous books is that I considered the first two experiences without taking the third one into account. By bringing to light this third experience, it seemed to provide a kind of guiding thread which, in order to justify itself, did not need to resort to somewhat rhetorical methods of avoiding one of the three fundamental domains of experience.[108]

Two questions remain: What are the modes of subjectivisation in the present? How can an analysis be undertaken which would allow being to be thought differently? These points graph a project that is firmly locked into the present, while utilising an historical method to undertake a problematization of self-as-Other possibility.

Discipline and Punish and *The History of Sexuality, vol. 1: An introduction* are both part of this project and they chart aspects of the modalities of power/knowledge, such as policing, governmentality, disciplinary techniques, etc., through which we constitute ourselves as subjects in the Modern age.[109] They are part of the analytic of the present. The *Use of Pleasure* and *Care of Self* operate on a different series of registrations as they examine the theme of how the Greeks and early Christians constituted and problematised themselves as subjects (*subjects*). This is presented as a measure of difference and dissimilarity with modern subjectivisation as well as in terms of continuities and similarities. This difference is posed not as an origin but as a possible opening for thinking the present differently.

As part of this work Foucault had begun to develop an informed perspective on the Middle Ages and, as is well known, had prepared but not published a work on this epoch. He was particularly interested in pastoral power and the role of confession in the Middle Ages in so far as they express a relation with oneself. The inquiry with which I am now engaged makes a modest attempt to participate in this project of a genealogy of the subject (*subject*). This work does not however stand in the place of Foucault's announced *Confessions of the Flesh*, which one hopes will eventually see the light of day.

I have argued in each of the preceding chapters that intellectual history, the history of philosophy and the history of ideas are unwilling or unable to analyse the role of the *Cogito* in their own methodological foundations and that they refer to a subject (*subject*) underpinned by either metaphysics, essentialism or a quasi-transcendentalism. But notwithstanding this it is also clear that it is possible that existentialist subjects, phenomenological subjects, Freudian subjects, *Cogitos*, materially exist as a reality-reference in the experiences of people's everyday relations with themselves. Foucault's argument is that they are effects of the power/knowledge network and it is precisely because of this that change is possible even at the most fundamental level of what we imagine to be our being:

> You see, that's why I really work like a dog and I worked like a dog all my life. I am not interested in the academic status of what I am doing because my problem is my own transformation. That's the reason also why, when people say, 'Well, you thought this a few years ago and now you say something else,' my answer is, [*Laughter*] 'Well, do you think I have worked like that all those years to say the same thing and not to be changed?' This transformation of one's self by one's own knowledge is, I think, something rather close to the aesthetic experience. Why should a painter work if he is not transformed by his own painting?[110]

In the next two parts of this inquiry I present a sketch of aspects of the technology of self in the Middle Ages. Each overlaps with the other and together they constitute a diagram of a moment when a fundamental reorientation of power/knowledge led to subjects (*subjects*) experiencing themselves in a novel way. With this in mind, perhaps Foucault's methodological themes need to be reframed before the work can be commenced:

> As a context, we must understand that there are four major types of these 'technologies', each a matrix of practical reason: (1) technologies of production, which permit us to produce, transform, or manipulate things; (2) technologies of sign systems, which permit us to use signs, meanings, symbols, or signification; (3) technologies of power, which determine the conduct of individuals and submit them to certain ends or domination, an objectivizing of the subject; (4) technologies of the self, which permit individuals to effect by their own means or with the help of others a certain number of operations on their own bodies and souls, thoughts, conduct, and way of being, so as to transform themselves in order to attain a certain state of happiness, purity, wisdom, perfection, or immortality.[111]

Is it only a moment of forgetful historicism that allows one confidently to write *Cogito?* where the subject (*subject*) is – neither placed under erasure, nor underneath the bar or delimited by a hyphen, but – put into question? This remains to be seen.

·3·

A diagram of the Middle Ages

The politics of primogeniture

The geographical location of this sketch and its chronology are narrowly defined. The epoch under consideration is roughly speaking from the tenth to the twelfth century and the geography is for most part north-western Europe. Both the chronology and the geography have enabled me to use the invaluable work of the *Annales* historians and in particular Georges Duby.[1] Key moments are marked by the circulation of the romances of Chrétien De Troyes, Abelard's *Historia Calamitatum*, Gottfried Von Strassburg's *Tristan*, the Fourth Lateran Council of 1215 and the consolidation of primogeniture as the dominant system of inheritance.

Historians suggest that with the collapse of the Roman Empire in the fifth century AD an essentially Germano-Celtic tribal, clan and retinue form of social organisation came to the forefront of social life. It found expression in multiple centres of power linked in a network of diffused and often temporary alliances. Production involved a widely variable balancing of subsistence agriculture and animal husbandry, always overlaid with the possibility of immediate and direct profit from warfare. Fundamental to social cohesion and interchange were blood relationships and ties of kinship which geometrically inscribed individuals into something of a cohesive entity of largely common aims and interests. It is precisely these lateral horizontal ties of kinship that were transformed by feudalism into an hierarchical system under the emerging domination of primogeniture.

The codes and regulations governing inheritance were varied depending on the local custom involved. In 500 AD Salic law asserted that: 'Salic land is no inheritance for a woman; rather, all land goes to the male sex – the brothers. . . .',[2] and again:

On the death of the father or mother the inheritance goes to the son not the daughter.... When a man has a son and a daughter and the son marries, has a son and then dies, the inheritance belongs to the son's son, that is the grandson, not the daughter.[3]

The Burgundian code (476–516 AD) proclaimed: 'If any one does not leave a son, let a daughter succeed.'[4] Visigoth law allowed that:

Husband and wife could jointly administer land either possessed before marriage; land acquired after marriage was considered community property, and the wife could claim a share. Furthermore when the husband died, the widow retained control of the family property and the inheritance of her minor children. Girls inherited equally with their brothers, even when the parents died intestate.[5]

On the whole the situation was a complex one allowing for continual amendments and changes, the overall criteria tending to emphasise its origins either in Roman or Germanic Law.[6] If there was a general underlying principle it was that of partibility: an inheritance would be split among those considered eligible by local law or custom. The important point to be made here is that perhaps up until the tenth century, there was no single system of inheritance and social identification; on the contrary, the situation was one of wide diversity, from those suggestive of maternal descent, to those of exclusively paternal descent.

David Herlihy's study 'Land, Family and Women in Continental Europe 701–1200'[7] indicates an increasing tendency in some regions to use matronymic names from the eighth century through to the period under study. His data in respect of women as alienators of land suggests that in some areas of north-western Europe women as inheritors and controllers of land were not the exception that they had previously been considered.[8] There is some literary support for this suggestion in the Celtic text, *Culhwch and Olwen*, when on her deathbed Culhwch's mother says to her husband:

I am going to die of this sickness, and thou wilt wish for another wife. And these days wives are dispensers of gifts, but it is wrong for thee to dispoil thy son. I ask of thee that thou take no wife till thou see a two-headed briar on my grave.[9]

There is an indication here that if Culhwch's father remarries, control of the family's wealth and estates will pass to Culhwch's new stepmother to the future exclusion of Culhwch. Indeed there are many references to the Celts' preference for matronymic names – King Conchobor Son of Ness, Gwyddyon, Sentata-CuChulain Son of Dectere.[10] Moreover the Irish Celts trace their ancestry back to the Tuatha De Danann, the tribe of the Goddess Danann.[11]

While there is no evidence of anything that indicates an overtly matriarchal form of social organisation, there is more than a suggestion that matrilineal descent did play a significant part in the pre-feudal period. It is also interesting to note that within a patriarchal structure that characterises its descent in matrilineal terms the central locus of inheritance disputes will tend usually to be between nephews and uncles all claiming matrilineal descent along the same uterine line, with secondary conflicts occurring between cousins, brothers and sisters. Some awareness of this seems to be present in medieval literature right into the twelfth century.

A brief survey of some of this literature will emphasise this point. In the Arthurian section of Geoffrey of Monmouth's *History of the Kings of Britain*, we find the main protagonists to be Arthur, Guinevere his wife, Gawain and Mordred, Arthur's nephews through his sister Anna.[12] It is Mordred the nephew who attempts to usurp Arthur with Guinevere's compliance and in so doing brings about the final collapse of Arthur's authority. In the fifteenth century in Malory's *Morte d'Arthur*,[13] Mordred appears as Arthur's illegitimate son, the process of social transformation being such that the nephew/uncle revolt has been transformed into the father/son revolt.

In an early medieval form of the story of Tristan and Isolde, the main protagonists are King Mark, his wife Isolde and nephew Tristan, the son of his sister Blancheflor.[14] Once again these relations are characteristic of the avuncular revolt, the revolt of the patriarchal matrilineage. However, in the thirteenth century *Tristan* by Gottfried von Strassburg, although Tristan is usually referred to as Mark's nephew, there are indications that this relationship is undergoing a transformation: 'Now as you have heard Noble Mark, his unsuspected father, acted with magnanimity, and there was truly a great need that he should.'[15] Later on King Mark says to Tristan:

> 'Tristan come here! I swear that if you like I will be your father by right of succession. I will give you this revenue: my land, my people, and all that I have is at your disposal.'[16]

The prevalence of nephew/uncle disputes in medieval literature suggests an awareness of patriarchal/matrilineal organisation, and whilst Gottfried von Strassburg maintains Tristan's position as both nephew and son, the general transformation of the relationships of both Mordred and Tristan indicates that the rebellion of nephews is becoming the rebellion of sons. This literary evidence combined with Herlihy's data suggests that women as inheritors and bearers of the matrilineage were an active part of medieval life up until the early twelfth century. At the other end of the scale was the system of paternal agnatic inheritance: combined with a patriarchal social structure it was fundamentally misogynistic, as was suggested in the early formulations of Salic law. Only sons could inherit, the central locus of disputes being between fathers and sons. There is nothing unconscious about this rebellion: to kill the father is an integral part of claiming an inheritance speedily from the moment of coming of age.

In drawing out these two extremes one can appreciate something of the diversity of inheritance practices and social identification. Feudalism brought about two significant changes: first, the end of partibility for patrimonial lands, and secondly, the uniform preference for inheritance along the male line only. These two transformations hinge upon the increasing acceptance of primogeniture along the male line as the sole inheritance practice.

Carolingian efforts towards political centralisation had gone part of the way to achieving this by a range of different strategies. The general movement included strengthening the indissolubility of marriage, dissuading from concubinage, and encouraging the production of legitimate heirs from one socially sanctioned conjugal unit. By the end of the ninth century monogamy had become the underlying principal if not the absolute rule for the Carolingian household:

> The introduction of monogamy changed the structure of the family and the descent of property, at least on the highest levels of society. The conjugal family consisting of husband, wife and children, emerged as the dominant economic unit. Concubines did not have economic rights and children born out of wedlock were barred from inheritance when there were legitimate offspring.[17]

In effect the number of potential inheritors was reduced and legitimacy became confined to the monogamous conjugal unit. This general tendency towards centralisation and uniformity in legal codes and the intervention of the Church in support of its own aims acted against the interests of women as active political figures: 'Women made a dynamic and creative contribution not only to social life but also to cultural, political and religious life whenever church and state were decentralised.'[18] If this view is correct one would suspect that with the collapse of the Carolingians in the late ninth century women again entered social and political life until the fragmenting impetus of the early feudal period itself became centralised in the mid-twelfth to thirteenth century. David Herlihy's work would again support this view, indicating that the most significant period of women's involvement in land was between 950 and the end of the eleventh century, steadily falling throughout the twelfth. In this respect it can be seen that primogeniture played a central if at times unexpected role, but before detailing this and its precise relation to feudalism a few comments need to be made on the general situation.

With the collapse of the Carolingians, partly due to internal contradictions and partly due to successive invasions of Hungarians, Moslems and

Vikings on all European fronts, north-western Europe was again propelled towards fragmentation and local self-sustaining centres of power based overtly on military prowess. This is a time when once again fighting men, 'bellatores', came to the forefront of social life.[19] Local horizontal ties of kinship, and the mutually protective exchange of vassalage cut across the remnants of centralised hierarchical relations that had marked the Carolingian period. However, the period of invasions and the ensuing disorder was relatively short lived. By the early tenth century the invaders were beginning to settle; in 911 the Viking Rollo and his Northmen were granted land 'for the defence of the realm'.[20]

It is evident that with the end of the invasions and the subsequent disorder, these local centres of power, encompassing a militarised nobility developed by warfare, pillage and financial opportunism, were subjected to a variety of forces that had the effect of confirming these warriors as agriculturalists. The interplay of these forces is not at all clear but major features of it are changes in climate and improved technology. It would appear from climatological studies and contemporary documents that from the mid-eighth to the twelfth century the European climate became warmer.[21] The impact of this on agricultural production would have been quite dramatic, as even an increase in temperature of one or two degrees would have made ploughing easier, halted the expansion of the forests and rendered the clearing of new land a good deal less arduous. In this way more land became available for agricultural production.

To this we may add the possible effects of some significant technological advances: the use of the padded collar and new harnessing techniques, three field crop rotation and finally the rapid expansion of the watermill and its adoption into widespread use for tanning, brewing, iron foundries and so on.[22] The overall effect was one of an increase in agricultural production at the moment the nobility was denied the possibility of accumulating wealth by force of arms. As new opportunities became available, the increased potential of land became evident. In effect the nobility was confirmed as a manorial/seignorial class and control of land and those who produced its surplus became central elements in the feudal economy. This reinforces the resistance of the early feudal period to centralisation, a resistance that became naturalised in the military fief, formally hierarchised and granted for life only, but in practice increasingly becoming informally a hereditary estate, marking a continual movement towards dissolution and fragmentation. It is here that a major socio-economic contradiction emerges; the production of the agricultural surplus vital for sustaining the nobility could be obtained only with difficulty from estates so subdivided and partitioned as to become uneconomic units of production. Lewis comments on this in relation to failing principalities in southern French and Catalan society:

And in each of the cases which we have examined, disintegration followed hard upon the division of the principalities or domains in question among a number of heirs, a process which was sometimes repeated a number of times. . . . Under such a system no principality could last for more than two generations at the most; and all political power and cohesion were lost in the resulting fragmentation which took place.[23]

Herlihy notes another manifestation of this problem at the level of village organisation:

Some time before 1059, at the little parish-village of Sainte-Radegonde, probably somewhere near Bordeaux, this rising 'mix up of land' (*oriente permixtione terrarum*) so crippled production that the village was abandoned, the inhabitants preferring to flee to a nearby forest and to try their hand at a fresh start.[24]

It can be seen that the partitioning of land to an uneconomic degree had become a serious one. To some extent the problem could be solved by the consolidation of holdings by direct purchase, but the basic issue remained: partible inheritances. This tendency towards fragmentation from the late tenth century posed a serious economic and political threat to the emerging surplus-dependent agricultural community, and it is in response to this that we can recognise the importance of primogeniture as it cuts across society as a whole, bringing together a mutual interest, to end partible inheritance.

To recapitulate briefly then, in north-western Europe at the so-called dawn of feudalism, there were vestiges of a number of different systems of inheritance which interacted in an unorganised way, varying from region to region. The effect of this was to produce a situation in which there were interminable abductions and murders pertaining to inheritance claims and land rights. This was to have a profound effect on the development of and need for medieval judicial institutions.[25]

As the Capetians' fortunes rose it would not have been lost to them that part of the failure of the Carolingians had been due to internal disputes among potential inheritors.[26] Whether this directly influenced Capetian policy is not clear, but central to their dynastic aims became the association of a single heir which ultimately was to develop into primogeniture:

Every King from Hugh (the first Capetian) to Louis VII at some time during his reign was to have his eldest son elected or acclaimed and then crowned. In this way a hereditary monarchy came into being, in practice if not initially in theory, a monarchy that unlike that of the Merovingians and Carolingians, no longer was divided among the sons of each succeeding king. It goes without saying that this development was of supreme importance because, for the first time, the king could pursue a policy of growth and consolidation without fear that division of the kingdom would render meaningless any gains made.[27]

This policy manifested what had been a tendency for the noble houses in general, to reorient their genealogical structure agnatically. Prior to the ninth century blood relations were traced horizontally along either the male or female line; at the turn of the tenth century familial lines tend to be traced vertically:

> The change was tied to a new familial order, the key to which seems to have been the hereditary transmission of the new property. The sons, or one of them, inherited; then the holding became indivisible, in order to preserve it, and primogeniture was introduced to that end; linked to these causes, the others, the patterns of names given, and later genealogies reflect a shift of stress to agnatic kinship.[28]

Against the general background of a movement towards a vertical genealogical structure and the emphasis on hereditary right to titles and estates, the Capetians in their attempts to transform the monarchy into a hereditary honour were embodying a general tendency in their contemporary society. From a general principle of agnatic association, the right of the eldest son to indivisible patrimonial lands emerged as the political and economic practice of the Capetians: 'At every succession the eldest surviving son received the crown and the undivided patrimonial lands. Cadets were married well, given territorial acquisitions, put into the Church, perhaps given money or disinherited.'[29]

It was the ability of the Capetians to avoid the fragmentation of estates endemic to the partible system, that provided for them a consolidated and stable base from which to pursue their dynastic aims as hereditary kings of France. Clearly they were not alone in pursuing these kinds of policy, for although there were some local variations, in general a comparison with the great noble houses of Normandy, Blois, and Burgundy indicates the common practice of passing down the undivided patrimonial lands to the eldest son.[30] For both the King and the noble houses, primogeniture prevented the perpetual subdivision of their estates among their kin and provided for them a political and economic stability with which at times to confront and resist each other. Even for the more lowly vassals, primogeniture had something to offer as it became central to their aims of transforming the fief from a lifelong tenure to a hereditary estate, positioning them as local centres of power of some strength. This appears to have been a widespread phenomenon: 'In the whole of Europe, in the eleventh and twelfth centuries, the military fief, as we shall see shortly, was transformed into what was to all intents and purposes an hereditary estate.'[31] In all these cases, be it king, lord or vassal, primogeniture provided security of tenure to land and maintained its economic viability.

The material effects of primogeniture on men in the twelfth century were quite dramatic; as succession was invested more frequently in the eldest son and his lineage, it became increasingly strategic to prevent lateral branches of the family expanding in order to prevent inheritance claims that were antithetical to the principle of primogeniture. Duby writes:

> it is indisputable that the outline of genealogies shows quite clearly, from the beginning of the 11th century at the latest, the tendency for family lineages to adhere to a single branch, an axis by which, so it appears the eldest son succeeded. Though favored by stiffening solidarity between blood relations, and masculine privilege, and probably even more by the new developments of matrimonial custom, this process of crystallization appears however, to be more the result of a prudent limitation of marriages. Obviously all the brothers had the same right of succession, but they did not share the inheritance on their father's death. Only one of them married and begat legitimate sons.[32]

The young men of the noble houses found themselves playing a fundamental role in both the acquisition and disposition of land by the marriage policies of familial houses. Under the influence of a pressure to restrict lateral expansion, these policies revolved around a select few within the family group. The other sons would have to find an heiress, enter the Church, or simply accept being disinherited.

There was then created a class of landless young knights, denied marriage and inheritance within this patrimonial group, and sent out into the world in an attempt to find an ever-decreasing number of heiresses. This situation is characteristic of many of the romances. For example, in Chrétien's *Le Chevalier au Lion*, also known as *Yvain*, three times Yvain saves a woman in danger, who is the inheritor of an estate that on each occasion is offered to Yvain by marriage. When Yvain does actually marry Laudine he does so on such a basis.[33]

To this class of landless wandering knights another group was added. With the rise of paternal/agnatic organisation and primogeniture, one aspect of its Oedipal dynamic came into play, and violent disputes between fathers and eldest sons became prevalent.[34] In response to this the father who felt threatened would force his son to leave the patrimonial home until he recalled him finally to hand over control of the family estates.[35] While these men were not dispossessed in the long term, they added to the number of men wandering about the countryside, and if by chance they managed to capture a wealthy heiress and increase their future potential power over two estates, then so much the better. This situation has been well documented by George Duby, in his celebrated article, 'Au XIIe siècle: les "jeunes" dans le société aristocratique dans la France du nord-ouest'. His conclusion seems particularly relevant:

> Such was the aristocratic youth of France in the late twelfth century, a mob of young men let loose, in search of glory, profit and female prey, by the great men of the noble houses in order to relieve the pressure on their expanding power.[36]

With the increasing implementation of primogeniture as a uniform system of inheritance, women were dispossessed of land, the basis of some semblance of economic and social freedom. However, it would appear that in the short term there may have been some advantages for women, since where there was no son to inherit, the principle of primogeniture may have overruled the general atmosphere of increasing misogyny. In this context one must be careful to make a distinction between the transmitter of landed inheritances, and the controller of the land. Many women inherited in the short term, but their status tended to be that of temporary guardians of an estate until they married and the control of it was transferred to their eldest son. These women are of course the prey of the landless knights already discussed, Laudine in Chrétien's *Yvain* being a literary example. This does not suggest a high status for women, since they could not autonomously associate with knights of their own choice but were still subject to the marriage strategies of their houses.[37] Laudine can only marry Yvain after lengthy discussions with her lords.[38] In the long term, women were dispossessed of land; as dowries took the form of movable property and without control of land – in a society when this was now everything – one might ask what they had to contribute to a social structure almost uniformly under the hegemony of paternal agnatic organisation and primogeniture?

Perhaps all that was left to them was their procreative power? To this a new dimension was added, an intensive and excessive investment in the purity of the procreative blood, which was reinforced by the conscious strategy of lineage building. A detailed study of the medieval concept of blood is perhaps overdue, but in the context of this chapter a few brief comments are appropriate. Under the regime of primogeniture the entire future of the lineage was invested in the eldest son alone, with his claims to inheritance being centred on the legitimacy of his blood. If a bastard crept into the family line, the entire patrimony could now be lost. Legitimate lineage now became more important, and the blood of the mother herself must now be maintained in an unadulterated state and directed towards the primary object of ensuring the legitimacy of male succession. To this end, a woman's body was constructed as the container of this pure blood, awaiting the introduction of seed for the production of male heirs. Something of this can still be seen even in the thirteenth century when Philip Augustus, while attempting to obtain an annulment from his wife Ingeborg, was urged to make a distinction between, '*commixio sexuum*', mingling of the sexual organs, and '*commixio seminum in vase muliebri*', mingling of the seeds in the female vessel.[39]

An increasing awareness of the importance of the blood became central to the practice of the lineage builders. The Capetians themselves emphasised the connection between blood right and sanctity, a blood right which they themselves traced through the uterine line. The *Chronicle of Tours*, presented to Philip V in 1317, vindicates Hugh Capet's accession in precisely this way.[40] But for the lineage builders the procreative blood did not simply have to be pure, it had also to be fecund. For the woman of the great noble house, many of her children died young, condemning her to an endlessly repeated cycle of childbirth. Henry of Bourbourg had seven sons by his second wife; the eldest died childless, two died young, one lost an eye and was barred from inheritance, and two entered the Church; only one married and was left to continue the lineage.[41] Not only must a woman give birth frequently but she must produce sons, as daughters left to inherit would carry the patrimonial lands to the control of another household. Louis VII had taken three wives, and was married for thirty years before producing 'a son and heir' at whose birth he proclaimed: 'And that ardent desire, that God would give us progeny of the better sex, inflamed also us, who had been terrified by a multitude of daughters.'[42] For women who produced no children, or only daughters, repudiations and annulments were an ever-present possibility.

Primogeniture is one of the axes of the transformation of the power/knowledge network in the Middle Ages, and without privileging it as an explanatory category outside the moment of its particular specificity, some points can be made:

1. Systems of inheritance imply and constitute the possibility of particular legitimate social relations (including sexual ones) at any particular time. They are intense moments of transfer on the power/knowledge network.
2. Systems of inheritance are part of and stand in relation to any given mode of production.
3. Systems of inheritance establish culturally appropriate procreative sexual activity and imply, constitute and exclude a series of relations not only with others but also with oneself.
4. Systems of inheritance are a most significant point at which the individual is also caught up in the juridical system. They are a point of interchange, of definition by the Law.[43]

We can therefore draw out the effects of primogeniture as it became the dominating inheritance system in the epoch under consideration.

First, primogeniture necessarily excluded women from active participation in political life, completing a process begun by the Carolingians and reflecting an increasing misogyny. Secondly, it fulfilled the immediate economic exigency of stopping the perpetual fragmentation of estates to a point where they were no longer viable in terms of agricultural production. Thirdly, the inheritance of the one as opposed to the many claimants ended the interminable family disputes that had pervaded the early medieval scene. Finally, it became the central feature of Capetian strategies to consolidate their resources and supremacy as hereditary kings of France.

In this way primogeniture halted the fragmentation and dissolution of authority that I described a little earlier and linked in a common interest the whole of the ruling aristocracy from king to vassal. This interest is to be understood as a transformation of the power/knowledge network and not as a result of individual agents; in other words it exists in the domain of Foucault's diagram – intentional but non-subjective.

Primogeniture set in motion a series of tactics and strategies between the Church and nobility, as a result of which legitimate sexual activity became centred on the confines of marriage.[44] The Church involved itself on the basis of its theological expertise that enabled it to intervene in the dynamic of sexual relations concerning the juridical question of the legitimate procreation of an heir, while the nobility had an interest due to its great investment in preserving the familial bloodline because: 'The mere suspicion of promiscuity in the lady of the feudal household and doubts about the legitimacy of her children which therefore arose could result in interminable lawsuits and destroy a great patrimony.'[45] We can see developing a collective anxiety from a theological perspective about the pleasure of the flesh, from a juridical perspective concerning the identity of a legitimate heir, and from a misogynistic–political perspective about the dangers of adulterous women.

The result of this was a densely constructed campaign across the culture as a whole to ensure the permanence of marriage, as, under the dominance of primogeniture, adultery was not simply a sin but was profoundly transgressive and rebellious.[46] It threatened the demands of pure blood and incited husbands to control and regulate their wives' sexual practices: a loss of control which involved the nightmare of a bastard destroying the patrimony and infiltrating the future integrity of the lineal bloodline.[47] In this way the question of social and legal identity was powerfully constructed around the question of sexual relations. But this was primarily an issue of pragmatics that was concerned to establish before God and the Law the legitimacy of the heir – thereby fusing theology, metaphysics and law.

This culminated with the Church intensifying its control of sexual practices as a result of the Fourth Lateran Council, which in 1215 changed the consanguinity prohibitions from the seventh to the fourth degree.[48]

While the immediate effect of this was to increase the number of marriages that could be annulled due to consanguinity, in the long term it strengthened the stability and permanence of marriage. Although many of the nobility were related to the seventh degree, or at least could claim to be if a repudiation or annulment was required, fourth degree relationships were in the first case easier to prohibit and, secondly, fewer of the noble families were related to that degree. The effect of this was to shift the possibility of annulment from consanguinity to adultery. This was to be decisive as disputes concerning consanguinity required a complex and detailed use of genealogical literature and moreover did not rest on the actual sexual practices of the couple involved. However, an annulment centred on adultery was subject to much more economic means of control; it simply required the physical observation of the couple (usually the wife) and functioned totally within the marriage economy. The Church which had initially been interested in taking over control of the marriage ceremony, now became directly involved in regulating sexual practices within marriage itself. An interplay of interests between the Church and nobility hinged on the developing consciousness of adultery. On the one hand, adultery allowed the Church to enter into the regulation of actual sexual activity within the conjugal unit, while on the other, for the nobility it represented a serious challenge to their aims of lineage building and the preservation of the pure unadulterated lineal bloodline.

The Fourth Lateran Council also instituted 'private' confession as the annual practice of all Christians. This served a double function. First, it bore witness to the creation of a dialogue between self and self around the question of the flesh, where the priest is not the object of the dialogue but a witness to it and the ultimate arbiter of its meaning. It is less a question of the specificity of the sexual but more a question of identity – how one constitutes oneself as a Christian. Secondly, as Foucault has suggested, it problematised the relation of self to flesh – although it should be said that the details of particular sex acts find their registration not only in their description but in the certainty for both the priest and penitent that the penitent has come to a true understanding of the technologies of self through which they are constituted.[49] It is not enough that the priest knows the truth of one's being, it is also that the penitent knows that the priest knows the truth of one's being – hence the contiguity with psychoanalysis.[50]

Primogeniture is part of an extensive transformation of the power/ knowledge network in the epoch under consideration. A transformation of both productive and material life that produced its own set of problems, tactics and strategies from which even the subject (*subject*) did not escape. It led to the widespread dissemination of a novel familial structure with sexual surveillance at its very heart, and constituted a series of relations between self and other – priest, wife, husband, father, family, brother, children, etc.

These relations in turn were problematised and the possibilities of new technologies of the subject (*subject*) were established.

The politics of truth

It is a commonplace among medieval historians to write about the 'twelfth century renaissance.'[51] Moreover, there are a number of highly respected texts that adopt this category as their organising principle: for example, *Renaissance and Renewal in the 12th Century*.[52] But perhaps we should question whether the category of the twelfth-century renaissance is an effective one for the purpose at hand. The medieval historian John O. Ward offers us a convenient starting point for our discussion:

> I would propose that the anti-discourse of the non-establishment intellectuals of the twelfth century, situated outside or on the margins of the developing nodes, centres, institutions, of truth and authority, is what we have come to know as 'humanism', as the so called 'Renaissance' features of 12th century society. This is not the humanism of R. W. Southern (MH p. 29 ff, which is but another name for medieval intellectual life) but a proto-humanism evincing patterns characteristic of the later Italian Renaissance, a mixing of Latin classicism, polemic, linguistic and stylistic experiment, intellectual precocity and the beginnings – if accidental – of philological acumen.[53]

Here we find a strong statement about the nature and content of the category 'twelfth-century renaissance', suggesting that in the intellectual life of the twelfth century we find a number of features that are either proto-events of the Italian Renaissance or are similar to the extent that we can include them in the general term 'renaissance'. In invoking the achievements of the Italian Renaissance, by virtue of a metaphorical association, a number of themes are implied, the rise of the individual, the birth of self (and all that this usually entails) and others, that are features of many twelfth century studies. Two examples come to mind, *Self and Society in Medieval France, The Memoirs of Abbot Guibert of Nogent*,[54] and *The Individual in Twelfth Century Romance*.[55] There is a danger in all this that the power of the metaphor of the Italian Renaissance will overlay my twelfth-century concerns and over determine its representation. One might then finding oneself writing of actors such as Abelard and Bernard as great individual adversaries, our explanations treating them as if they are modern minds, rationalist and mystic respectively, engaged in debates that emerge from a specifically proto-humanist culture.[56] I have previously suggested in my discussion of Foucault's concept of the *œuvre* that this kind of approach is already embedded in discursive structures and may not necessarily lead to the most productive historical work being undertaken.[57] In this context Ward notes that the very category of authorship and its attribution to particular individuals largely arose post-twelfth century. In fact in the early medieval period, texts circulated quite successfully without having names appended to them, so great care must be taken when the role of the author is allowed to function in twelfth-century studies:

> They [medieval historians] have sought to identify possible influences, sources and antecedents for their constructed 'author', on the supposition that a particular 'author' might have read this or that, or heard it read out, and chosen to copy, incorporate, imitate, adapt it in the context of his/her own motivation for 'authoring' a piece of writing. Such a process leads them to establish 'novel' or 'pioneer' writers/thinkers, who are alleged, for various reasons, to have been the 'first', to read, copy, incorporate, imitate etc. a particular source or antecedent. On this basis they construct genealogies of things they, in their own day, think important, or, worse, things that nineteenth century scholars thought important. In so doing, they clothe the manuscripts or fragments that frequently circulated anonymously, or at best nominally and often erroneously author-attributed, with the full model of authorship, and reduce the cultural phenomena they are assessing to a conscious history of ideas based on the notion of the author as an inferred construct.[58]

Ward's warning is a timely one as there would be little point in allowing this study to offer a long, continuous, diachronic history that legitimises and temporalises those fundamental humanist categories that I was so anxious to criticise and destabilise in the Foucauldian exegesis. So it is apparent that I will need to establish another way of discussing those issues I will be highlighting and examining. A lead has already been given in the above quote from Ward, and which is continued here in more detail:

> The key to this 'humanism', however, is not so much a shift of consciousness on the part of 'an age as a whole', not a swing of the pendulum of fashion or whim, but the collapse of what Foucault calls the 'political economy of truth', the breaching of the monopolistic domination of literacy by the established institutions of truth – episcopacy and monastery, together with their schools and traditional aristocratic recruitment fields.[59]

This is an interesting and important conceptualisation for this inquiry. I have already discussed some aspects of the sociological basis of this in my examination of the effects of primogeniture on the young men of the twelfth century. But Ward's point is rather more significant, as he argues that what was at issue in the twelfth century was the control and regulation of an emerging discourse in a society that at the time was undergoing social change at a pace that was disturbing its cohesiveness. Crucial to this process was the widespread effect of increasing literacy, and if I adopt Ward's thesis, with some reservations, it allows me to open up the discussion and reorientate it in terms of the emerging discursive practices of the twelfth century:

> Put simply, literacy (in all its senses) 'created' mechanisms of power, which came to operate in the areas of sexual and religious attitudes (homosexuality, heresy), intellectual enquiry and state omnicompetence (Baldwin/Hollister p. 868). What created 'literacy'? This is in part a false question, but the following seems clear: the dimensions of competition in society from *c.*900 on were in successful process of continuous enlargement, and literacy, as a mode of control of discourse the potential for which had always been present and had indeed been utilized by the church and, through the church, sporadically by the state, was at hand as a complex of mechanisms, in process of effervescence due to the scale of intellectual dispute and controversy since the eucharistic and investiture controversies of the eleventh century. This phenomenon of controversy was itself due to the multiplication of the number and size of knightly families from *c.*1000 AD on, and perhaps also to the effects of primogeniture.[60]

Malcolm Parkes' study 'The literacy of the laity', charts the spread of literacy among the laity in the twelfth century, and he notes the expansion of literacy through the emerging middle class, down even to peasants, as the skills of literacy became increasingly significant in the emerging business economy.[61] This view is given some general support from studies that have analysed the distribution of documents, and it has been suggested that from the whole of Anglo-Saxon period only some 2,000 charters and writs survive, while from the thirteenth century: 'tens of thousands of such charters and writs survive; this estimate is no more precise because the documents have never been systematically counted.'[62] Even allowing for regional differences and the uncertainties of documentary survival, it is apparent that the twelfth century stands out as a period of rapid expansion of literacy and the fundamental skill that goes with it, writing. This amounts to a major transformation of the mode by which power/knowledge is distributed.[63] The twelfth century, then, has a peculiarly specific relation to writing in the history of Western culture, and this raises a number of important considerations.[64] Literacy demands the adoption of a number of skills not necessary to the non-literate community, and as literacy itself spread its influence, a number of new technologies for organising power/ knowledge were implemented:

> The great codifications of the period – Peter Lombard's *Sentences*, Abelard's *Sic et Non*, Gratian's *Decretum*, and towards the century's end, Huguccio's *Magnae Derivationes* – went hand in hand with new methods for organizing knowledge. And these were reflected in codices, not only in clarity of form,

expression, and genre, as well as the separation of text and commentary, but also in the design and functionality of manuscripts themselves. Richard and Mary Rouse note: 'Innovations on the layout of the manuscript page are surely the most highly visible of all the twelfth-century aids to study – such techniques as running headlines, chapter titles in red, alternating red and blue initials and the gradation in size of initials, cross-references, and citation of authors quoted.' To these one may add the beginnings of alphabetized indexing.[65]

It is also noted by Duby that 'genealogical tables' were designed to prove the identity of the individual as legitimate heir. In many ways the reduction of the consanguinity prohibitions in the twelfth century in practice, if not in law until the thirteenth century, made this process more certain and the resulting identity of the subject (*subject*) it composed more defined.[66] The *Decretum* also contained a questionnaire to help with the analysis of sins and the apportioning of their gravity and was part of a process whereby the mode of production of information and its dissemination was re-organised.[67]

As part of the transformation and redistribution of power/knowledge, two major discussions emerged in the twelfth century. First, how can the veracity of texts be established? Secondly, what is the relation between language, texts and the reality-reference?

Two examples from the twelfth century give us a sense of the importance of the issue of oral versus written evidence. Henry I was in a dispute with Anselm of Canterbury that could be decided only by the Pope. Henry's emissaries were three bishops, who returned (or so they claimed) with a privately given oral assurance of support for Henry, while Anselm's messengers, who were two monks, returned with letters from the Pope. As the two communications were contradictory some attempt to validate their authenticity was necessary. The supporters of Anselm argued that weight should be given to the letters under the papal seal and not 'to the uncertainty of mere words', while Henry's side replied that the words of three bishops should be relied on rather than 'the skins of wethers blackened with ink and weighted with a little lump of lead'.[68] The outcome of the dispute is not important, but it serves to illustrate the emerging conflict between written and oral testimony.

> The rule that oral witness is preferable to documents, like the rule that seisin is superior to a charter, shows how cautiously – and perhaps reluctantly – written evidence was accepted. Much important business continued to be done by word of mouth. Bearers of letters were often given instructions which were to be conveyed *viva voce*, either because that was convenient and traditional or because the information was too secret to write down.[69]

It is clear that on the first point of discussion the whole issue of the authenticity and the authenticating of documents played an important part in twelfth-century intellectual life. Given that many twelfth-century documents were unauthored and undated (at the very best reference may have been made to a contemporary event), the failure of any external temporalised chronology meant that establishing authenticity was often technically a very difficult task.[70] In the case of a will or a donation of land, this could be quite crucial:

> An outward and visible sign of wealth and a check upon the 'wrongful' disposition of property, it enshrines the wishes of the individual holder as against the demands of the potential heirs. It is in effect the written version of the 'dying words', the permanent expression of the deathbed wish. As such it became an instrument for the alienation of property not only to 'irregular' heirs (mistresses rather than wives) but also to organizations such as the church.[71]

Furthermore there is some evidence to suggest that literacy as a technological skill, and the problems that it exposed for medieval society had a considerable impact on the cultural patterns of the twelfth century, as a 'literate/written' consciousness, driven to be secure in its own identity, came into being. So what can we say about the general category of the 'literate/written' consciousness?

In his study *The Implications of Literacy* Stock argues that the twelfth century is a crucial turning point in the emergence of a literate culture and consciousness. He suggests that the orientation of the major philosophical and theological discussions around the central issue of the relation between 'language texts and reality' is an indication that there was already emerging a 'semiotics of culture', underlying a general methodology where: 'Phenomenal manifestations of meaning were looked upon as a series of signs and symbols which could be interpreted once one broke the code of their grammar, logic and rhetoric.'[72] According to Stock we can see this process at work in the *Monologion*, which is marked by its supposition of a widespread abstractly literate audience, so much so that it indicates that:

> The audience within the mind is in principle oral; the wider public is presumed to be dependent on writing. Through the latter, Anselm becomes one of the first authors to conceive of a reading public in the modern sense. Indeed, the assumption of an abstract audience helps to guide the presentation of his thoughts as the *Monologion* progresses.[73]

Stock argues that the 'reawakening to the potential of literate communication' can be redescribed within the terms of contemporary semiotics as the emergence of the distinction between *langue* and *parole*, which was organised around the distinction between:

an inner linguistic model, based upon Latin's explicit grammar, and common, at least in theory, to many members of a group, and an outer, speaking-capacity, chiefly associated with the vernaculars, which demanded individual performance and flexible social allegiances.[74]

Semioticians may disagree with Stock's association of *langue* and *parole* with inner and outer but the conclusion that he draws is an important one for this study.[75] He argues that the effects of texts being embedded on to oral discourse forced the culture as a whole to redefine itself by allowing the construction of a number of opposites – 'popular/learned', 'custom/law', 'things/linguistic ideas', 'synchrony/diachrony', 'sense/experience', and so on.[76]

The major sites where this process of redefinition occurred were the monastic and cathedral schools, which at this intellectually volatile time were engaged in a struggle for supremacy. This struggle was not just one of effectively defining these new concerns and their intellectual limits, but also about who could share in this knowledge, its dissemination, proliferation and popularisation. On the one hand, there is the question of authorisation and, on the other, the content of the intellectual speculation.

The issue of the authorisation and regulation of discourse manifests itself in a number of different ways, first, at the level of direct competition between the monastic and cathedral schools, which increasingly came to be addressing themselves to two different groups of scholars. The monastic schools were concentrating on providing literacy and theological skills appropriate for the clergy who would take up residence in a monastery. The cathedral schools were becoming sites of training for those clergy who would not take up the life of the cloister but would require bureaucratic skills, and would be associated with the household of the sovereign or the powerful and wealthy nobility. It would be inappropriate to see this division as a dichotomous one, as these two seats of medieval learning were not mutually opposed, nor mutually exclusive.[77] However, another dimension of this is that the traditional distinction between *clericus*, *litteratus*, *laicus* and *illitteratus*, breaks down:

> By the twelfth century *clericus* meant *litteratus*, *laicus* meant *illitteratus*, and vice-versa. . . . More important in the present context is his observation that a learned knight would be called a *clericus*, because that implies that a person described as *clericus* in a document was not necessarily a member of the clergy. Such a person is just as likely to have been an educated layman.[78]

The *Historia Calamitatum* makes explicit references to both 'clerks' and 'scholars' and there is no doubt that this emerging group was important to the life of a *magister*. Furthermore, it has been argued that the Church and the French crown had an interest in centring as much of the intellectual activity as possible in Paris where it would be easier to regulate: 'Both the French king and the pope wanted it thus, reckoning that if theological research was centered in one location, the work would be easier to control and the atmosphere more stimulating.'[79]

It is at this time of a 'theoretically' fluid situation that, in the first quarter of the twelfth century, a burst of new intellectual activity takes place, and repeatedly the discursive mechanisms modify themselves against emerging strategies and tactics to ensure the maintenance of a stable and effective system of regulation and authorisation. The figure of Peter Abelard is exemplary in this respect, as initially equipped with the then new dialectically based technique of *disputatio* he brings himself into a direct conflict with the traditionally based technique of *lectio*. It had been the practice selectively to read aloud a passage from the Scriptures and then provide the appropriate glosses on it from the early Church writers.[80] Abelard directly challenged this, suggesting that through the technique of *disputatio* it was possible to remove the inconsistencies that had always been recognised in the early Christian writings, be they theological or philosophical. It was this methodological approach that formed the basis of his initial conflict with William of Champeaux.[81]

As a result of this methodological challenge William was forced to change his position twice and this led to his eventual retirement from teaching in Paris. However, Abelard was not granted an official position but rather was forced to open his own school, which is a commentary both on initial attempts to establish the system of authorisation and on its apparent fluidity at this time. In effect for some time Abelard was able to bypass it, and was able to teach solely on the basis of his reputation attracting enough students to pay for his services. After briefly returning to Brittany he then studied theology under Anselm of Laon, and after experiencing great disappointment began to teach theology. His first commentary related to an obscure passage in Ezekiel. Anselm's response to this is an interesting one:

> It was largely through their insinuations, as we afterwards proved, that Anselm lost his head and curtly forbade me to continue my work of interpretation in the place where he taught, on the pretext that any mistake which I might write down through lack of training in the subject would be attributed to him. When this reached the ears of the students, their indignation knew no bounds – this was an act of sheer spite and calumny, such as had never been directed at anyone before; but the more open it was, the more it brought me renown, and through persecution my fame increased.[82]

A similar incident occurs after Abelard has entered the Abbey of St Denis, when he begins to lecture on theology:

This roused the envy and hatred of the other heads of the schools against me; they set out to disparage me in whatever way they could, and two of them especially were always attacking me behind my back for occupying myself with secular literature in a manner totally unsuited to my monastic calling, and for presuming to set up as a teacher of sacred learning when I had no teacher myself.[83]

Abelard's own analysis of the motivations underlying this are not relevant but what is, is that under an emerging system of authorisation, a *magister scholarum* had certain juridically validated powers. While at this time a *licentia docendi* was not required from the person responsible for the schools or a diocese to teach, it does appear that a *magister scholarum* could forbid someone from teaching within a local area.[84] Indeed the whole development of the *licentia docendi* gives some support to the general thesis about the regulatory mechanisms that were emerging in the first half of the twelfth century:

> In the twelfth century each of these phrases can be exemplified. The scholastic commentary, *sententia* and *quaestio* (Constable/Benson pp. 143, 165ff, 173 etc.), representing discourse validated by the *licentia docendi* and the emergent machinery of the cathedral school *cum universitas*, manifest the valorised techniques and procedures for obtaining truth. . . . The status of those who were charged with saying what counted as true was a vital issue: witness the struggles over the *licentia docendi* in the first half of the 12th century, the papacy's determined attempt to dominate the schools and nascent universities, the progressive tendency to let the special fields of law and theology determine the nature of truth.[85]

Also it is to be noted that Anselm of Laon is concerned that as the 'authorised' teacher he would be held responsible for Abelard's 'erroneous' opinions. The figure of Abelard operating as the 'peripatetic' scholar, wandering from teacher to teacher, setting up schools whenever and wherever the mood took him, and always attracting large numbers of students, was acting in a way that was inconsistent with the emerging mechanism of regulation. In contrast to these political systems of regulation, Abelard offered a methodological regulation, which continually brought him into conflict with the emerging orthodoxy. As a proponent of a system of belief based on a rigorous methodology, he is constituted by an intellectual movement in the first half of the twelfth century that was redefining both its relation to discourse and its mechanisms for authorisation and control amid the transformation of the power/knowledge network. He represents the masters who associate their task with that of the second person of the Trinity by redefining the meaning of the Trinity itself:

Take Abelard, for instance, who scrutinized the mystery of the Trinity; he reverts to Augustine's notion of correspondences among the three persons and the three categories – *mens, notitia, amor* – which he alters by substituting another triad for the latter: 'power,' 'wisdom,' and 'charity.' Here 'wisdom' is the attribute of the second person. The image of Jesus in the West has its own history. In that history the present period was one of preparation for the replacement of the image of the Lamb of the Apocalypse and the Redeemer of the Synoptics by the new image of the Teacher, at least in intellectual circles. Could one ask for a more striking sign of the rise of the masters, who, during the first half of the twelfth century, made up for the decline of monasticism by bringing down the temples of the old high culture?[86]

It is his theological contribution to the analysis of the Trinity that leads to his first condemnation at Soissons as a participant in a struggle amid an emerging politics of Truth. At Soissons, no theological evidence could be found to condemn him, and yet he was condemned for the following reason:

> They said that the fact that I had dared to read the treatise in public and must have allowed many people to make copies without its being approved by the Pope or the Church should be quite enough to condemn it, and that the Christian faith would greatly benefit if an example were made of me and similar presumption in many others were forestalled.[87]

This again is in fact the central issue at the Council of Sens and after Abelard's condemnation there in 1140, the Archbishops at Sens who condemned him wrote to the papal Curia giving their reasons for their action:

> Therefore, since throughout France, in towns, villages, and castles, by scholars not only within the schools, but in the roads and public places, disputes are carried on about the Holy Trinity and the Nature of God; and that not only among learned or passable instructed persons, but among children even and simple and ignorant persons; besides all this, many propositions are put forth by these disputants, not less contrary to reason than to the Catholic Faith, and to the doctrine of the holy Fathers; and since, though frequently warned by those who thought more justly on these matters that they should lay aside those foolish fancies, those persons showed themselves more ardent still; and, relying on the authority of their master, Peter Abelard, and especially upon his book entitled *Theologia*, as also of other treatises of his of a similar kind, persisted more and more in sustaining and defending these dangerous novelties, to the detriment of many souls; we, though distressed and alarmed, as were many others, at this state of things, were fearful to meddle with these difficult questions.[88]

This is a clear expression of the issues of regulation and authorisation that I have been discussing. The major concern here is the proliferation of discourse – and a transformation of the principles on which knowledge is based. Certainly theological issues remain, but it is the widespread discussion of Abelard's work that is the major problem, and it is this that primarily leads to his condemnation.

The question of authorisation was important to the first half of the twelfth century, and was paralleled by the emergence of discourses that constituted a series of problematisations that became a site of a struggle for regulation.

This brings me to the second of the major discussions of the twelfth century, the relation between language, texts and an understanding of the reality-reference. This is where the question of 'realism' (under the guise of the discussion concerning universals) emerges again and will be detailed in the remainder of this chapter. Given the interdisciplinary nature of this work and for the reader not familiar with the background to this debate, I will outline a brief history of the intellectual situation that dominated western Europe prior to the so-called intellectual revival or renaissance of the twelfth century.

Initially reference must be made especially to Augustine of Hippo. There are three aspects of his work that I will briefly consider to allow an appropriate evaluation of the novelty of the twelfth-century philosophical and theological debates which I will be discussing. These are Augustine's view of sin, his attitude to the relation between faith and belief, and his critique of scepticism. Augustine's account of sin was based on the idea that it was the acts themselves that were sinful – the state of mind of the agent involved did not come into consideration. Human nature itself through the operation of original sin was fundamentally sinful and earthly life was a battle with concupiscence balanced by a capacity to love God. This meant that human action had no relation to a preconceived end of the intellect but was motivated '*a tergo* by immediate and blind desire'.[89]

While I will be arguing that it is the Augustinian principle *Credo ut intelligam* (I believe in order that I may understand)[90] as the first principle which is steadily undermined from the eleventh century, this does not imply that Augustine was crudely anti-rational in the sense of disallowing the intellect the pursuit of scholarly enquiry. Augustine's own training in 'pagan' philosophy had equipped him particularly well to engage in both the philosophical and theological discussion of a number of difficult issues, and he was anxious to use his intellect to critically attack those doctrines of which he disapproved. His arguments for the existence of God, and the existence of the soul are not relevant to the present discussion, although at a general level it should be noted that they involve well-constructed, 'rationally' based arguments that utilise a number of easily recognisable 'pagan' techniques.[91] That this should be so is hardly surprising as the early

Christian Church was attempting to convert pagans and heathens to its ranks. What could be a more effective technique than to represent early Church doctrine in an argumentative and philosophical structure that would have been recognisable and convincing to potential converts. So in Augustine's work rational argument is used to 'prove' a number of points essential to Church doctrine and is presented in a form that adopted pagan philosophical techniques: a dialogical structure, examples taken from mathematics, geometry and so on.

His critique of scepticism directed against the New Academy, while supposedly being composed before his baptism, offers an example of his philosophical skill. Although acknowledging that the problem of illusions and dreams, and the uncertainty and possibility of deception, raise doubts about the foundations of knowledge, Augustine suggests that even to be deceived is to presuppose existence; if we did not exist we could not be deceived.[92] So while we may be deceived about the everyday conditions of our existence we cannot be deceived about the fact that we exist.

> I know most certainly that I exist and know and love. About such truths I fear no arguments from the Academy's sceptics. 'What if you are deceived?' they protest. If I am deceived, I exist! For one who does not exist, cannot be deceived. Consequently I exist even if I am deceived.[93]

Augustine's second line of attack on scepticism suggests that it presupposes a criterion of truth:

> To be conscious that I am deceived presumes some awareness of what constitutes reality. And the cardinal principle which is thus revealed is the principle of non-contradiction or, in positive terms, of coherence. We may not know what quality a thing in reality possesses. But we know that it cannot both have a particular quality and not have it. The same cannot both perish and be immortal; if the world contains only four elements it cannot contain five. This principle gives a positive guide to knowledge, a clue to its general nature. But again the question arises whether it gives any but a formal content to knowing apart from reference to sense-experience.[94]

From this basis Augustine is able to develop a philosophical system that uses the concept of the inner knowledge of 'understanding' to defend his onto-theological views with their basis in Neoplatonism and a mind/soul–body/flesh separation:

> There are two types of things that one can know; one comprises what the mind perceives with the aid of the bodily senses, the other what it perceives on its own. While the babblings of these philosophers have some relevancy in regard to the former, they are completely powerless to cast doubt on what the

mind on its own perceives to be most certainly true, such as the aforementioned, 'I know that I live'.[95]

However much Augustine's philosophical reasoning may have been crucial to the development of early Church doctrine, by the early medieval period, the association between a critical philosophy and theology had largely broken down and was reinterpreted as the overly simplistic medieval interpretation of *Credo ut intelligam*. Something of this can be seen in the eleventh-century transubstantiation controversy. From the ninth century on, it had increasingly become the view that during the Mass, the bread and wine were literally changed into the body and blood of Christ.[96] Berengar of Tours in the mid-eleventh century began to challenge this view, arguing that the *Sacramentum* in Augustine meant *sacrum signum* and this indicated that there was a difference between *res* and *signum*, the object and the sign by which it was consecrated.[97] Berengar's opponents led by Lanfranc argued that a portion of the 'real' body and blood of Christ was produced in the bread and wine.[98] Berengar argued that if this were the case, then the existence of the first material would cease and be replaced by that of the second, which would be evident to the senses. By a skilful and judiciously selective use of Augustine he was also able to indicate that it was possible both to defend the view that the sacraments were divinely inspired mysteries and that they could be interpreted logically.[99]

Berengar was condemned at the Council of Rome in 1059 by Hildebrand and Lanfranc, without being given the opportunity to further defend his view; he later replied to this in the *Opusculum*:

> The bread and wine, he repeats, despite their sacramental value, remain on the altar after consecration, for they can be felt, seen, and tasted. Radert, Humbert, and Lanfranc, in his view approach the eucharist in too fundamentalist a fashion, accepting a crude equation between the letter of the text and events in the real world. If the eucharist is to have any genuine meaning, one must get beneath the surface senses and therefore employ methods in interpretation. This was the approach of Ambrose, Jerome and Augustine, which now, he feels needs to be reinstated.
>
> However, Berengar is not content as were the fathers with separating the logic of texts from that of reality. He claims that the one can be imposed upon the other. His philosophical method is essentially a series of deductions based on the relations between words, phrases, and syntax. This logic in turn is assumed to apply to the realities which lie behind the verbal arrangements, whose formalistic and conventional qualities he nonetheless recognizes. He thus reasons from texts to reality, that is from words to things.[100]

There are two issues to be drawn out of this incident. First, it indicates the beginning of the reinterpretation of the 'rational/logical' Augustine.

Secondly, at this time such intellectual activity was not acceptable to the Church. None the less a process had begun which was to come to fruition in the following century, and which had opened up the issue of the relation between 'language, texts and reality' and had polarised the debate. On one side were those dialecticians who saw the need for a rational/logical basis to belief, and on the other were those who considered the simplified Augustinian doctrine of *Credo ut intelligam* unchallengeable.

The next figure to be considered is Anselm of Bec and Canterbury.[101] The full title of Anselm's work *Proslogion* is the *Proslogion: or Faith Seeking Understanding*; it begins with a prayer for understanding: 'I do not seek to understand in order that I may believe, but I believe in order that I may understand.'[102]

Anselm is clearly not setting out to undermine the Augustinian formula, indeed the concentration on the importance of 'understanding' is wholly Augustinian. However, Anselm reintroduces the question of an acceptable theological/philosophical reading of the Augustinian corpus in such a way that it is not condemned (as had been the work of Berengar) by the Church orthodoxy, and which indeed pushes a philosophical reading of Augustine to new limits. So while in the *Monologion* his arguments are still based on Augustinian Neoplatonism, Anselm manages to systematise two Neo-platonic ideas in a way that had not previously been undertaken:[103] that 'the source of things cannot be distinct from the source of their existence'; and 'the causal argument for the existence of changing things'. In Anselm the existence of God is always presupposed and then after a subjective, consciously based moment of 'understanding' occurs in the strict Augustinian sense, it can be deduced and explained:

> Anselm, it is said, was a mystic, and his *fides quarens intellectum* is the progress from a mystical or an intuitional knowledge. God is present to Anselm's inmost consciousness, and the mind, starting from the fact of its presence, goes on to analyze and deduce.[104]

None the less the *Proslogion* and *Monologion* make important contributions to medieval intellectual life in that they legitimise the reintroduction of philosophically based discussion – and the philosophical reading of Augustine – into popular theology and in this way vindicate the earlier work of Berengar. Anselm's proof of the existence of God is an important contribution to this general process and will be examined in some detail.[105]

After initially making a formulaic Augustinian confession of faith Anselm argues that there could be a fool who might deny the existence of God, and he constructs an argument to counter this possibility. The position that he adopts is fundamentally that of the Neoplatonist suggesting that the fool, when responding negatively to the definition of God as 'something greater than which we conceive of nothing greater', shows that he understands what is meant by the definition in his refusal of it: 'Even the fool then must be convinced that in his understanding at least there is something than which nothing greater can be conceived, for he hears this, he understands it and whatever is understood is in the understanding.'[106]

Given the fundamental Neoplatonist principle that greater cannot be inferred by the lesser and the logical principle of non-contradiction, Anselm argues that the thing that cannot be conceived of as being greater, cannot only exist in the understanding:

> For if it were there only, one could also think of it as existing in reality and this is something greater. If the thing than which none greater can be thought were in the mind alone, then this same thing would both be and not be something than which nothing greater can be conceived. But surely this cannot be. Without doubt then there exists both in the understanding and in reality a being greater than which nothing can be conceived.[107]

Anselm concludes his argument with a prayer of thanks to the understanding, 'For now I understand by your light what I once believed by your grace', and this sums up both his attitude to the intersection between philosophy and theology and the beginnings of the small shift in emphasis that he is instigating. Belief still has primacy but philosophy can now be legitimately used to support it. A reply was forthcoming to Anselm's initial position from Gaunilon, who argued that Anselm's use of the 'understanding' was ambiguous and imprecise, and that there was a difference between understanding something when it is heard and what already is in the understanding in the Augustinian, Neoplatonic sense:

> For anyone whose words I understand can mention all sorts of dubious or unreal things. And I still think such things are in my understanding in the same way as this being is, or even more so if I am deceived and believe such words, as often happens.[108]

Gaunilon goes on to argue that our understanding comes from our ability to recognise familiar general categories and from the general ability to make positive or negative statements about a particular instance:

> By reason of the special or general knowledge I have of what a man is or what men are, I could think of this individual in terms of that reality itself which a man is. And still it might be that the man I conceived of was nonexistent, for example, if the man who spoke of him were lying, for I was not thinking of him according to that reality that would make him just this man but in terms of what is true of any man whatsoever.[109]

As Gaunilon points out this is not true of the case of God, where an understanding of non-existence would not be of the same sort as of the non-existent man:

> since I can think of the latter [man] in terms of some real and familiar thing, whereas I can only think of the former [God] in terms of mere words and one can never or scarcely think of anything real in this signification rather than the word itself we think of. The words (i.e. the sounds and syllables) are real enough. Neither is it like the case of one who does not know the actual signification of the word, but when he hears the word in his mind tries to imagine what it would be. And it would be surprising if he were to arrive at the truth in this fashion.[110]

Gaunilon finally shows that the idea that what can be 'understood as being the most excellent' must also exist in reality is a fallacy. He gives the example of the imaginary 'Fortunate Islands', that when described as the most perfect and excellent imaginable enter the understanding:

> If one were to try to prove to me that this island in truth exists and its existence should no longer be questioned, either I would think he was joking or I would not know whether to consider him or me the greater fool, me for conceding his argument or him for supposing he had established with any certainty such an island's existence without first showing such excellence to be real and its existence indubitable rather than just a figment of my understanding.[111]

Anselm's reply to Gaunilon reasserts his original arguments and underscores them with the principle of faith when his arguments begin to fail: 'But for proof that the consequent is false, I appeal both to your faith and to your conscious experience.'[112] Gaunilon had forced the beginnings of a reassessment of Neoplatonism, and moreover the exchanges between him and Anselm were carried on in the spirit of philosophical and theological enquiry which was to dominate the twelfth century. But curiously in his defence of Neoplatonism, it is the textual technique that Anselm used rather than the arguments themselves which had considerable consequences.[113]

In his major works, Anselm assumes a conversational *persona* with himself 'which both internalizes a textual methodology and anticipates a written product.'[114] This introduces a relation with the text that according to Stock, has a number of consequences for him:

1. For Anselm, the text also acts as an intermediary for discussion within his own mind; that is, words in the mind constitute a mental text, and this in turn eventually gives rise to a real written text. 2. The written text also acts as an intermediary between Anselm and his real and fictive audiences. It is a focal point for both dialogue and with his brethren and, *in abstracto*, with a putative

reading public. 3. While achieving these positive purposes, text production is nonetheless a reductive process.[115]

Thus Anselm stands at the intersection of two opposing trends: his extreme idealism firmly places him within a longstanding Church tradition; at the same time, he both defines a new series of relations to the written text and adds to its importance by associating it and its philosophical/theological purpose with the mind of God:

> Moreover, Anselm proceeds by analogy from words and things to the created and the creator. For God, words, which are normally the mental images of objects, are the inner realities of the objects themselves, logically and therefore temporally prior to them in the creative process. He sees in God the verbalisation (*locutio*) of a perfect grammar of texts. . . . It does not follow that for Anselm to exist is merely to be thought to exist. Rather, to exist is in large part to exist in thoughts capable of logical expression, for which the model is a text.[116]

Having examined the major sociological and philosophical issues that constituted the intellectual field at the beginning of the twelfth century, I am now in a position to consider the work of Peter Abelard and its connection to the reorientation of the relation between 'language texts and the understanding of reality' – that passes under the title of the 'twelfth-century renaissance' or the 'twelfth-century intellectual revival', but in fact was part of the transformation of the power/knowledge network and a rearrangement of the politics of truth that constituted the possibility of a new technology of self and leads to the composition of a unique technology of the subject (*subject*).

·4·
Drawing the subject

As I mentioned previously Abelard's intellectual work came to public attention when he was studying under William of Champeaux, and made some important contributions to the debate on 'universals'. As we have already seen, the 'universals' debate and the resulting confrontation between Lanfranc and Berengar had an impact on medieval theology in the eleventh century. It emerged again under the influence of Roscelin (who is thought to have been one of Abelard's early masters), who argued that those who adopted the theory of universals and its necessarily presupposed realism were in fact confusing 'words' and 'things'. This was not an entirely new position; however, Roscelin forced the consequences of this through with an unprecedented rigour and argued that universals did not exist, rather there were only 'individuals' or particular instances. It was a case of confusing a 'thing' (*res*) with *flatus vocis*, a breath of wind, a verbalised sound. This had severe implications for the doctrine of the Trinity as it implied that the three persons as the one God – universal – was a logical impossibility; there must be three particulars, that is, three independent Gods. This also had a further consequence, although it was not one drawn out by Roscelin, nominalism: 'that any analysis or classification of the individual beings of our experience was a matter of words, not of things, in the well-known dichotomy'.[1] It was this dichotomy that dominated medieval thought at the time that Abelard entered the debate.

The overall problematic emerged out of a well-known passage in Boethius who translated into Latin the Greek writer Porphyry's *Introduction to Aristotle*. At a particular point in the translation, Boethius had written:

> Now concerning *genus* and *species*, whether they have real existence or are merely and solely creations of the mind, and if they exist, whether they are material or immaterial, and whether they are separate from the things we see or are contained within them – on all this I make no pronouncement.[2]

As David Knowles points out, for five generations these words had remained unchallenged, but then in the eleventh century and continuing into the twelfth they were at the centre of a continuing controversy. The issue was one that concerned the nature of 'reality'/things (*res*). At the level of language, when we refer to Socrates as a man we refer to a nature that includes 'man-ness'. However, at the logical level we refer to him as an individual or substance, one of a species who share a number of common qualities and a common name. Socrates the 'particular' can be given his name by the process of ostensive definition, but how can the qualities of 'man-ness' or 'humanity' or any of the other substantive qualities be attributed to him? Further, what philosophical weight can we give to these various categories that we 'isolate' for the purposes of argument or classification? Moreover is a different mental process involved in the two cases of the individual and the universal?

> Granted that any mental perception is valid, we have a direct perception of the individual man. But by what process do we recognize and define in thoughts and words the resemblances between two individual beings which lead us to say that each is a man or a rose? Is it merely a visual process? Or an intuitive one? Or some kind of recognition or memory or inward light? Or is it what we call an abstractive process of the reason? But this is not the end of the problem. What in the last resort, are the individual being and its 'nature'? Are they no more than mental divisions of one thing? Is the individual more real than its nature? Or is the 'nature' the only reality, and if so, what is the relationship between it and the individual? Or, if they are both real and extra-mental, what is their relationship and how does the mind achieve knowledge of them?[3]

At a more general level this raises a number of difficulties in relation to a whole range of abstract categories, such as justice, truth, God, church, state, and so on. Do they have an independent existence or are they just the result of the classificatory operation of our language or even our minds?[4] 'Are they purely mental images and convenient terms or are these images and terms expressive of metaphysical reality outside individual minds?'[5]

We have already seen the nominalist response to this problem (Roscelin) so now it is appropriate to contrast to it the 'realist' position of William of Champeaux. William initially held that the universal which was a substance was present in each and every individual/particular.[6] This leads to an extreme form of realism, whereby the 'nature' of a being is essentially present in every individual.[7] This is the point at which Abelard enters the debate, by addressing himself to problems alluded to in Boethius' translation of Porphyry and drawing out three specific issues from Boethius:

1) Whether genera and species subsist i.e. are substances in the 'real' world or whether they only exist in the men's minds i.e. in the understanding?
2) If they exist in the world of things (*res*) are they corporeal or incorporeal?
3) If one and two, then are they in sensible things, i.e. objects or are they separate from them?[8]

Abelard adds to these issues another problem: How can things be made to agree? How can universal nouns deal with particular objects as being the same 'thing'?

> namely, whether genera and species, so long as they are genera and species, must have some thing subject to them by nomination, or whether, if the things named were destroyed, the universal could still consist of the meaning only of the conception, as this noun *rose* when there is not a single rose to which it is common.[9]

This issue strikes at the very heart of the universals/realism debate. If genera and species have an essential relation to essences in objects, what would they refer to if their referent did not exist; for example, in the case of the word 'rose' when no roses exist? Abelard details the opinions of the familiar sources on the questions raised, finding some useful contradictions in Boethius and summarising the positions of Aristotle and Plato. He suggests that Aristotle held that species and genera subsist in sensibles (objects) but are understood outside them, and Plato held that genera and species exist outside objects and are understood outside them. Then he proceeds to discuss the questions raised and argues that the issue is whether the universals genera and species 'apply only to words or to things as well,' bearing in mind that universals are predicated of many, while individuals/particulars are predicated of one. Suggesting that Aristotle at times attributes universals to both words and things, Abelard argues that for Aristotle nouns are universals, while *genus* is that which is in a thing that makes it the specific sort of thing that it is. Abelard counters this by claiming that there is a distinction to be made between signifying and a signified. Signifying applies to 'words,' while to be signified applies to 'things', a view that according to Abelard can also be found in Aristotle. Since nouns are 'accidental' in their relation to objects, they cannot be universals by relation to an essence, but only because they fall into the category of universals as being predicated by many. Therefore it is their role as signifiers and not as signifieds that determines their status:

> However, it is not properly called species since a noun is not substantial but accidental, but it is decidedly a universal since the definition of the universal applies to it. Hence it follows that words are universals whose function it is to be predicates of propositions.[10]

Abelard suggests that there is an important distinction to be made between a 'universal' and a 'collection of things'. He gives the example of a house or Socrates as being predicated of all their many separate parts but not being granted the status of a universal but rather simply being a 'collection of things'; this is summarised by Weinberg as follows:

> Abelard has little difficulty in showing that this theory will not stand. The universal is that which is naturally apt to be predicated of many. But a collection, as a collection, cannot be predicated of any of its members because it lacks the sort of commonness required for this. Moreover, any individual can be considered as a collection since it consists of parts, so that, for example, Socrates would be a universal. Again, if a universal is nothing but a collection, any arbitrarily designated collection will be a universal. Again, a collection is not logically prior to its parts so that its members cannot be characterized until the collection is formed.[11]

Furthermore if one accepts the essentialist view of the existence of universals it becomes apparent that this leads to a ridiculous position. When all the 'accidental' or 'particular' qualities that separate Aristotle from Socrates have been taken away they become 'essentially' the same man. If one follows Boethius and argues that universals never exist in a pure form but only in various forms in their state as accidents, a consequence of this is that they can never be experienced but only understood. Abelard refuses to accept this argument, suggesting that this account of universals leads to 'contraries' in the same universal. For example, the universal 'animal' includes both rational and irrational animals, men and asses. One can argue that it is the combination of various categories that constitute the universal, so that blackness and whiteness combine to form the same essence – which from one view is black but another white. This is not allowed by Abelard who utilises these pre-suppositions to prove that Socrates and an ass would be the same:

> That too is shown thus: rationality and irrationality are truly in the same individual because they are in Socrates. But since they are in Socrates at the same time, it is proved that they are in Socrates and in the ass at the same time. But Socrates and the ass are Socrates. And Socrates and the ass are indeed Socrates, because Socrates is Socrates and the ass, since obviously Socrates is Socrates and Socrates is the ass. That Socrates is the ass is shown as follows according to this opinion: whatsoever is in Socrates other than the forms of Socrates, is that which is in the ass other than the forms of the ass. But whatever is in the ass other than the forms of the ass, is the ass. Whatever is in Socrates other than the forms of Socrates, is the ass. But if this is so, since Socrates is himself that which is other than the forms of Socrates, then Socrates is himself the ass. The truth of what we assumed above, namely, that

whatever is in the ass other than the forms of the ass is the ass, we may indicate
as follows, for neither are the forms of the ass the ass, since then accidents
would be substance, nor are the matter and forms of the ass taken together
the ass, since then it would be necessary to say body and not body were
body.[12]

In response to Abelard's initial attack, William of Champeaux modified
his theory of realism, arguing that each individual did not have the same
essence substantively but could be classified as the same by virtue of their
'indifference' from each other.[13] Abelard attacks William's new position
arguing that in its essentially negative formulation it becomes almost
meaningless:

> There are, however, those who take *agree in man* negatively, as if it were
> said: Socrates does not differ from Plato in man. But this likewise can be
> said, that he docs not differ from him in stone, since neither of them is
> stone. And so no greater agreement between them is noted in man than
> in stone, unless perchance some propositions precede it, as if it were stated
> thus: They are man because they do not differ in man. But this can not stand
> either, since it is utterly false that they do not differ in man. For if Socrates
> does not differ from Plato in the thing which is man, he does not differ from
> him in himself. For if he differs in himself from Plato, but he is himself the
> thing which is man, certainly he differs from him also in the thing which
> is man.[14]

Having satisfied himself that universals do not exist in objects Abelard
moves on to the question of the relation between universals and language –
'it remains to ascribe universality of this sort to words alone' – and devotes
his attention to the other side of the realist/nominalist dichotomy. Abelard
claims that a 'universal' word is a word that is singly predicated of many,
whereas a 'particular' word is predicated of only one. The problem of
'universals' is fundamentally one of meaning, which is caused by the
strength of the predicative function of 'universals'. This predicative function is not unquestionable, as clearly there are cases of incorrect – in terms
of meaning – uses of a correct predicative structure:

> If anyone should say man is a stone, he has not made a proper construction of
> man and stone in respect to the meaning he wished to demonstrate, but there
> had been no fault of grammar; and although so far as the meaning of the
> proposition is concerned, this stone is predicated of man, to whom clearly it is
> construed as predicated (as false categories do have their predicated term),
> still in the nature of things stone is not predicable of man. We merely note
> here the great force of this predication while defining the universal.[15]

Furthermore there is no way of establishing exactly what 'universals' might refer to. For example universal nouns such as justice have no common basis for agreement on which such a universal could be based: 'since universals could not name things as they agree in something, for there is no something in which they agree, universals seem to derive no meaning from things, particularly since they constitute no understanding of thing.'[16] If they cannot constitute meaning by signifying the subjects of individual/particular cases, universals fail the first principle that they must have a subject of which they are the predicate:

> For even if Socrates alone be sitting in this house, and if because of him alone this proposition is true: *A man sits in this house*, nevertheless in no wise is the subject transferred by the name of the man to Socrates, except in so far as he is also a man, otherwise sitting would rationally be understood to inhere in him, so that it could be inferred clearly from the fact that a man sits in this house, that Socrates sits in it. In the same way, no other man can be understood, in this noun man, nor can the whole collection of men since the proposition can be true of only one. Consequently, man or any other universal word seems to signify no one thing since it constitutes the meaning of no thing. But it seems that there can not be a meaning which does not have a subject thing which it conceives.[17]

Abelard has rejected the claims of the extreme proponents of the realist/nominalist dichotomy and now goes on to address the question that if universals are neither exclusively essences or words, then what are they?

> But now let us inquire carefully into these things which we have touched upon briefly, *namely, what that common cause by which the universal word is imposed is, and what the conception of the common likeness of things is, and whether the word is called common because of a common cause in which the things agree or because of a common conception or because of both at once.* [Italics in original][18]

Abelard argues that a distinction must be made between the operation of the senses and the understanding and suggests that sight only perceives 'bodies' or what is in 'bodies', while the 'understanding' does not require the presence of 'bodies' in order to function. He gives the example of a tower that is destroyed and is no longer present to the senses and yet is still the object of the understanding:

> the understanding is a certain action of the soul by which it is called intelligent or understanding, but the form to which it is directed is a certain imaginary fictive thing, which the mind constructs for itself when it wishes and as it wishes.[19]

Universals become general categories in the understanding that do not require a corporeal existence. The category 'man' produces a general conception that is common to all men, but particular to none, whereas the noun 'Socrates' produces a particular form in the mind which 'expresses the likeness of a certain person'.

> Wherefore *man* is rightly said to signify neither Socrates nor any other man, since none is specified by the meaning of the word, although nevertheless it names particulars. *Socrates*, on the other hand, must not only name a certain particular, but also determine the subject thing.[20]

So according to Abelard universals are neither essences nor merely words but are conceptions formed out of the mind's ability to abstract. They must not be treated as objects but neither are they simply empty 'breathes of wind'. What is taken for the *substance* man is comprised of infinite forms that include animal, body, etc., which are abstracted from all the possible attributes of particular cases. Corporeity is abstracted from a number of other forms, animations, sensuality, whiteness and so on. Universals first involve this process of abstraction and then are co-joined into the universal category. They are not objects or words but are the result of abstraction and conjunction. For Abelard a universal is not the name of a thing, nor does it denote a thing. It points to a way of being, it is a linguistic and ontological status rather than the essential part of an object.

Abelard is now in a position to answer the questions that he posed at the beginning of the *Glosses on Porphyry*:

1. Universals nominate individual objects that exist, they are not simply a matter of empty opinion, 'nevertheless, they consist in a certain sense in the understanding alone and naked and pure, as has been determined'. So it is not a question of attempting to resolve the realist–nominalist dichotomy at all, as 'the words can be taken in absolutely the same sense on both sides, by the resolver and the inquirer, and then it is made a simple question not by opposition of the prior members of two dialectical questions, to wit, these: whether they are or are not, and again whether they are placed in the sole and naked and pure understanding or not'.[21]

2. Universal names are both corporeal with respect to the nature of things and incorporeal with respect to the manner of their signification, 'because although they name things which are discrete, nevertheless they do not name them discretely and determinately'.[22]

3. Universals are only universals in the sense they are in the understanding, and have arrived there by the process of abstraction and conjunction, 'they signify both sensible things and at the same time that common conception which Priscian ascribes particularly to the divine mind'.[23]

4. Even if all the noun objects were destroyed, in the case of there being no roses, the universal 'rose' while no longer nominating would still signify understanding, '. . . . as for example the name of the rose when there are no longer roses, but it would still, nevertheless, be significative by the understanding, although it would lack nomination; otherwise there would not be the proposition: there is no rose'.[24]

Abelard concludes his summary on the *Glosses on Porphyry* with a brief summing up of what he sees as the main issue:

> It must be noted, however, that although the definition of the universal or of the genus or the species includes only words, nevertheless these nouns are often transferred to their things, as when it is said that species is made up of genus and difference, that is, the thing of the species from the thing of the genus. For when the nature of words is examined with respect to signification, it is a question sometimes of words and sometimes of things, and frequently the names of the latter and the former are transferred reciprocally. For this reason most of all, the ambiguous treatment of logic as well as grammar leads many, who do not distinguish clearly the property of the imposition of nouns or the abuse of transference, into error by the transference of nouns.[25]

Abelard's work on the theory of universals has a number of important consequences for this inquiry:

1. His general argument that a great deal of the confusion has been caused by poor argument and bad philosophical training demands that a more effective methodology be utilised. This no doubt fed into the emerging philosophical scholasticism he himself promoted.

2. His view of Conceptualism demands that the concepts of 'understanding' and 'meaning', play a crucial role, and the site of this 'understanding' is the *individual* correctly trained philosophical consciousness. Without going into detail here, it is appropriate to note that Abelard's solution to the problem of universals had some similarities to Aristotle's, even though at this time the relevant Aristotelian texts, *De Anima* and the *Metaphysics*, were not available to him.[26]

3. Abelard represents those who had an unsurpassed confidence that dialectic when 'correctly' applied – and the question of this 'correct' application is a crucial issue here – would without a doubt lead to the Truth. This implied that theology as an expression of religious Truth 'must conform to dialectical practice' and was a major challenge to the Augustinian first principle *'Credo ut intelligam'* as the *first* principle.[27] Further evidence of this emerges from the distinction that he established between understanding (*intelligere*) and comprehending (*comprehendre*)

which allowed him to identify a distinction between faith and cognising or manifesting: 'Faith', he writes, 'is called an estimation of things not apparent, whereas cognition is an experience of those things by their very presence.'[28] As Weinberg argues that while this is an affirmation that faith necessarily involves some understanding it also suggests that it would be ridiculous for a teacher not to understand the things that they wish to teach.

4. In his logical work on the problem of universals Abelard established a distinction between the word itself as a physical entity, *vox,* and *nomen* (which he later termed *sermo*), the word as having logical content or meaning: 'When a universal term, such as 'man', is predicated of the members of a class, it is predicated according to this logical content. It is the *sermo,* not the *vox,* which is predicated. And it is to *sermones* alone that universality can properly be ascribed.'[29] This is a crucial distinction as it raises an important issue. When in the utterance of a 'meaningful expression does meaning actually take place'?[30] Abelard claimed that meaning is not established until the last element of the utterance had occurred (*in ultimo puncto prolationis*). If this is the case, then the part of the discourse that is not evident at the time of a particular utterance does not 'on that account lack potential significance.'[31] Meaning arises out of what is not spoken as much as out of what is spoken and Stock concludes from this that what we have in Abelard's work at this time is a distinction that is similar to Saussure's between *langue* and *parole.*[32]

To produce understanding one must signify through words which have a dual character. As sound (*voces*) they act on our senses. As signs (*signa, sermones*) they are interpreted, but what is interpreted is not an object (*res*) it is a *quasi res* which expresses 'the manner in which things relate to each other'.[33]

When internalized in the mind, the same sentence represents not things said (*dicta*) but things in the form of intellections (*res in intellectu*). Words, in Abelard's view, are not created on account of images, which merely act as a bridge between the senses and the mind. They are the verbalizations of man's inner conceptions of reality. As meaningful sounds, words or sentences indicate their meaning in speech, as texts, and as thoughts.[34]

The place of the subject (*subject*) is central to Abelard's theory of language and his solution to the problem of universals. It is the 'subject' that abstracts from things to words and deconstructs what initially appear as unities and then recomposes them into general categories. His emphasis on the importance of the place of the subject in language enabled him to break down the original realism/nominalism dichotomy and relocate the terms of the debate. This can also be seen in his logical work which re-emphasised the relation between words and things. A relation that turned on the nature and place of the linguistic and phenomenal subject which imparted meaning/ understanding and was both the subject and object of the methodology. So Abelard's approach called into question the place, structure, and function of the subject (*subject*). In doing this he problematised not simply realism, idealism or nominalism but the structure of the relationship between them, and in so doing found a way to step outside the philosophical debate of his day by using his methodology to problematise the whole debate rather than by trying to settle it on one side or the other.

This methodology developed by Abelard was 'methodological scepticism' bound by dialectics. He explains this most clearly in a celebrated passage in *Sic et Non*, which was written as an educational manual for his students. There existed a number of such manuals from the twelfth century, such as Gratian's *Decretum* and the standard mid-twelfth century orthodox textbook on theology, Peter Lombard's *Sentences*. However, Abelard's *Sic et Non* differs in one important respect, as he refused to reconcile the contrary opinions as had been the traditional practice but left their resolution to the reader.[35]

In the Prologue to *Sic et Non* he argues that there are two sources of possible error in the Bible and patristic writings. First because authors, copyists and translators were human it was possible that they made mistakes. Secondly, the meaning of words themselves change and so old-established interpretations could not be relied on:

> And so what wonder is it if, lacking the presence of that Spirit through whom these things were written and pronounced and by whom they were conveyed to the writers, we lack understanding of them, for unaccustomed modes of expression and different meanings for many of the same words greatly hinder our understanding of them, since the same word is used to mean first one thing and now another? Indeed, just as each word abounds in levels of meaning, so also each meaning can be expressed by many words.[36]

Often writings were 'attributed' incorrectly so one could not simply accept a statement on the grounds of its attributed source; Abelard quotes Jerome on this point:

> May she be aware of all apocryphal statements; and whenever she might want to read them, not learn truth of dogma, but out of reverence for their names, let her know that they were not written by the men whose names are assigned to them, and that one needs great prudence to seek for gold in the mire.[37]

Furthermore, even in everyday speech things are spoken of which are not Truths in the theological sense of the word so a distinction must be made between eternal truths and linguistic conventions:

As a final point, the use of daily speech is according to the judgement of the corporeal senses, and many things are spoken of otherwise than they are in themselves. For although there is in the entire world no place which is altogether a vacuum, since it is filled with air or some body, nevertheless we say, in a word, that in the chest in which we perceive there to be nothing in view there is a vacuum. He who judges a thing according to how he sees it says that the heavens are sometimes starry, sometimes not, that the sun is sometimes hot, sometimes not at all, or that the moon sometimes gives off more or less light and sometimes does not give off any light, when nevertheless these things which do not always appear to us to be the same remain always the same in themselves. What wonder is it then if some things were also sometimes uttered and even written by the holy fathers on the basis of opinion rather than on truth?[38]

According to Abelard, therefore, it was likely that some of the gospels and patristic writings contained mistakes and errors that would prevent particular passages from being understood. He argued that this should be acknowledged and something should be done to attempt to correct the errors and provide for understanding. The model teacher was Jesus himself in the persona of the *Magister*, who taught that Truth was the outcome of inquiry, and so Abelard gathered together all the contradictory statements from Church writings and challenged the reader to seek the Truth. This would only be achieved by 'assiduous and frequent questioning', an Aristotelian principle, but to this Abelard adds another:

> For by doubting we come to inquiry, by inquiring we grasp the truth, according to what even Truth himself said, '*Seek and you will find, knock and it will be opened to you*'. Truth furnished us moral instruction by his own example when he chose to be found at the age of twelve, sitting and questioning in the midst of doctors. By his questioning he appears to us as a pupil rather than, by preaching, as a master, although there is in him, nevertheless, the full and perfect wisdom of God.[39]

This clear statement of methodological scepticism is repeated in Abelard's other works, in particular in the *Glosses on Porphyry* which we have already discussed and *A Dialogue of a Philosopher with a Jew, and a Christian* :

> Christian, 'In fact, in every discipline controversy arises in regard to the written word as well as in regard to the opinions expressed, and in any disputation the giving of a reason is firmer than a display of authority. The question of what is really the truth is not an issue for the building up of the faith, but rather it is a question of what can be held by opinion: and many questions arise concerning the words of the authority itself, so the judgment must be rendered on them before it is rendered by means of them. After reasonable judgment has been rendered, even if the solution is not rationally

conclusive but appears so, no further question remains since there is no doubt left.'[40]

This raises a number of issues that need some discussion. As has already been argued in relation to Abelard's logical work, his theory of language and the nature of meaning presupposes a certain specific notion of the subject (*subject*). This emerges directly out of his methodology where his reference to the principle of 'doubt' has a fundamentally self-reflective base in that it refers to the 'subject' or consciousness that does the doubting. We have already seen how the question of authorisation is an important one for twelfth-century intellectual work, and if we bear in mind the transformations in the politics of truth I have already outlined we can appreciate the full dimensions of Abelard's approach.

Some commentators have suggested that in fact his methodological scepticism was really not all that radical and usually these kind of comments are based on his *Confession of Faith* made at the very end of his life.[41] This view obscures the importance of his intellectual contribution and the way that this was received in the twelfth century by his contemporaries. I would suggest that his methodological scepticism challenged the fundamental principle of early medieval learning. Instead of the master glossing on countless texts utilising numerous references, which is an educative process that requires a long learning apprenticeship, Abelard offers a simple and singular method that can speedily settle any debate. No longer is extensive knowledge of the vast corpus of Christian literature required. Instead, his method founded on immediate subjective experience can settle any question and it is precisely this subjective emphasis in Abelard's approach that concerns his contemporaries:

> William (of Saint Thierry) strongly protested against the subjective character of Abelard's teaching which 'estimated that faith is an estimate' ('aestimans fidem aestimationem esse') and which disclaimed certitude. Abelard, he wrote, likes to dispute everything and to think everything over ('disputare' – 'putare'); with his 'nobis videtur' – 'it seems to us' – he treats theology as if it were dialectic.[42]

Bernard made much the same complaint in his letter to the Pope following Abelard's condemnation at Sens:

> while he is presumptuously prepared to give a reason for everything, even of those things which are above reason; he presumes against reason and against faith. For what is more against reason than by reason to attempt to transcend reason? And what is more against faith than to be unwilling to believe what reason cannot attain? For instance, wishing to explain that saying of the wise man: *He who is hasty is light in mind*, he says that a hasty faith is one that believes before reason, when Solomon says this not of faith towards God, but

of mutual belief amongst ourselves. For instance, on the very threshold of his theology (I should rather say his stultology) he defines faith as private judgement; as though in these mysteries it is to be allowed to each person to think and speak as he pleases, or as though the mysteries of our faith are to hang in uncertainty amongst shifting and varying opinions, when on the contrary they rest on the solid and unshakeable foundation of truth. Is not our hope baseless if our faith is subject to change.[43]

Bernard quite rightly points out the consequences of Abelard's methodological scepticism. If faith is detached from a universal correspondence to Truth and becomes a matter of private judgement from among a variety of opinions – including even those of the unlettered or unlearned – then the nature of faith and the mysteries themselves must be radically altered. Bernard's response to Abelard is revealed in his profession of faith which immediately follows the above passage, and he concludes 'For faith is not an opinion, but a certitude'.

For Abelard this is simply not good enough as it threatens to stop intellectual advancement, and intellectual advancement is a condition of human existence. In the persona of the philosopher in *A Dialogue of a Philosopher with a Jew, and a Christian* he argues that 'understanding' has advanced throughout the ages except in the area of faith, where the highest expression of faith is to hold to the common understanding of 'the unlettered as well as the lettered'. The result of this is to block intellectual inquiry: 'Surely the result of this is that no one is allowed to inquire into what should be believed among his own people or to doubt what everyone affirms, without fear of punishment.'[44]

Abelard considers that Bernard's view is just crudely anti-intellectual and only serves the interests of those who are incapable of learning. He suggests that it is a form of insanity born out of pride and presumptuousness:

These even frequently burst into such insanity that they are not ashamed to declare that they believe what they admit they are unable to understand, as if faith consists in the utterance of words rather than in the understanding in the mind, and as if faith were more a matter of the mouth than of the heart. Hence, they take the greatest glory in their apparent belief in what can be neither expressed in words nor conceived by the mind. The attachment of each to his own school of thought even makes them so presumptuous and proud that whomever they see separated in faith from themselves, they judge to be estranged from the mercy of God, and with everyone else condemned, they will declare that they alone will be blessed.[45]

Knowledge, for Abelard, can never be an evil, given that it leads to understanding. In fact its advance and increase is an important part of any religious system. In *letter 7* of the letters of direction to Heloise, Abelard cites the case of one who mouths the appropriate religious words without experiencing understanding in the mind, and suggests that without the addition of understanding, praying and prayers bring no merit but are just empty breaths. He gives the example of simple and illiterate people who pray for evil things by mistake thinking they will receive merit:

> for example, in the words 'that we may so pass through temporal things that we lose not things eternal', many are easily confused by the similarity in sound, so that either they say 'that we lose things eternal' or 'that we admit not things eternal.'[46]

This is possible because of the similarity of the two phrases in Latin: 'Instead of saying *ut non amittamus aeterna* some say *ut* nos *amittamus aeterna*, others *ut non* admittamus *aeterna*.'[47] It is for this reason Abelard tells Heloise that all nuns should have knowledge of Latin, and he refers to illiteracy in contemporary monasteries in a highly contemptuous fashion:

> And so we very much wonder what prompting of the enemy brought about the present situation in monasteries, whereby there is no study there on understanding the Scriptures, but only training in singing, which is no more than the forming of words without understanding them: as if the bleating of sheep were more useful than the feeding of them.[48]

Abelard considers that the ability to pronounce letters or doctrine without the accompanying 'understanding' is as useless as illiteracy and believes this to be an intolerable situation.[49] He claims that one of the main motivations for his theological writing was to meet a demand of his students:

> who were asking for human and logical reasons on this subject, and demanded something intelligible rather than mere words. In fact they said that words were useless if the intelligence could not follow them, that nothing could be believed unless it was first understood, and that it was absurd for anyone to preach to others what neither he nor those he taught could grasp with the understanding: the Lord himself had criticized such 'blind guides of blind men'.[50]

If we draw together Abelard's work on logic and his methodological scepticism, two things become increasingly clear. First, his approach undermines the Augustinian first principle of faith before understanding. When his contemporaries interpreted his work in this way they were absolutely correct. Secondly the place and the nature of the 'subject' (*subject*) becomes increasingly evident. Parkes suggests Abelard completes the process undertaken by Anselm and conceives of himself as a textual subject and presents himself in this way for a literate audience. This raises two important points. If an emerging subjective sense is vital to Abelard's work, what is it founded on and where is it clearly manifested? Certainly some sense of the importance of subjective experience is evident in his theory of Conceptualism as I have already described it. This same theme emerges from his methodological scepticism. But should we expect to find some clearer articulation of what the subject of a Conceptualist epistemology and methodological scepticism is?

This is what emerges from his ethical work, *Scito Te Ipsum,* or *Know Thyself.*[51] This is a novel text in medieval intellectual life. The subtitle *Know Thyself* is a direct reference to the Delphic oracle and Abelard's other references to it as *Ethica* redirected the question of ethics to pagan texts rather than those of the patristic writers. To the twelfth century the *ethici* were the pagan moralists who had developed a rational ethics, so by using this subtitle Abelard was attempting to open up a new set of pagan references for medieval ethics.[52] In *Know Thyself,* Abelard presents an 'intentionally' based ethics. For him the question of 'acts' is made secondary to that of intentions. In part he is extending Augustinian arguments but for Augustine, while the role of the will was not irrelevant to the state of 'sin', it was in the last analysis secondary to the state of the 'acts' themselves. Abelard pushed this argument to its logical conclusion, suggesting that:

> Will is too equivocal a word; it may mean concupiscence and our desires, but in this sense an evil will does not constitute sin unless consent is given to it. Properly speaking therefore consent to an evil will constitutes sin, not the will for evil. Abelard's purpose in this as in much else seems to have been to reorganize the language of traditional discussion.[53]

The effect is that Abelard is one of the first medieval writers to bring a discussion of the philosophical basis of an ethical life back into the intellectual domain. He argues that the question of 'acts' or will must be reorientated around the issue of intent. He supports this view by offering a number of examples that show instances which under the Augustinian model would be interpreted as sinful, while under his are not. He arrives at this view by arguing that God cannot be offended by acts as they can have no bearing on his existence as God. Therefore sin can only be contempt of God and so natural pleasures cannot be sinful in themselves:

> I think, from all this that no natural pleasure of the flesh should be imputed to sin nor should it be considered a fault for us to have in us something in which when it has happened the feeling of pleasure is unavoidable. For example, if someone compels a religious who is bound in chains to lie between women and if he is brought to pleasure, not to consent, by the softness of the bed and through the contact of the women beside him, who may presume to call this pleasure, made necessary by nature, a fault?[54]

Abelard claims further that 'sin' is of the soul whereas 'acts' are of the body. It is only consent that occurs in the soul and can therefore have an impact on it. Conversely without consent there is no possibility of sin occurring.[55] He gives the example of someone who in ignorance has intercourse with his sister. This is undoubtedly transgressing the law and yet everyone would agree he is not a transgressor because there was no consent, showing that even in law there is a distinction between an act and consent to that act. Therefore prohibitions are not applied to deeds themselves but in consenting to those deeds.[56] This coincides with Abelard's view of divine ordinance which suggests that the devil is only allowed to do what God allows him to:

> Christian continues, 'Therefore, since it is clear that nothing comes about without God's permission, indeed nothing can occur if he resists or is unwilling, and since it is certain that God never permits anything without a reason and does nothing except rationally so that his permission as well as his action are reasonable, surely he is not ignorant of why they must be done even if they are evils or done evilly, since he sees why he permits each single thing to occur which does occur. For it would not be good that they be permitted unless it were good that they be done; nor would he be perfectly good who would not thwart what would be not good to happen, since he is capable of doing so. Plainly he would be blameworthy if he consented to an action whose occurrence would not be good. So it is clear that whatever happens to be done or not to be done has a rational cause why it is done or not done. Therefore, it is good that it be done or good that it not be done even if it is not done well by him who does it, or if it is evilly not done by the one who does not do it, that is, it is omitted with an evil intention. And so it is even good that evils exist or occur although the evils themselves are in no way good.'[57]

This leads him into a position of determined optimism:

> The world, if it is the temporal manifestation of a 'good' and rational World-Ground, must be the best possible world; this means that in it all genuine possibility must be actualized; and thus none of its characteristics or components can be contingent, but all things must have been precisely what they are.[58]

God then allows both good and evil to exist in the world and subject acts are often outwardly indeterminate in relation to the question of good and evil. What is important is the intention of the individual agent in relation to those acts:

> Works in fact, which as we have previously said are common to the damned and the elect alike, are all indifferent in themselves and should be called good or bad only on account of intention of the agent, not, that is, because it is good or bad for them to be done but because they are done well or badly, that is, by that intention by which it is or is not fitting that they should be done.[59]

This acts as a counter to the deterministic optimism of God's relation to the world in allowing the existence of evil. God allows the existence of good and evil; however, intentions in the form of the responsibility of the self over-determine actions and prescribe whether they contribute to good or evil in the world. This in no way restricts God's nature, in allowing or disallowing existences, nor does it make God directly responsible for the individual response to what is created. It becomes solely a question of individual intentions. Abelard follows through the logic of his presentation arguing that the Jews did not commit a sin in the part they played in the death of Jesus.[60]

This view also has three other consequences that were something of a problem for Abelard's contemporaries. First, it allowed him to argue that when the keys were presented to Peter and his descendants the power that went with them only applied to bishops with the correct intentions but not to 'bad' bishops who could and should be disobeyed. Secondly, he suggests that in the form of the address that Christ used it did not apply necessarily to all the Apostles present but only those with the appropriate good intentions:

> For when one says 'them' or 'you' (these being demonstrative pronouns) the speech is aimed, according to the intention of the speaker, either equally to all present or to some of them whom he has selected, just as these quotations should be referred not to all the apostles in general but only to those who were chosen. And it seems that we should perhaps think likewise of his statement: 'Whatsoever thou shalt bind upon earth shall be bound also in heaven', in which it thought the opinion is entirely the same.[61]

Thirdly, in the *Ethics*, Abelard strongly argues in favour of private confession which at this time in the twelfth century was not compulsory in opposition to the practice of public penance. He suggests that while the power to forgive was that of the priest it would not mark the moment of divine forgiveness, 'if sorrow and inner contrition had already preceded the act of confession'.[62]

In spite of these reservations it can be seen that Abelard's support of private confession was entirely in keeping with his ethical view. The previous system of confession, based as it was on the Augustinian concept of 'public acts' that were part of a list of sins and a public penance, contrasted strongly to the concept of a private confession and private penance. In the latter case an essential part of the confessional process is the examining of the intentions of the agent in relation to the act committed. Indeed no act in the sense of an action in the world is necessary; thought alone can constitute sin and require the penance.

It is of some relevance here that only a little over forty years after the death of Abelard, in 1215 at the Fourth Lateran Council, private confession was made a required annual practice of all members of the Catholic Church. There can be little doubt that this was a significant point in the development of a general concept of an inner morally responsible self.[63] Foucault argues that the effects of this were crucial in as much as the practice of private confession – particularly in so far as it concerned matters of sex – turned 'subjects' back on themselves to produce a truthful discourse about themselves and their sexuality.[64] He makes the following comment on the significance of the Lateran Council of 1215:

> We have since become a singularly confessing society. Whence a metamorphosis in literature: we have passed from a pleasure to be recounted and heard, centering on the heroic or marvellous narration of 'trials' of bravery or sainthood, to a literature ordered according to the infinite task of exacting from the depths of oneself, in between the words, a truth which the very form of the confession holds out like a shimmering mirage. Whence too this new way of philosophising: seeking the fundamental relation to the true, not simply in oneself – in some forgotten knowledge, or in a certain primal trace – but in the self-examination that yields, through a multitude of fleeting impressions, the basic certainties of consciousness.[65]

It would appear that there is in the twelfth century the composition of something that we can describe as an 'intentional self' or a subject (*subject*) that refers to itself as the foundational basis of its knowledge. Abelard's *Ethics* is important in this respect but we also find references to intentionality in the letters of Heloise to Abelard, and even in the work of Bernard. Although the consequences of Abelard's argument in relation to the power of the 'keys' and the role of the Jews in the death of Christ and various other details may have been controversial, the general intentionality thesis does not seem to have been particularly problematic. However, his articulation of it in the striking terms that we find in the *Ethics* has suggested to some scholars that he deserves a special place in the disclosing of the human subject.[66] Without a doubt his rigorous application of the principle of the Delphic oracle 'know yourself' introduced a new tone into early medieval intellectual life as he moved the focus away from exteriority, a world of acts, and redirected it 'towards the realm of informed, individual judgement'.[67]

I want to suggest that in Abelard's work, be it in the level of the general methodology or in its specific application to logic, linguistics or ethics, there is a consistently developing theme of the self-reflecting subject (*subject*) a subject that is fundamentally transparent and turned back on itself as the foundation of knowledge. This had the cumulative effect of reversing those Augustinian principles that had dominated early medieval intellectual life until the twelfth century. (Faith over philosophy and actions over intentions.)

Abelard's logical and ethical work opens up a fracture which is occupied by a technology of the subject (*subject*) that is transparent to itself. However, his reliance on methodological scepticism as his general technique poses for him a difficult problem. On the one hand, his epistemological/ontological foundation demands the certainty of subjective experience, on the other, his methodology continually acts to undermine it. Methodological scepticism even in its dialectical form has a tendency to become scepticism per se. Too much 'certainty' of self undermines the possibility of methodological scepticism at all, making the application of the sceptical method simply degenerate into subjectivist assertions. As we have already seen Augustine also faced this problem and offered a partial solution to it. He argued that to assert one's own existence even as a being able to be deceived about anything, is to implicitly acknowledge one's own existence as a being capable of deception. 'If I am deceived, I exist! For one who does not exist, cannot be deceived. Consequently I exist even if I am deceived.' Augustine's second response to scepticism was that it already presupposes a criterion of truth. The ability to perceive a deception already implies an awareness of what constitutes the truth. To simultaneously presuppose the truth and argue 'deceptively' for its contrary is to involve a contradiction. Given that the principle of non-contradiction is fundamental to Augustine's intellectual schema the sceptic maintains an indefensible position.

Abelard does not have such a strong position from which to respond to scepticism. First, the reactivation of Aristotelian dialectics had legitimised the kind of methodological scepticism that was discussed in detail previously. This was qualitatively different from what Augustine had opposed, since this time it was emerging from within the Church and was not being proposed by the 'heathens' of the New Academy. Secondly, if all his arguments failed Augustine could make one further move past – *Si fallor sum*, 'Though I doubt, I am aware of myself existing when I doubt' – resorting to *Credo ut intelligam*.[68] As we have seen, the effect of Abelard's work was both to undermine and invert this principle: ' "Anyone who loves me", says Truth, "will heed what I say." But who can heed the words or precepts of the Lord by obeying them unless he has first understood them?'[69]

Furthermore the technique of Abelard's *Sic et Non* in questioning 158 of the Church's central doctrines and leaving them unresolved expanded the dimensions of what could be questioned and what was beyond question. This was acting on Anselm's already well-known proofs for the existence of God, but Abelard's determined pursuing of the consequences of dialectical doubt introduced a new philosophical rigour into medieval intellectual life. This rigour necessarily turned back onto the subject (*subject*) of the methodological practice, which raised a problem for Abelard that was unknown to Augustine. If faith is not to be accorded the position of the first principle, then the danger of methodological scepticism is that it threatens the subject – on which the whole epistemology is now founded – with uncertainty. Abelard's solution to this is to find a new technology of certainty and experience of the subject (*subject*) that supports it – a place from which to philosophise that is relatively secure and which with transparency as its presupposition overcomes the wavering induced by the oscillation between the Yes and No, between being and not being. It is this place that emerges from Abelard's autobiography, *The Historia Calamitatum*.

Before beginning the discussion of the details of *The Historia Calamitatum*, two issues need to be addressed: the question of authenticity and the definition of the category 'autobiography'.

First, in the 1950s there was some controversy among medieval scholars as to the authenticity of the Abelard and Heloise letters, including *The Historia Calamitatum*. The proponents who doubted their authenticity did so on the following major grounds: that there was no manuscript prior to the second half of the thirteenth century; that there were problems of style; and that the psychological presentation of Heloise was unconvincing.[70] Then a number of 'newly' discovered older manuscripts made the first point rather less significant, the stylistic criticism was shown to be based on work that was subsequently discredited, and the problems of the picture of Heloise were resolved 'by advances in historical knowledge in conjunction with literary analysis'.[71] The debate remained dormant until the 1970s when the question of authenticity was again raised by Benton. Once again there were alternative defences for the authenticity of the Heloise letters that met each of his objections.[72] Questions of dating, authenticity and authorship are difficult ones for medieval scholarship in general and they do not apply simply to the Abelard-Heloise letters. That to date there has been no manuscript found from the twelfth century is not an isolated case. Given that often twelfth-century documents originally only existed in small numbers, 'the vagaries in the manuscript tradition for particular works should not be treated as statistical data susceptible of sophisticated mathematical analysis'.[73] Although the question of the authenticity of the Abelard-Heloise letters emerges from time to time and probably will continue to do so, on balance it can be agreed that:

> While no definite conclusion can be drawn regarding the authenticity of the letters, tentative ascription must rest on weight of evidence. Until any more solid evidence for any other authorship is available, Abelard and Heloise still have the best claim as the authors of the letters ascribed to each. The problems created by the other ascriptions that have so far been suggested are at least as great as the problems obtaining with this original ascription.[74]

This is also the view held by most of Abelard's commentators and defenders:

> Yet it must be said that historians questioning the genuineness of the letters have been unduly selective. The other written exchanges between Abelard and Heloise are also very substantial. In particular, the *Problemata Heloisae* which Abelard answered at length is not known in manuscript earlier than the thirteenth century. Moreover, the hymn collection which Abelard composed for the Paraclete is not found in any manuscript earlier than the late thirteenth century, and the hymns were only selectively adopted by the nuns. The problems raised by the letters should be studied in association with the other documents that testify to the numerous and highly cultivated exchanges between Abelard and Heloise and to the development of the observances of the Paraclete.[75]

In the last analysis the debate can be allowed to rage. As was discussed previously the 'question' of attributing a text to a certain author is not without its own theoretical and intellectual problems. Furthermore, if it could be shown that the *Historia Calamitatum* was in fact a thirteenth-century work not by Abelard at all, the points about to be made would not be weakened. This is because my contention all along has been that the texts discussed were integrated into a transformation of the power/knowledge network that I have analysed in terms of the 'Politics of primogeniture' and the 'Politics of truth'. The solutions they proposed were solutions to problems raised by an environment which demanded such solutions and which constituted alternative problematisations – including the problematisation of self. What is important is that the discourses I have discussed so far and the *Historia Calamitatum* came into existence within a relatively short number of years – not to whom they can be exclusively and definitively attributed. Having made that point clear it is my contention that the content and philosophical structure of the *Historia Calamitatum* is consistent with the work already discussed under the *nomen* of Abelard and was part of problematising the subject (*subject*).[76]

Turning now to the second issue for discussion, the question of 'autobiography'. How are we to define and distinguish it from other similar textual practices? In the twelfth century the model autobiography was Augustine's *Confessions*, and yet I will argue that this is not an autobiography in the modern sense – in the sense that the *Historia Calamitatum* will be referred to as an autobiography. Rather it is a work of hagiography, an idealised biography of the pre-conditions for a saintly life. This is a contentious view. Radice in her introduction to *The Letters of Abelard and Heloise* argues the following: 'In this sense the *Historia* is a search for identity and a personal autobiography comparable with those of St Augustine, Cellini, St Teresa and Rousseau.'[77] Running counter to this argument we have the opinions of Cantor:

The description of personal idiosyncrasies would be regarded as proud, sinful arrogance. Augustine's *Confessions* was the last autobiography written before the twelfth century, and even it is not strictly an autobiography, for the bishop of Hippo was concerned with revealing himself only as Everyman. In the early middle ages there was very little biographical writing worthy of the name. A mass of hagiographical literature followed conventional patterns, forcing its subjects into preconceived moulds and turning them into plaster saints.[78]

and of Gilson:

Moreover, Augustine's masterpiece was a sort of spiritual autobiography rather than the story of his own life. Peter Abelard's intention was different. In the Confessions, the central figure in the story was God; Abelard occupies the very centre of his own narrative. As though trouble were his natural element and with his own career and his adventures as a knight-errant in the schools of philosophy, he was always willing to challenge any adversary.[79]

It would seem that when Radice writes of 'comparability' she is failing to disassociate the 'comparable' as always possible between two objects and the 'same' something altogether quite different. The spiritual autobiographies of St Teresa and Augustine are nothing like the autobiographies of Cellini, Rousseau and Abelard the major difference being that Augustine's model of the *Confession* is based on the principle of *Confessio*:

The *Confessions* are one of the few books of Augustine's, where the title is significant. *Confessio* meant, for Augustine, 'accusation of oneself; praise of God'. In this one word, he had summed up his attitude to the human condition: it was the new key with which he hoped, in middle age, to unlock the riddle of evil.[80]

Augustine's *Confessions* aims to praise divine goodness and mercy and he is concerned to reveal his life only in so far as it relates to the fortunes of Christianity as a whole: 'Far from being obsessed by his individual *ego*, Augustine is always looking at himself in the light of divine perfection in order to disclose his real nature and authentic status.'[81] This autobiographical model was well known to Abelard's contemporaries and demanded the Augustinian formulaic confession as its organising principle. The opening of the *Confessions* was the model for spiritual autobiographies: 'Can any praise be worthy of the Lord's majesty? How magnificent his strength! How inscrutable his wisdom.'[82] And the disclosure of the subject (*subject*) that follows is explicitly offered to God: 'I wish to act in truth, making my confession both in my heart before you and in this book before the many who will read it.',[83] and 'O Lord, my Helper and my Redeemer, I shall now tell and confess to the glory of your name how you released me from the fetters of lust which held me so tightly shackled and from my slavery to the things of this world.'[84]

Guibert of Nogent, Abelard's twelfth-century contemporary, strictly adheres to the Augustinian 'confessional' formula:

> I confess to Thy Majesty, O God, my endless wanderings from Thy paths, and my turning back so often to the bosom of Thy Mercy, directed by Thee in spite of all. I confess the wickedness I did in childhood and in youth, wickedness that yet boils up in my mature years, and my ingrained love of crookedness, which still lives on in the sluggishness of my worn body.[85]

Guibert's editor, Benton, comments that Guibert's reflections do not constitute an autobiography as he addresses his book to God: 'Who "knoweth the secrets of the heart", and wrote it for the edification of his readers and to provide material for sermons.'[86] It would appear, then, that Augustine, St Teresa and Guibert did not write what we would consider to be autobiographies in the present sense of the term, which presupposes that the text is not totally mediated by a relationship with God. On the whole one is inclined to disagree with Radice's analysis on the grounds that it does not account for this crucial distinction, and to consider the *Historia Calamitatum* as an expression of what we might refer to as a modern (whatever that might mean) autobiographical textual voice:

> Abelard's autobiography, The History of My Calamities, was the critical turning point in the twelfth-century rediscovery of personality. Abelard revels in his idiosyncrasies and delights in revealing to the world the peculiar facts of his own life, even those which could not be socially approved. In fact, like so many later biographers, he may have made his experiences appear more dramatic and startling in retrospect than they actually were. The important point is that Abelard wished to reveal himself to the world as a unique individual whose biography could not be confused with anyone else's.[87]

Perhaps the distinction is now clear enough in reference to traditional hagiography but does not take into account the development of the medieval chronicles, and this point now needs addressing. The most familiar of the early medieval chronicles is Gregory of Tours' *The History of the Franks*.[88] This text was composed well before the period of this study, in the sixth century, and details the events from the Creation to contemporary political life in the Frankish court with which Gregory was intimately involved. In the preface Gregory tells us what motivated him to undertake his task:

> In fact in the towns of Gaul the writing of literature has declined to the point where it has virtually disappeared altogether. Many people have complained about this, not once but time and time again. 'What a poor period this is!' they have been heard to say. 'If among all our people there is not one man to be

found who can write a book about what is happening today, the pursuit of letters really is dead in us!'
I have often thought about these complaints and others like them. I have written this work to keep alive the memory of those dead and gone, and to bring them to the notice of future generations.[89]

It would appear that there is some similarity here with the 'intentional' style of the *Historia Calamitatum*. However, this similarity soon disappears as Gregory begins his account of the history of the Franks with a detailed account of the Creation.

The first twenty-six chapters of Book 1 deal with matters of early Church history up to and including the story of the Evangelists. It is only in the last part of the first book that events which have a direct bearing on the history of the Franks are included. Furthermore Gregory begins Book 1 with a formulaic confession of faith and it becomes apparent that the object of the *History of the Franks* is to explain how Christianity came to the court of the pagan Frankish kings and displaced their old heathen religion and showed it to be false. Even when Gregory deals with events of which he had personal knowledge he does not reveal that interiority and inner voice that we find in the *Historia Calamitatum*. We never read of how Gregory 'feels' about the issues of which he writes. His commentary, for that is really what the *History of the Franks* is, is a list of events that directs the reader's relation to them according to their place as significant in the conversion of the Frankish kings to Christianity. Gregory concludes his work with a list of the Bishops of Tours who preceded him and writing of himself at the end of *The History of the Franks* says:

All unworthy as I am, I, Gregory, have been the nineteenth Bishop. When I took over Tours cathedral, in which Saint Martin and all these other priests of the Lord had been consecrated to the episcopal office, it had been destroyed by fire and was in a sorry state of ruin. I rebuilt it, bigger and higher than before, and in the seventeenth year of my episcopate I re-dedicated it.[90]

Even the most superficial reading of *The History of the Franks*, supports the view that while it is an interesting and important text it does not manifest the same interiority, sense of self or subject (*subject*) that can be attributed to the *Historia Calamitatum*. However, it does provide the basis of the 'chronicling' that will occur throughout the early medieval period and it is these later chronicles that can be seen as closer to the style of Abelard's 'autobiography'.

Two of the most famous of the chronicles by Joinville and Villehardouin were written in the mid-thirteenth century and so are outside the chronology of our study; however, some brief comments are in order.[91]

Joinville's *Life of St Louis* follows the formulaic introduction that we find in Gregory:

> In the name of God Almighty we have now put down in writing some part of the pious sayings and good teaching of our saintly King Louis, so that those who study this book may find such things introduced in their proper sequence, and may thus derive more profit from them than if they had been recorded among his deeds. From this point onwards we begin, in the name of God and in the name of King Louis, to speak of the things he did.[92]

Joinville's work is the archetypal medieval chronicle of which there are many other examples. Given that its subject matter is not only a king but also a saint, it operates as literature somewhere between Church hagiographies and the political biographies typical of twelfth- and thirteenth-century kings and princes. The function of these biographies was often to legitimise the existence of various households as ruling families. Not only does Joinville not reflect on his own relation to the events that he recounts, he fails to provide us with any sense of interiority or subjectivity that we can attribute to the object of his study, Louis. If there is a sense of self in Joinville's work it is the self of the eyewitness, the reporter, not that of the contemporary autobiographer:

> I wish to make known that I myself actually saw and heard a great part of what I have told you concerning the saintly king. Another considerable part of it is based on what I found in a certain book, written in French, which I have incorporated in this chronicle. I am drawing your attention to this so that those who hear this book read may have full confidence in the truth of what it says I saw and heard. As for the other things recorded here, I offer no guarantee of their truth, because I did not witness them myself.[93]

Joinville himself refers to his work as a chronicle and although the *Life of St Louis* is an important text for medieval studies and raises a number of significant issues that could be pursued at another time, it does not qualify within the limits of my definition of an autobiography.

Villehardouin's *Conquest of Constantinople* is even more of a chronicle than Joinville's work. The *Conquest of Constantinople* records the events of the Fourth Crusade in the style of the chronicle and does not allow the chronicler's own thoughts and intentions to intrude into the story. Villehardouin presents an eyewitness account of the events but minimises the part that he played in them. It is not the story of his individual life of the kind that we find in Abelard's text, it is rather an attempt to write a chronicle from what we would now consider to be an objective point of view. Whatever intrudes into the text does so only in terms of its relation to the Fourth Crusade.

Even if these comments are restricted to a matter of degree, Abelard's autobiography exhibits a conception of the subject (*subject*) and interiority so far not usually found in contemporary documents in the twelfth and thirteenth centuries. The *Historia Calamitatum* is one those moments when the subject (*subject*) reflects upon their own activity through the medium of a text. It does have resonances with the previous use of notebooks, diaries and chronicles of other epochs, but its reflexive intensity is much greater.[94] We can separate it from similar strategies in the following ways:

1. Unlike a diary or a chronicle the *Historia Calamitatum* is not just a collection of events that the subject observed. Importantly the subject (*subject*) reflects on the meaning of the events at some chronological distance from them.
2. Unlike Augustine's *Confessions* the relation of subject (*subject*) in the *Historia Calamitatum* is not mediated by God but only by their self-reflection.
3. Unlike the memoirs of Guibert of Nogent, in the *Historia Calamitatum* only events that the subject directly participated in are included and reflected upon.
4. The prime function of the *Historia Calamitatum* is not to act as an exemplar but is a point of transmission where what is transmitted through a dialogue with oneself is a particular construction of the subject. In other words it is a technology of the subject (*subject*) that is at stake.
5. The *Historia Calamitatum* is framed in relation to Abelard's ethics and their theme of *Know Thyself*.[95] From within the framework of an ethics based on consent not acts, it posed two questions: Who is responsible for the life of the subject (*subject*) that I am? How did I become the subject (*subject*) that I am?
6. These two questions frame a diagram where the writing of self in the *Historia Calamitatum* is an ontological technology that is novel to the Middle Ages and is a particular historical event in the history of Western culture.
7. In so far as the *Historia Calamitatum* serves as a conjunction between material practices of self, and reflection on those practices, the subject (*subject*) as experienced is anchored in the reflexive reactivation of this materiality.

This is not a moment when one can speak of the liberation of the universal subject of humanism as if it had waited from the dawn of time for this moment to be brought into the light of day, where it stayed until Nietzsche's relentless and disruptive questioning. The subject (*subject*) as it emerged in the twelfth century was the direct effect of transformations in the power/knowledge network – of material and discursive practices some of which I have previously outlined. If it seems that the *Historia Calamitatum* speaks to us with a voice closer to our own than other texts of the twelfth century it is not because it refers to any universal structure of the subject (*subject*), be it scientific, metaphysical or transcendental, it is because of its particularity and emergence as a specific historico-cultural event.[96]

The *Historia Calamitatum* is presented in the form of the *consolatio,* a letter of consolation to a friend, and opens with the rhetorical convention required by a *consolatio*:

> There are times when example is better than precept for stirring or soothing human passions; and so I propose to follow up the words of consolation I gave you in person with the history of my own misfortunes, hoping thereby to give you comfort in absence. In comparison to my trials you will see that your own are nothing, or only slight, and will find them easier to bear.[97]

This opening, conscious of its 'classical' style, is quite unlike those other contemporary texts where the subject's life is presented as an exemplar being offered up to God as demanded by the '*confessio*'. Quite to the contrary, this is not a confession at all, since Abelard rarely, if ever, sees his actions as sinful, except in one or two rather striking cases and even then it is not clear that they are examples of 'sin'.[98] Having completed the conventional opening to the *Historia Calamitatum* Abelard details his genealogy and recounts the details of his life covering the period from 1119 to 1132. He tells us how he renounced his inheritance as the first born son and decided to pursue a philosophical career instead of the military one that his training had prepared him for. Indeed military metaphors abound both in the *Historia Calamitatum* and in the personal letters to Heloise:

> I took my school outside the city to Mont Ste Geneviève, and set up camp there in order to lay siege to my usurper. The news brought William back to Paris in unseemly haste to restore such scholars as remained to him and his community to their former monastery, apparently to deliver from my siege the soldier whom he had abandoned.[99]

and:

> As in the army camps of the world, so in the camp of the Lord, that is, in monastic communities, people must be appointed to be in authority over the rest. In the army there is one commander over all, at whose bidding everything is carried out, but because of the size and complexity of his duties he shares his burdens with several others and appoints subordinate officers to be responsible for various duties or companies of men.[100]

Throughout the *Historia Calamitatum* we are witness to intentions behind actions, even when this requires the inclusion of material guaranteed to shock and disturb:

> I was amazed by his simplicity – if he had entrusted a tender lamb to a ravening wolf it would not have surprised me more. In handing her over to me to punish as well as to teach, what else was he doing but giving me complete freedom to realize my desires, and providing me an opportunity, even if I did not make use of it, for me to bend her to my will by threats and blows if persuasion failed? But there were two special reasons for his freedom from base suspicion: his love for his niece and my previous reputation for continence.[101]

In one of the letters from Abelard to Heloise we are shown that Heloise was coerced to conform to Abelard's will, which makes the intentions he declares above all the more insidious:

> You know the depths of shame to which my unbridled lust had consigned our bodies, until no reverence for decency or for God even during the days of Our Lord's Passion, or of the greater sacraments could keep me from wallowing in this mire. Even when you were unwilling, resisted to the utmost of your power and tried to dissuade me, as yours was the weaker nature I often forced you to consent with threats and blows. So intense were the fires of lust which bound me to you that I set those wretched, obscene pleasures, which we blush even to name, above God as above myself; nor would it seem that divine mercy could have taken action except by forbidding me these pleasures altogether, without future hope.[102]

This confirms an ambivalent attitude to women which has a number of consequences for this self-reflexive autobiographical subject (*subject*). In general what is rearticulated is the position of Jerome which supports the view that women were responsible for the Fall and must therefore accept the blame for original sin and the failure of men to lead lives not marked by restraint of the passions. To some extent this is also accepted by Heloise.[103] However, Heloise maintains that in spite of this their action did not constitute a sin:

> Wholly guilty though I am, I am also, as you know, wholly innocent. It is not the deed but the intention of the doer that makes the crime, and justice should weigh not on what was done but the spirit in which it is done.[104]

An important issue needs mentioning here. We know from a number of sources that Heloise was a remarkable scholar in her own right, so it is not necessarily clear who was responsible for some aspects of Abelard's doctrine. Heloise's contribution, not simply as a student but also as a philosopher, to the development of those views and work that we attribute to Abelard has never to my knowledge been adequately discussed. Perhaps the paucity of such relevant material as would allow this discussion to take place accounts for this failure. None the less one might well be more cautious in maintaining Heloise's role as a passive recipient of Abelard's doctrine, as in a number of places in the *Historia Calamitatum* and the *Letters* the indications are that she won a number of philosophical debates with Abelard.[105] As we read the *Historia Calamitatum* and the *Letters* an important point emerges. At the moment of the production of this technology of self, the autobiographical subject (*subject*) that supports it: a) is composed around sexual practices; and b) is not as 'certain' as its epistemological foundations demand. I will now examine these issues individually.

The question of sex is absolutely central to the *Historia Calamitatum* and the Abelard-Heloise letters. Perhaps the most crucial event in Abelard's life is the seduction of Heloise and his subsequent castration. Furthermore Abelard consciously sets out to seduce Heloise from the outset and pursues this task relentlessly. In a sense he is being confronted with a problem that had emerged out of the history of the early Church, the education of women. The conversion of women to the early Church had demanded their instruction in the Gospels and this necessarily brought them into contact with teachers who professed a celibate life. Two examples that Abelard was fond of quoting were St Jerome and Origen. Each responded to this in different ways, and in neither case opted for the practice of seduction. However, due to the demands of increasing literacy and the need to provide potential nuns with an education appropriate to their vocation and social status, the education of women had re-emerged as an important issue in the twelfth century. Abelard's letters of direction to Heloise for the establishment of a 'rule' designed explicitly for women emphasises this point. Heloise, however, while not being the exception, was the unusual case of being a highly educated woman even before her instruction by Abelard. We are told in the *Historia Calamitatum* that she could already write and Abelard considered this one of her main attractions:

> Knowing the girl's knowledge and love of letters I thought she would be all the more ready to consent, and that even when separated we could enjoy each other's presence by exchange of written messages in which we could speak more openly than in person, and so need never lack the pleasure of conversation.[106]

Some twelfth-century sources suggest that Heloise could read Greek and

Hebrew as well as Latin whereas Abelard read neither Greek nor Hebrew, and we are given the impression by Abelard that her education made her 'worthy' of his attention which is why he set out to seduce her through the educative process.[107] The practice of homosexual seduction as part of the process of acquiring a love of knowledge has its own history from the Greeks through to the medieval monasteries of Abelard's day.[108] While Abelard was fond of quoting Jerome's and Origen's approach to women his intentional seduction has little to do with these early Church fathers. Jerome had taken his female students with him into exile while simultaneously developing a misogynist theology. Origen had castrated himself in order to end rumours about his relations with his women students.

A fundamental problematising of sex played a continuing part in Heloise's life even after she entered religious life and was prioress of the convent at the Paraclete:

In my case, the pleasures of lovers which we shared have been too sweet – they can never displease me, and can scarcely be banished from my thoughts. Wherever I turn they are always there before my eyes, bringing with them awakened longings and fantasies which will not even let me sleep. Even during the celebration of the Mass, when our prayers should be purer, lewd visions of those pleasures take such a hold upon my unhappy soul that my thoughts are on their wantonness instead of on prayers. I should be groaning over the sins I have committed, but I can only sigh for what I have lost. Everything we did and also the times and places are stamped on my heart along with your image, so that I live through it all again with you. Even in sleep I know no respite. Sometimes my thoughts are betrayed in a movement of my body, or they break out in an unguarded word. In my utter wretchedness, that cry from a suffering soul could well be mine: 'Miserable creature that I am, who is there to rescue me out of the body doomed to this death?' Would that in truth I could go on: 'The grace of God through Jesus Christ our Lord.'[109]

If this remains important to Heloise throughout her life, Abelard takes an alternative course as a result of the events that followed the seduction of Heloise. After Heloise's uncle Fulbert finally discovered their relationship he forced a separation, but this enforced absence did not bring about the intended result as it:

inflamed our passion even more; then we became more abandoned as we lost all sense of shame and, indeed, shame diminished as we found more opportunities for love making. And so we were caught in the act as the poet says happened to Mars and Venus.[110]

Further complications followed as Heloise became pregnant and was sent by Abelard to his home country Brittany where she subsequently gave birth to a son, Astrolabe. There is a hint here in the *Historia Calamitatum* that in part, in sending Heloise to his own country Abelard was ensuring that Fulbert would not attack him with Heloise in the hands of a potentially hostile family: 'If he killed me or did me personal injury, there was a danger that his beloved niece might suffer for it in my country.'[111]

After the birth of Astrolabe Abelard returned to Brittany and decided to marry Heloise. The *Historia Calamitatum* then details the arguments for and against marriage, with Heloise being resolutely opposed to any marriage and offering effective arguments in defence of her view, which include an appeal to practical grounds:

> What harmony can there be between pupils and nursemaids, desks and cradles, books or tablets and distaffs, pen or stylus and spindles? Who can concentrate on thoughts of Scripture or philosophy and be able to endure babies crying, nurses soothing them with lullabies, and the noisy coming and going of men and women about the house? Will he put up with the constant muddle and squabble which small children bring into the home? The wealthy can do so, you will say, for their mansions and large houses can provide privacy and, being rich, they do not have to count the cost nor be tormented by daily cares. But philosophers lead a very different life from rich men, and those who are concerned with wealth or are involved in mundane matters will not have time for the claims of Scripture or philosophy. Consequently, the great philosophers of the past have despised the world, not renouncing it so much as escaping from it, and have denied themselves every pleasure so as to find peace in the arms of philosophy alone.[112]

Heloise wins the argument but fails to change Abelard's mind and after returning to Paris they were married in a secret ceremony in the presence of Fulbert. Heloise returned to Fulbert's house and Heloise and Abelard could only manage occasional secret meetings. Maintaining this secrecy was important for Abelard since although he was not a priest his career as a magister and clerk would have been undermined by his marriage. Fulbert failed to adhere to an agreement to keep the marriage secret and news of the marriage began to spread. Abelard's response to this was to order Heloise to the convent of Argenteuil and after protesting violently she finally agreed.[113] It is here that the events of Abelard's life take an unusual turn. Scandalous relationships between clerks or even priests and women were common in the twelfth century, indeed this is the time when the Church was attempting to enforce celibacy on the clergy. Fulbert's response to Abelard, however, was extraordinary:

At this news her uncle and his friends and relatives imagined that I had tricked them, and had found an easy way of ridding myself of Heloise by making her a nun. Wild with indignation they plotted against me, and one night as I slept peacefully in an inner room in my lodgings, they bribed one of my servants to admit them and there took cruel vengeance on me of such appalling barbarity as to shock the whole world; they cut off the parts of my body whereby I had committed the wrong of which they had complained. Then they fled, but the two who could be caught were blinded and mutilated as I had been, one of them being the servant who had been led by greed while in my service to betray his master.[114]

The barbarity of the act of which Abelard complains with some justification is not why these events are surprising. This kind of punishment was not unusual. Aelred of Rievaulx cites the example of a man who was castrated by nuns for making one of their community pregnant.[115] Clanchy also gives the example of a similar case:

The proclamation to which Matthew gives most attention likewise occurred in 1248, when the king 'ordered it to be proclaimed as law by the voice of a crier' that henceforward no man might castrate another for fornication except a husband in the case of his wife's adulterer. The reason for this was that John le Bretun had castrated the Norfolk knight, Godfrey de Millers, for lying with his daughter.[116]

What is so unusual in the case of Abelard is that at the time of his castration he was married to Heloise:

The punishment you suffered would have been proper vengeance for men caught in open adultery. But what others deserve for adultery came upon you through a marriage which you believed had made amends for all previous wrong doing; what adulterous women have brought on their lovers, your own wife brought on you.[117]

Abelard's response to his castration was to enter the monastery of St Denis and he undertook to devote his life to the teaching of theology. It is at this stage that he began to compare himself to Origen in something of a curious 'disavowal' of the role he played in his own downfall. He then started to criticise the depravity and lax lifestyle of the monks of St Denis and following the publication of *On the Unity and Trinity of God* was condemned at the Council of Soissons.

It was only after his castration that Abelard re-examined his life and developed his interest in theology and his concern to find a method capable of discovering the Truth. Without appealing to a psychological or biographical point of view, it is evident that the question of sex and sexual practices plays an important role in the articulation of the textual voice of Abelard and Heloise in the *Historia Calamitatum* and their letters. This might suggest that the reflexivity that the technology of the autobiographical self both presupposes and articulates is fundamentally orientated around sexual practices.

The second issue that needs to be discussed is the certainty and coherence of the subject (*subject*) that is found in the *Historia Calamitatum*, the *Letters* and some of Abelard's other work. Both Abelard's epistemology and ontology demand the production of the transparent autobiographical voice that we find in the *Historia Calamitatum* and the *Letters*. As this subject (*subject*) is founded on the apprehension of its own certainty this tends to undermine the 'doubt' necessary for methodological scepticism. However, without the operation of doubt in the method it simply becomes a crude principle of 'subjectivist assertion'. Either the subject is so secure that the method cannot function or it becomes so unstable that an infinite regression of doubt occurs which ultimately causes the transparent subject to disintegrate and madness follows.

Abelard appears to be aware of this as a possible consequence of his method because references to madness appear not only in the *Historia Calamitatum* and the *Letters* but throughout his work. In *A Dialogue of a Philosopher with a Jew, and a Christian*, at the very moment that Abelard is establishing the defence of reason for solving theological and philosophical problems the question of madness intervenes:

Christian: 'Now for the first time I see that you have become shamelessly rash, wrangling rather than philosophizing. Indeed fearing that you may seem to be compelled to confess what is clearly the truth, you turn to the insanity of the most obvious falsehood and are of the opinion that all good men are equally good and all guilty men are equally guilty, and all are deserving of the same glory or punishment as well.'[118]

and:

Christian: 'Who, finally, does not understand that it is the height of insanity to say that all sins are equal?'[119]

At a number of important places in this dialogue Abelard allows the Christian to attack an argument on the grounds that it is not rational and therefore is insane. As the location of rationality in Abelard's work is the soul, to be insane is to be soulless, to be without that condition that makes one a human. Not only is the threat of insanity a consequence of the adoption of methodological scepticism, at some general level it appears that it has a more direct application to Abelard's life. Passages in the *Historia*

Calamitatum strongly suggest that Abelard exhibits symptoms of what we would now term paranoia and psychosis:

> I am still in danger, and every day I imagine a sword hanging over my head, so that at meals I dare scarcely breathe: like the man we read about who supposed the power and wealth of the tyrant Dionysius to constitute the supreme happiness until he looked up and saw a sword suspended by a thread over his own head and realised what sort of happiness it is which accompanies earthly power. This is my experience all the time; a poor monk raised to be an abbot, the more wretched as I have become more wealthy, in order that my example may curb the ambition of those who have deliberately chosen a similar course.[120]

and:

> but it is within the cloister that I have to face the incessant assaults – as crafty as they are violent – of my sons, that is, of the monks entrusted to my care, as their abbot and father.[121]

and again:

> But if the Lord shall deliver me into the hands of my enemies so that they overcome and kill me, or by whatever chance I enter upon the way of all while absent from you, wherever my body may lie, buried or unburied, I beg you to have it brought to your burial-ground, where our daughters, or rather, our sisters in Christ may see my tomb more often and thereby be encouraged to pour out their prayers more fully to the Lord on my behalf.[122]

While it is the case that occasionally an abbot was indeed murdered by the monks under his charge, Abelard seems to respond out of all proportion to the threat at hand. If one carefully rereads the *Historia Calamitatum* bearing in mind that it was written well after his castration, it becomes evident that this autobiographical technology and the subject (*subject*) that sustains it is unstable and marked by paranoia. This has been noted even by some of Abelard's more conservative commentators: 'but he is so vague when writing about his continued dangers and apprehensions of further charges of heresy that one wonders if he was developing a persecution complex.'[123]

My emphasis is slightly different as I do not want to allow a psychologistic account of this, but a philosophical one. My view is that Abelard's response to his situation is both material and philosophical. His system of methodological scepticism has destabilised the very subject (*subject*) that it needs to operate. As a result of this he is confronted with paranoid fears and he reacts in the manner of a psychotic. The inner/outer or real/personal distinctions collapse and reality is made to agree with his individual subjective philosophical perspective. He system builds. He creates a world dominated by his own philosophical and methodological system. This psychotic solution becomes associated with the autobiographical technology, and the subject (*subject*) that sustains it.

One of the most respected studies of medieval philosophy is David Knowles's *The Evolution of Medieval Thought* and he says of the philosophical period under discussion: 'No medieval thinker started like Descartes or Kant, to build up a great system from the postulates of his own mental experience; philosophy could be received from others and taught like any other subject.'[124]

This view of the early medieval period is entrenched with medieval scholars. As I have been attempting to show, the philosophical system of Abelard when considered as a system, which is how we consider the works of Descartes, Kant and so on, does presuppose a particular subject (*subject*). Both the system and the subject on which it is based constitute a series of problems and possible solutions that are relevant to a number of debates in contemporary philosophy in the twelfth century. Abelard does not manage to solve the tensions that his system sets up. His methodological scepticism always strains at the coherence of the subject (*subject*) that it both requires and yet systematically undermines. At its inauguration in the *Historia Calamitatum* the transparent self is not transparent in isolation simply through reflexive self-knowledge but is transparent because of its relation to its specific history, the technology of autobiography and psychosis. This suggests the possibility of the composition of a textual and philosophical autobiographical subject (*subject*) from a different perspective to that of Stock, but one which still agrees with much of his work:

> *The influence* of literate ways of thinking has now been traced through heresy, reform, sacramental theology, and the philosophical attitudes towards texts. These changes within medieval cultural life, it was proposed, were not only produced by a renaissance of higher disciplines. They also revealed a new balance between oral and written communication, adapted, as it were, to the needs of different branches of thought. Culture, therefore, was reborn, while the forms through which it expressed itself emerged as self-conscious instruments of analysis.
>
> Just as, for Abelard, the mind acquired the capacity through the use of language to structure the raw data of the senses, so written statements began to act as reference points for giving meaning to everyday human relations.[125]

and:

Experience in other words became separable, if not always separated, from ratiocination about it; and the main field of investigation turned out to be, not the raw data of sense of the platonized ideal of pure knowledge, but rather the forms of mediation between them. This set of changes resulted in a rebirth of hermeneutics as a critical philosophy of meaning, in a renewed search for epistemological order, and in a widespread interest in diachrony, development, and processual evolution. Understanding as a consequence began to emerge from the accumulation of reiterated experience, even though, as was recognized, the tools of methodological analysis were not given in each concrete set of events; and an understanding formed of similar elements links the contemporary reader to the past through the preservation of those very written artefacts which originated new patterns of thought and action themselves.[126]

To date I have initiated a number of arguments concerning the twelfth century that need further elaboration. I have suggested that there was a transformation of the power/knowledge network along three axes: systems of inheritance, the politics of truth, and technologies of the subject (*subject*). I have suggested that as primogeniture emerged as the major inheritance system for at least the nobility, a number of social phenomena occurred. Women were often dispossessed of land and those that were not became the objects of the attention of landless knights. With the narrowing of lateral ties the family itself became focused on the monogamous heterosexual couple, and the protection of the integrity of the lineal bloodline took on an unprecedented significance. This combined with an expanding monogamy to produce an increasingly misogynist society.

I have also argued that transformations occurred to the way in which knowledge was produced, transmitted, circulated and regulated. And I have suggested that these changes problematised technologies of the self, of the subject (*subject*) which we can see operating in texts of the epoch, including works attributed to Abelard.

As the masculine line began to dominate at a wider social level, at the level of philosophy a subject (*subject*) was redefining itself as self-reflexive, transparent, the arbiter of all knowledge and fundamentally psychotic. At an anthropological level we have the emergence of a patriarchally ordered society, while at the philosophical level we have the construction of a dialectically based transparent subject. Two issues emerge from this. Did popular literature reflect these changes? What are some of the possible relations between this ordering of society and the construction of the subject of the technology of autobiography?

In order to discuss these issues further I shall now consider the literary work of two of Abelard's near contemporaries, Chrétien de Troyes and Gottfried von Strassburg. Abelard died in April 1142 and Chrétien is thought to have composed his major works in the 1170s, some 28 years later. It is almost inconceivable that he would not have known of Abelard's work – particularly so because many people believe that the name Troyes was attributed to him due to the time spent in the region. Troyes was also where Abelard's Paraclete was built and where Heloise died in 1163. I am bringing Abelard and Chrétien together not to suggest that Chrétien's work was derived from Abelard's, which cannot be known, but simply to suggest that as Abelard and Chrétien shared the same social milieu they may have shared some of its intellectual concerns. If, as I have argued, it was the social and institutional changes in the milieu that are significant in the construction of the autobiographical subject (*subject*), then one might expect the work of Chrétien also to reflect some of these changes. This is not to be a definitive study of Chrétien, but a use of his work to remake some of the points I have already made in a wider context.

In Chrétien's *Erec and Enide* we are presented with three representations of the status of women: woman as maiden, woman as wife and woman as widow. Each of these roles confronts the social order mediated by the narrative voice of Chrétien – a voice that has found a novel place within language from which to speak, as Chrétien places himself within the text as its organising principle and its arbiter of what is right: 'So Chrétien De Troyes maintains that one ought always to study and strive to speak well and teach right',[127] and goes on to detail his unhappiness with those who get the story wrong: 'a story, which those who earn a living by telling stories are accustomed to mutilate and spoil in the presence of kings and counts'.[128] The importance of speech, and in particular the need for speech to be right or appropriate is established by Chrétien in the opening page of the story. Throughout the text of *Erec and Enide* Chrétien as the narrator will intervene and reconstitute the text around the fundamental issue of speech and silence and the rightness of the text. Both at the level of the story being told and at the level of the characters' rightness of behaviour Chrétien regulates the actions of his characters around the principle of the narrator's speech and silence about moments of textual speech and silence.

A short way into the narrative the problem of speech is directly raised as Erec, Guinevere and an unnamed maiden are riding together in the hunt for the White Stag. They come upon a knight, a dwarf and a damsel. Guinevere wants to know their identity and asks the maiden, the daughter of a king, to find out who they are:

'Dwarf,' says she, 'let me pass. I wish to speak with yonder knight for the Queen sends me hither.' The dwarf who was rude and mean, took his stand in the middle of the road, and said: 'You have no business here. Go back. It is not meet that you should speak to so excellent a knight.'[129]

The maiden ignores the dwarf's rebuke and tries to pass him, but he whips her forcing her to return to Erec and Guinevere. Erec then approaches the dwarf and is whipped by him and being unarmed is forced to return to Guinevere saying:

> 'I did not dare to strike or touch him; but none ought to reproach me, for I was completely unarmed. I mistrusted the armed knight, who, being an ugly fellow and violent, would take it as no jest, and would soon kill me in his pride.'[130]

A number of themes emerge here that are repeated throughout the tale. First, the problem of identity and, in particular, knowing the name of the other so that their behaviour is predictable. Secondly, the question of when it is appropriate to speak and when it is not. Thirdly, Erec fears social reproach from his peers if he does not act correctly, as the speech of the other takes on the dimension of censure. In failing to defend the maiden in his company, even allowing for the fact that he is unarmed, Erec has allowed the maiden, the Queen and himself to be the victims of an insult. Guinevere and the maiden do not reproach him but from that moment until the end of the tale the fear of reproach and the right to speak become its major organising principles.

Erec follows the knight and the dwarf hoping to borrow arms and overcome the knight in a final confrontation. In the course of this pursuit he finds lodgings in the house of Enide's father. Enide does not participate in the conversation that follows between Erec and her father but becomes the object of it, and even at the moment of her betrothal to Erec we are told:

> The maiden sat quiet; but she was very happy and glad that she was betrothed to him, because he was valiant and courteous: and she knew that he would someday be king, and she should receive honour and be crowned a rich queen.[131]

Enide silently accompanies Erec to the tournament where he meets the knight that he is pursuing and manages to overcome him in battle saying:

> 'Vassal, I am he who was in the forest yesterday with Queen Guinevere, when thou didst allow thy ill bred dwarf to strike my lady's damsel. It is disgraceful to strike a woman.'[132]

If we reconsider the original incident it is apparent that the knight's offence was not that he allowed his dwarf to prevent the maiden from speaking to him when he did not wish it, but in allowing the dwarf to strike her. In spite of the fact that she was the daughter of a king, her speech was not seen to be socially valid by either Erec or the knight he had just overcome. She may be shut up but not beaten up. The ironic force of the tale will be that Erec has to come to terms with exactly the same problem in relation to his wife Enide. There is something about speech, and in particular, the speech of women, that is threatening enough to the emerging social order that it allows Chrétien to bring this irony into play:

> She could not have been happier, and showed it plainly, making no secret of her joy. All could see how gay she was, and throughout the house there was great rejoicing for the happiness of the maiden they loved.[133]

Even at this moment of apparent happiness and pleasure curiously Enide says nothing, at least not in the first person, the persona closest to the narrators. We do not know how she expressed her joy, we only know that her speech about it is not allowed to intrude either in to the narrative or the internal structure of the tale. In the characterisation of women to date, whether as the daughter of a king, or in the case of Enide the daughter of a poor vasavour, the speech of women has little or no value. Enide as maiden has no say in her betrothal, she is speechless as she is placed within an increasingly masculine society. However, with her changed status after her marriage some change might be expected in her social recognition.

After success at the Pentecost tournament Erec obtains leave from Arthur to return to his father's court and tensions begin to emerge:

> He [Erec] made of her his mistress and his sweetheart. He devoted all his heart and mind to fondling and kissing her, and took no delight in other pastime. His friends grieved over this, and often regretted among themselves that he was so deep in love.[134]

This is a recurring theme in the romances. Too much devotion in marriage strains the social order. Erec no longer takes part in the tournaments, and his companions start to believe that he has gone soft and that his body is being weakened by his relationship with Enide. The connection between sexual activity and the loss of physical vigour has its own history to the present day and it is outside the scope of this work to analyse it here. However, its force as a social construction at the time that Chrétien was composing *Erec and Enide* was such that it allows him to present Enide speaking for the first time in the tale:

> 'Everyone used to say not long ago that in all the world there was known no better or more gallant knight. Now they all go about making game of you – old and young, little and great – calling you a recreant. Do you suppose it does not give me pain to hear you thus spoken of with scorn? It grieves me when I hear it said, and yet it grieves me more that they put the blame for it on me. Yes, I am blamed for it, I regret to say, and they all assert it is because I have so

ensnared and caught you that you are losing all your merit, and do not care for aught but me. You must choose another course, so that you may silence this reproach, and regain your fame; for I have heard too much of this reproach, and yet I did not disclose it to you. Many a time, when I think of it, I have to weep for very grief. Such chagrin I felt just now that I could not help myself from saying that you were ill-starred.'[135]

Enide finally speaks out both as a wife and as a representative of the wider social order. She accuses Erec of being a recreant, the opposite of the courteous knight. The recreant is the ill-mannered, discourteous knight who is always defeated by the courteous knight of Arthur's court. The effect of Erec's marriage and his distraction by its pleasures is that he has disavowed those principles of courtesy, valour, honour and so on that made him a respected knight. Enide as wife has taken on some of the dimensions of Eve as seductress, as Erec has given up the nomadic life of the true Arthurian champion and by his behaviour disrupted the court of his father. This takes us back to my account of Duby's view of the place of young men in their fathers' houses in the twelfth century that I discussed earlier. The epitome of the Arthurian chivalrous knight is the alienated nomad. We rarely see a group of singularly minded knights together unless they are under the watchful eye of Arthur himself. This is not surprising since a band or troop of knights would have been a potential army capable of serious opposition to a society undergoing rapid social change that was in many ways excluding them. The potential danger of a band of young vigorous men may have been such that it was forced out of Chrétien's text; when we do meet even a small group of knights like this, they are invariably defeated by the single hand of the Arthurian knight.

While Enide regrets and laments her folly at speaking, Erec makes the arrangements necessary for them to leave his father's court and then says to her:

'Ride fast', he says, 'and take care not to be so rash as to speak to me of anything you see. Take care never to speak to me, unless I address you first. Ride on now fast and with confidence.'[136]

Enide is placed in a situation of total dependency on Erec, but as she laments she sees three knights about to attack Erec and kill him and so she warns him. He treats her very harshly and this situation of threat, warning and anger from Erec is repeated a number of times until finally Erec says:

'This once again I will pardon you: but another time restrain yourself, and do not turn around to watch me: for in doing so you would be very foolish.'[137]

After many adventures Erec is finally seriously wounded and collapses in front of Enide who believes him dead and says:

'A grievous mistake I made in uttering the word which has killed my lord –
that fatal poisoned word for which I must justly be reproached: and I
recognise and admit that no one is guilty but myself: I alone must be blamed
for this.'[138]

She has now internalised the denial of her right to speech by the emerging
social order and is in the social place of being a widow. Her status as wife
was no better than as a maiden. In some ways it was worse because as a
maiden she was at least living among her family. As a wife she has been taken
away from her home, first to Arthur's court and then to Erec's father's court
where she is without the comfort and support of familiar people around her.
Finally she has been forced by her husband to be placed in a position of total
dependence on him as she is made to lead the life of the nomadic Arthurian
figure.

Her position deteriorates even further as a widow when she falls into the
hands of an amorous Count who in spite of her protestations simply claims
her as his own. This situation forces her to speak out once more:

'I care not what thou say to me, or what thou do! I fear not thy blows, nor yet
thy threats. Beat me and strike me, as thou wilt. I shall never heed thy power
so much as to do thy bidding more or less, even were thou with thy hands
right now to snatch out my eyes or flay me alive.'[139]

As a widow Enide has no place at all. In anthropological terms she has no
exchange value. The sound of her voice suddenly brings Erec around from
his faint and they make good their escape and are reconciled as Erec says:

From this time on for evermore, I offer myself to do your will just as I used to
do before. And if you have spoken ill of me, I pardon you and call you quit of
both the offence and the word you spoke.[140]

Her recovery of social position by means of a reversion to the status of wife,
however, does not now alter her fundamental state of helplessness and
speechlessness, and she offers no more warnings to Erec. Her speech and all
that goes with it – desire, consciousness and so on – are prohibited by a
social system reorganising itself along stricter patriarchal lines. This
prohibition even intrudes into the narrative voice as Chrétien says:

They have had so much pain and sorrow, he for her, and she for him, that they
now have their satisfaction. Each vies in seeking to please the other. Of their
further sport I must not speak.[141]

The only function permitted to Enide is sexual activity with the objective being the production of heirs. A cycle has been completed; as a maiden, as a wife and as a widow Enide is subjected to the desire of men: father, husband, abductor. Her value as an independent being is to be found as a producer of children, of heirs. At the very end of the tale even her thoughts must become those of Erec:

> Erec stoops over before Enide, whose heart was in great distress, although she held her peace: for grief on the lips is of no account unless it also touch the heart. And he who knew her heart said to her: 'Fair sister, dear, gentle, loyal and prudent lady I am acquainted with your thoughts.'[142]

Now not only is she not allowed her own speech, she is also denied independent thoughts as well. As wife she mirrors her husband, her only difference is to be found in her reproductive role. It should be remembered that when Erec first sees Enide this is how Chrétien describes her:

> Her eyes were so bright that they seemed like two stars. God never formed better nose, mouth, and eyes. What shall I say of her beauty? In sooth, she was made to be looked at: for in her one could have seen himself as in a mirror.[143]

In *Erec and Enide* Chrétien documents the attitude of a society undergoing a period of rapid social change reflecting on its attitude toward the relation between men and women. Enide is systematically deconstructed and then recomposed as a companion suitable for the chivalrous knight. She is made into the object of the look of the other and placed in a totally passive position. In Enide, Erec comes to see himself except with an added procreative potential. As Erec and Enide become joined in the narcissistic androgyny they represent, a series of social relations were being redefined in a culture reidentifying itself along patriarchal and hierarchical lines. Speech and silence mark the limits of social cohesion at the historical moment when their regulation moves from an onto-theological imperative to a personal sexed inter-subjective level. The concentration and limiting of the role of women to a procreative function becomes increasingly evident in the later romances and with it an increasing concern with the lineage-damaging potential of adultery.

Gottfried Von Strassburg's *Tristan*, written in approximately 1210, only five years before the Lateran Council and some sixty years after the death of Abelard, offers an excellent example of this:

> So it was with Tristan and Isolde. As soon as they were debarred from their pleasures by watchers and guardians and denied them by prohibitions, they began to suffer acutely. Desire now tormented them in earnest with its witchery many times worse than before. Their need of one another was more

painful and urgent than it had ever been. The ponderous load of cursed Surveillance weighed on their spirits like a mountain of lead. This devilish machination, Surveillance, enemy of Love, drove them to distraction, especially Isolde. She was in desperate plight. Tristan's avoidance was death to her. The more her master forbade her any familiarity with him, the more deeply her thoughts were embedded in him.

This passage goes on to connect Gottfried Von Strassburg's attitude towards Isolde with the Church's theological attitude to women:

Women of this kind are children of Eve, who flouted the first prohibition. Our Lord God gave Eve the freedom to do as she pleased with fruits, flowers and grasses, and with all that there was in Paradise – excepting one thing, which he forbade her on the pain of death. Priests tell us that it was the fig-tree. She broke off its fruit and broke God's commandment, losing herself and God. But indeed it is my firm belief today that Eve would never have done so, had it never been forbidden her. In the first thing she ever did, she proved true to her nature and did what was forbidden! But as good judges will agree, Eve might well have denied herself just that one fruit. When all is said and done, she had all the rest at her pleasure without exception, yet she wanted none but that one thing in which she devoured her honour! Thus they are all daughters of Eve who are formed in Eve's image after her. Oh for the man who could forbid all the Eves he might find today, who have abandoned themselves and God because they were told not to do something![144]

There are many echoes here of the fundamental attitudes that I suggested are to be found in *Erec and Enide*, and something of the effects and density of the genre of the romance as a whole on medieval life can now be seen. The landless knight could pursue fantasies of marrying an heiress or subverting the power of his lord through his wife. Women were provided with a role of household duties, confined largely to a model of sexual activity as acceptable only after marriage. The potentially damaging consequences of adultery for the lineage builders of the great houses overlaid the concept of the married woman with a dangerous and threatening element. The Church and the nobility could then use the resulting fear and paranoia to undertake programmes of regulation, sexual surveillance and lineage building.

But equally as significant as this is the development of the subjective narrative voice and the sense of interiority that pervades many of these texts. As I have mentioned earlier, Foucault suggests that the Lateran Council of 1215 and its injunction that all Christians should go to a private annual confession both reinforces and is constituted by a new sense of interiority that began the process of one's 'truth' being located in one's sex. 'The truthful confession was inscribed at the heart of the procedures of individualization by power.'[145]

In the romances this sense of the subject (*subject*), transparency, self-reflexivity, and interiority is often found. Chrétien as narrator brings this to the fore as he manipulates and reflects on both the actions of the characters in the story and the veracity of his version of the tale:

> Thus Chrétien concludes his romance of the Knight with the Lion; for I have never heard anymore told of it, nor will you ever hear any further particulars, unless some one wishes to add some lies.[146]

Furthermore the characters in Chrétien's romances often battle with themselves in a form of dialectical argument in order to force the truth out of a given situation. In *Yvain*, also known as the *Le Chevalier au Lion*, we find an example of this.[147] In a remarkable passage Laudine whose husband has recently been killed, has to decide whether or not to marry Yvain her husband's killer and she engages in a long dialectical conversation with herself about the intentions and motives of all the people involved in the incident:

> The lady, too, is in great perplexity all night, being worried about how she should defend the spring; and she begins to repent of her action to the damsel, whom she had blamed and insulted and treated with contempt. She feels very sure and certain that not for any reward or bribe, nor for any affection which she may bear him, would the maiden ever have mentioned him, and she must love her more than him, and that she would never give her advice which would bring her shame or embarrassment: the maid is too loyal a friend for that. Thus, lo! the lady is completely changed: she fears now that she to whom she had spoken harshly will never love her again devotedly; and him whom she had repulsed, she now loyally and with good reason pardons, seeing that he had done her no wrong. So she argues as if he were in her presence there, and thus she begins her argument: 'Come,' she says, 'canst thou deny that my lord was killed by thee?' 'That', says he, 'I cannot deny. Indeed I fully admit it.' 'Tell me, then, the reason of the deed. Didst thou do it to injure me, prompted by hatred and spite?' 'May death not spare me now, if I did it to injure you.' 'In that case, thou hast done me no wrong, nor art thou guilty of aught toward him.' Thus by her own arguments she succeeds in discovering justice, reason and common sense, now that there is no cause for hating him; thus she frames the matter to conform with her desire, and by her own efforts she kindles her love, as a bush which only smokes with the flame beneath, until some one blows it or stirs it up.[148]

The work of Robert Hanning supports the view that the twelfth century is a time when a novel sense of self was experienced and although I disagree with some of his more general comments which appear to legitimise the origin of a rather more nineteenth-century bourgeois individual, many of his examples from the twelfth century are useful:[149]

The rise of chivalric romance after the middle of the twelfth century created a narrative from within which the chivalry *topos* could thrive, and within which, therefore, the ideals of courtly society could be fully and self-consciously explored at the level of metaphor. The romance plot lacks any context larger than the lives of its protagonists: it permits the simultaneous presentation of external, heroic adventures and of an inner world on which the self-awareness born of love permits the control of marital impulses.[150]

Just as in the philosophical work of Abelard, the other aspect of this search for the rational truth via dialectics is the danger of madness. This is ever present in the romances in two forms: rashness and madness as a loss of reason. Rashness is often found in the behaviour of the unchivalrous or discourteous knight and is something which threatened the new ordering of sensibilities that was emerging. I have already discussed rashness in speech in relation to *Erec and Enide* but if one aspect of this is its control through a dialectical argument prior to action, it always has a potential to become a complete loss of rationality which sees the humanity of the individual become the animality of the beast. In *Yvain*, Yvain becomes animal and with a loss of reason degenerates and becomes a beast. He throws off his clothes and disappears into the forest, foraging for food:

Then such a storm broke loose in his brain that he loses his senses; he tears his flesh stripping off his clothes, he flees across the meadows and fields, leaving his men quite at a loss, and wondering what has become of him. However, he had no recollection of anything that he had done. He lies in wait for the beasts in the woods, killing them, and then eating the venison raw. Thus he dwelt in the forest like a madman or a savage, until he came upon a little low-lying house belonging to a hermit, who was at work clearing his ground.[151]

It is the discovery of the humanity in the lion that reduces the animality in Yvain and restores him to his proper function in the chivalrous society. I am suggesting that the kind of transformation I have drawn out for society at large, and for philosophy in particular, can be traced through the literature of the time and the work now completed allows a slightly different interpretation of the function of the romances.[152]

Nowadays there seem to be at least three competing, though not necessarily mutually exclusive, scholarly interpretations of the romance/ courtly love cycle. First, that it reflected the high status of women in medieval life, as is suggested by the concurrent appearance of the cult of the Virgin.[153] Secondly, that the courtly love/romance cycle expressed fundamentally Oedipal relations in as much as the love of the knight or the squire is that of a repressed desire for the mother. In this view the genre is discussed and interpreted in psychoanalytic terms.[154] Thirdly, the genre was written for the landless knights, fulfilling their dreams of either capturing an heiress, or undermining the prestige of their lord by their association with his wife.[155]

The problem with the first view is that the historical evidence does not indicate that women were in a privileged position at this time. On the contrary all the indications are, as I have shown, that women were largely being dispossessed of an active socio-economic position. Far from experiencing an enhanced social status under feudalism, the social position of women was deteriorating, since deprived of the independent control of land, they were being locked into household duties, socially imprisoned by their role of guardianship of the lineal purity. Furthermore the central element of courtly love was as a rule that the women must be married, serving to strengthen the view that for women sexual activity even of the illicit kind had to be prefigured by marriage. In this way two groups of women were created, virgins and wives, both being denied access to socio-political life, confronted with a system of thought that either confined them to marriage or household duties, or presented them with an ideal of impossible human conduct.[156] So while the first view has some interpretative value, it seems to jar with the historical evidence, which indicates that women did not have a high social status – if this is to be measured in the terms of active social participation – but rather were suffering a decline in their social position.

The second view does not necessarily exclude the theme of the high status of women, and in this respect would suffer from the difficulties previously mentioned. Even if this is not the case, a further problem emerges. As we have shown previously, there are certainly a number of difficulties in using psychoanalytic categories uncritically and, furthermore, if they are used 'absolutely', they emerge as providing an a priori framework that could be seen to distort the data to confirm the theory. This view would then have some difficulty in explaining the rise of the genre at a particular period, unless it could be shown that feudalism itself produced a social structure especially well explained by psychoanalytic categories not taken as a priori, but as historically specific events.

The third view while explaining the usefulness of the genre to a specific group does not seem to explain its proliferation and density throughout the nobility as a whole.[157] Perhaps part of the confusion and difficulty derives from a tendency to treat the genre as if it were characterised by a uniform theoretical and interpretative position. The earlier romances of Chrétien seem to fit the 'landless knight' view much better than the later ones, which directly involve a relationship with a married woman. This second kind are fundamentally structured around the actuality or possibility of adultery. It is here that we can add another view of the genre as a whole to those previously mentioned. Given the endemic fear of adultery as the destruction of the lineage-building strategies being pursued by the noble houses, the more the romances proclaimed the ideal of adulterous love, the more paranoid the nobility became about the sexual practices of their houses, and the more they demanded their regulation and surveillance. In this way the myth of the adulterous woman served a culture becoming increasingly repressive and anti-feminist. The regulation of sexual practices within the conjugal household provided for a fusion of the immediate interests of both Church and nobility.

Without privileging primogeniture, it is possible to establish that dramatic changes in inheritance patterns took place between the tenth and twelfth centuries. They were implicated in the restructuring of the familial unit towards that of the patriarchal nuclear family, a family structure with sexual surveillance at its very heart.

A more general thesis could be made that the movement towards interiority and a new technology of the subject (*subject*) which I analysed in terms of philosophy in the eleventh and twelfth centuries, is found in the popular literature of the day . In philosophy I have suggested that out of the conflict largely between a medieval version of realism and idealism a novel sense of the subject (*subject*) is to be found in the work of Abelard. We also find in the work of Chrétien some indications of the emergence of a similar model: in the voice of the narrator, in the dialectically applied logic of the characters in the tale, and so on. Both are events that took place against a significant transformation of society which I have analysed.

My argument is that the construction of the autobiographical self-reflective transparent subject (*subject*) in the twelfth century and its basis in the transformation of the power/knowledge network and the material practices of the epoch allow us to think differently about how intellectual history, the history of philosophy and the history of ideas usually present some salient features *of their own history*.

·5·

Subversions of the subject

Cogito ergo sum[1]

At the beginning of this inquiry I suggested that students in first-year courses at university are typically given a sketch of the history of philosophy from the Greeks, to the early Christian philosophers and patristic writers, the most notable being Augustine, then the late Medieval period which is usually scholasticism, then finally the philosophical and epistemological revolution of Descartes in the seventeenth century which laid the foundations for the scientific revolution and the birth of philosophy as 'science'. I suggested that this is complemented by a secondary view which adds a different emphasis and argues that the history of late medieval Europe is marked by an increasing secularisation, as is eventually manifested in the Protestant revolution and the basis of knowledge in 'self'. This tendency finds its first expression in philosophy in the work of Descartes. In both these cases the role of Descartes as an innovator, or as a victor over the narrow-mindedness of medieval scholasticism is rarely challenged by holders of different theoretical persuasions, and becomes the pre-condition for the category of the 'modern age'. Hans Blumenberg in his book *The Legitimacy of the Modern Age* challenges both these views of the work and the importance of Descartes and argues that this importance is an effect of the history of philosophy itself:

> The categories that Descartes provided for the modern age to use in understanding itself, which make him the favored thinker of every account of its origin, are those of methodological doubt and an absolute beginning founded only on itself. Methodological doubt is a cautious procedure; it is meant to be distinguished from the dogmatic negation that already knows

160

what should ultimately be rejected, and must demonstrate that; instead, it restricts itself to regarding all judgments that it produces to exclude the very hypothesis that would enable us to understand why this undertaking is considered necessary and is carried out at a particular point in history.[2]

Blumenberg questions the status of Descartes' methodological doubt, and points out the sense of contradiction involved in the apparently sudden historical emergence of 'doubt' as a method, based as it is on a supposedly consistent attribute of rationality available to all human beings (something that will be discussed later). He suggests that *Discourse on Method* and the *Meditations* attempt to conceal their own historical foundations by effacing any references to the previous use of 'methodological scepticism'. The experiment in reason which Descartes claims he is inaugurating: 'poses for itself under conditions of artificial difficulty in order to gain access to itself and to the beginning it proposes for itself.'[3] Blumenberg argues that the Enlightenment philosophers unequivocally accepted Descartes' approach as foundational, and incorporated it in to their own account of the historical coming in to being of 'rational self-consciousness'. As a consequence of this all theorists of the 'modern age' view resist any attempt to show the basis of Descartes' work as profoundly medieval:

> Thus a claim was made to the absolute beginning of the modern age, the thesis of its independence from the outcome of the Middle Ages, which the Enlightenment was to adopt as part of its own self-consciousness. The exigency of self-assertion became the sovereignty of self-foundation, which exposes itself to the risk of being unmasked by the discoveries of historicism, in which beginnings were to be reduced to dependencies. The weak point of modern rationality is that the uncovering of the medieval 'background' of its protagonists can put in question the freedom from presuppositions of which it claimed to have availed itself as the essence of its freedom.[4]

A close examination of Descartes' work appears at times consciously to conceal any traces of the history of methodological scepticism from it, the most striking example of this being his claim that he was not initially aware of Augustine's use of methodological scepticism and the corresponding principle 'I know that I live', which I discussed previously. Descartes refers directly to this in a letter to Colvius in November 1640:

> I am obliged to you for drawing my attention to the passage of St Augustine relevant to my *I am thinking, therefore I exist*. . . . He goes on to show that there is a certain likeness of the Trinity in us, in that we exist, we know that we exist, and we owe the existence and the knowledge we have. I, on the other hand, use the argument to show that this I which is thinking is an immaterial substance with no bodily element. These are two very different things. In itself

it is such a simple and natural thing to infer that one exists from the fact that one is doubting that it could have occurred to any writer. But I am very glad to find myself in agreement with St. Augustine, if only to hush the little minds who have tried to find fault with the principle.[5]

Perhaps Descartes is correct in distinguishing his work from Augustine on the basis of the mind/body division, which I will discuss later, but still there are two surprising things about these comments. First, it is almost inconceivable that Descartes' own training in scholasticism failed to familiarise him with Augustine's argument in relation to scepticism. Secondly, while here Descartes claims to have no prior knowledge of the relevant passage in Augustine, in other letters he uses both Augustine and Aquinas to defend his position. In a letter to Mersenne on 21 April 1641, he says the following:

> Those who say that God continually deceives the damned and that he might similarly be continually deceiving us, contradict the foundation of faith and all our belief, which is that *God cannot lie*. This is stated over and over again in so many places in Augustine, St. Thomas and others that I am surprised that any theologian denies it.[6]

Thus at a most crucial point in the development of Descartes' theory he denies the appropriate knowledge of the history of philosophy, while at the same time being quite happy to invoke aspects of this history and indicate his wide-ranging knowledge of it when it suits him. I can allow Descartes the benefit of a doubt, but Blumenburg is rather less generous:

> Descartes painstakingly effaced and disavowed the traces of his historical background in order to constitute the myth of the radical beginning of reason. In the *Discours de la Méthode* he dated the beginning of his doubt regarding the tradition back to La Flèche and passed over his crucial encounter with Isaak Beeckmann in Breda in 1618; he avoided (at the least) any answer to the reproach that his *Cogito* argument had already been formulated by Augustine, and the question of a possible dependence has remained undecidable down to the present.[7]

Without giving this sentiment my entire support it can be used to raise a number of questions about Descartes' work and the way it was accepted by the Enlightenment and subsequent intellectual historians, historians of philosophy and historians of ideas. Exactly how does Descartes' epistemology and theology differ from the Medieval period and in particular from the work of Abelard, as it was assessed previously? And exactly how much does Descartes owe to Augustine and Anselm?

But before examining these specific issues let me take up the general question of the Enlightenment's reception of Descartes. Some accounts of the history of philosophy base their definition of what makes a philosophy 'modern' on the theory that the Enlightenment marks a fundamental shift in the course of human history. This is demonstrated by the emergence of the concept of 'rationality' as an essential private part of human consciousness, which first finds philosophical expression in Descartes. This view then looks to Enlightenment philosophers and, in particular, what they have to say about history and the unfolding of rationality, and the work of Descartes as its starting point. So Descartes holds a double position in this discourse: he is the pre-condition of the 'modern', which exhibits a continuity up to the present age; he is also an object of study of the Enlightenment and provides for them the condition of possibility for their own attempt to distinguish themselves from the Medieval period.

These two different though contiguous projects fuse in a general history of rationality that can be abbreviated in the following way. The Modern age from the Enlightenment to the present is characterised as the age in which 'reason' the 'natural vocation of man definitively prevailed'.[8] A problem immediately emerges: if reason is in some way the natural vocation of humanity, then why was its appearance so delayed? Or alternatively, if it is subject to a discontinuous history, then what are the conditions of its appearance and disappearance and the principles of its recognition? If reason is identical with human existence, then it should be evident throughout human history; if it is discontinuous, then one cannot make the strong claims about reason since the seventeenth century that are often made for it. It is possible to avoid these problems by resituating the problem around a historical process whereby one describes 'the prehistory of the age of reason as the natural impotence or the forcible suppression of the power of rationality'. This is supported by a host of metaphors and allusions about the end of the darkness of medieval superstition and the coming to light of reason, which, as Blumenberg argues, are in the last analysis somewhat implausible metaphors.[9] However implausible they may be at the level of metaphor, the process that they constitute seems even more unlikely and leads to a fundamental contradiction in the interpretation of Descartes' work:

> The idea of a continuous upward progress of rationality contradicted the fundamental ideas of the radical, revolutionary self-empowerment of reason as an event of epoch-making, unexpected suddenness. The idea of reason liberating itself from its medieval servitude made it impossible to understand how such a servitude could ever have been inflicted upon the constitutive power of the human spirit and could have continued in force for centuries. Another dangerous implication of this explanation was that it was bound to inject doubt into the self-consciousness of reason's definitive victory and the

impossibility of a repetition of its subjugation. Thus the picture of its own origin and possibility in history that the epoch of rationality made for itself remained peculiarly irrational. In the Enlightenment's understanding of history, the relation between the Middle Ages and the modern age is characteristically dualistic, and this is expressed more than anywhere else in the conception formulated by Descartes of an absolute, radical new beginning, whose only prerequisites lay in the rational subject's making sure of itself, and for which history could become a unity only under the dominance of the method.[10]

Blumenberg points out some of the difficulties of the history of the foundations of the Enlightenment and the Modern age. If reason is a constitutive feature of humanity and suddenly liberates itself in the work of Descartes from the darkness and superstition of the Medieval period, how can the subjugation of the human spirit through those generations when reason did not rule be explained? And how can its future existence be guaranteed? The very possibility of its 'discontinuous' existence would demand techniques of analysis rarely if ever proposed by the proponents of reason and the Modern age. There is then, as Blumenberg suggests, something irrational about the history of rationality as it is usually presented. Furthermore, if the mark of the 'coming to light of reason' is self-certainty then Descartes may well not be either the first or most significant proponent of this perspective. Certainly Augustine would have a strong claim, and I would suggest as a result of my previous work, Abelard has an even stronger one. What is at stake in the theory of the 'modern' being based on Descartes is that a particular kind of contemporary philosophy embedded in a contemporary debate folds back on to Enlightenment attitudes to the Medieval period, and constructs a history where Descartes serves a profoundly 'a-historical' role.[11] As I have suggested earlier Descartes denies that he is dependent on medieval philosophy but I am not convinced, and I will now discuss the nature of this dependence in some detail.

It is an important feature of the contemporary acceptance of Descartes that he is represented as the first modern dualist. Descartes himself distinguished his work from Augustine precisely on the grounds that its importance was to be found in his separation of the existence of the mind from its dependence on the body. There is one major problem with this view, which is usually overlooked. Descartes' distinction between mind and body is profoundly medieval and must be considerably modified in order to make it fit into contemporary debates about materialism, idealism, empiricism, realism, and so on. In fact it may be inappropriate to call Descartes a dualist at all in terms of the contemporary mind/body debate. Perhaps he should be seen as a tri-ist faced with a trilemma? The basis for this is that Descartes usually uses mind to mean soul, although on occasions when writing of anatomy he uses the word brain to indicate the grey matter under a skull, but this is not mind. So he retains three categories mind/brain/body. The Cartesian division between mind and body is in fact the medieval one between soul and flesh that was mentioned previously in relation to Augustine and Neoplatonism. The mind which is the soul, is the source of understanding and is that incorruptible part of human existence that is immortal and certainly can exist without the body, or at least with a transformed one in the afterlife. Descartes' apparent inconsistency emerges from his failure to redefine his terminology as he claims he will do, in a way that will allow him to escape from the history of philosophy and scholasticism that was his intellectual heritage.[12] I am not arguing that he ought to be able to do this, or that this is a measure of his failure. However, the point needs to made that to argue that Descartes somehow escapes from medieval superstition by an 'act of reason' demands a highly idiosyncratic and specific reading of both the history of philosophy and his philosophical corpus which I do not share. On the contrary, Descartes' philosophy can be read as attempting to come to terms with a number of medieval problems to which, in some ways, he does not offer as sophisticated a response as the one I attributed to Abelard.

Let me begin then by examining what Descartes says about the mind/body division and offer some supporting evidence for my claim that this is a re-inscription of the medieval distinction between soul/flesh:

From this it follows that the human body may indeed easily enough perish, but the mind [or soul of man (I make no distinction between them)] is owing to its nature immortal.[13]

I am not more than a thing that thinks, that is to say a mind or a soul, or an understanding, or a reason.[14]

And although possibly (or rather certainly, as I shall say in a moment) I possess a body with which I am very intimately conjoined, yet because, on the other side, I have a clear and distinct idea of myself in as much as I am only a thinking and unextended thing, and as, on the other, I possess a distinct idea of body, inasmuch as it is only an extended and unthinking thing, it is certain that this I [that is to say, my soul by which I am what I am], is entirely and absolutely distinct from my body, and can exist without it.[15]

The above quotations are taken from the *Meditations on First Philosophy*, and indicate that Descartes in elaborating the mind/body distinction was reformulating the medieval distinction between soul and flesh. The mind/soul is the fundamental site of the Neoplatonic notion of understanding and is comprised of an infinite universal substance or essence. Immediately after the *Cogito* argument Descartes says that he is:

a substance the whole essence or nature of which is to think, and that for its existence there is no need of any place, nor does it depend on any material thing; so that this 'me,' that is to say, the soul by which I am what I am, is entirely distinct from body, and is even more easy to know than is the latter; and even if body were not, the soul would not cease to be what it is.[16]

This substance is in fact something like a medieval universal, and as such it is consistent that this mind/soul could exist independently of any body, but this mind/soul is not the same as the brain. So according to our more medieval reading of Descartes, his work is less than epistemological in the modern sense and rather more a theology or theogony, the fundamental object being to continue Anselm's project of proving the existence of God. In *The Discourse on Method* Descartes' claim is that he has proved the existence of God and soul, not brain and soul.[17] If the repository of thought and understanding is the mind/soul, then in what terms does Descartes refer to the third element of his project, the brain?

And finally what in all this is most remarkable of all, is the generation of the animal spirits, which resemble a very subtle wind, or rather a flame which is very pure and very vivid, and which, continually rising up in great abundance from the heart to the brain, thence proceeds through the nerves to the muscles, thereby giving the power of motion to all the members.[18]

I further notice that the mind does not receive the impression from all parts of the body immediately, but only from the brain, or perhaps even from one of its smallest parts, to wit, from that in which the common sense is said to reside, which, whenever it is disposed in the same particular way, conveys the same thing to the mind although meanwhile the other portions of the body may be differently disposed, as is testified by innumerable experiments which it is unnecessary here to recount.[19]

Descartes describes the process of receiving data in this way. Sense impressions are received in the sense organs and pass along by means of nerves to the brain where they excite a movement in the brain which will be felt in the mind. At this stage it is clear that the brain and mind are separate. In the passage between the brain and the mind a number of other processes can take place: memory, ideas, understanding and so on, until 'pure understanding' is finally experienced in the mind/soul. Given that 'soul' is the mark of God's work in the construction of human beings, it is God that guarantees the relationship between the brain and the mind/soul:

It is true that God could have constituted the nature of man in such a way that this same movement in the brain would have conveyed something quite different to the mind; for example, it might have produced consciousness of itself either in so far as it is in the brain, or as it is in the foot, or as it is in some other place between the foot and brain, or it might finally have produced consciousness of anything else whatever; but none of this would have contributed as well to the conservation of the body.[20]

The problem that Descartes has is to attempt to describe the precise relation between the mind/soul and the brain. In an attempt to do this he argues that the soul/mind is not a localised phenomena but is distributed throughout the body while still maintaining a fundamental indivisibility. Soul is therefore a universal located in the body. This view is close to the medieval conception of God where God is infinite/everywhere, has no precise location, and yet can be a particular as opposed to universal presence, anywhere. How then is it possible to account for the relation between soul/mind and body/brain? Descartes argues that while soul is distributed throughout the body infinitely and indivisibly, it has a particular point of contact with it:

But in examining the matter with care, it seems as though I had clearly ascertained that the part of the body in which the soul exercises its functions immediately is in nowise the heart, nor the whole of the brain, but merely the most inward of all its parts, to wit, a certain very small gland which is situated in the middle of its substance and so suspended above the duct whereby the animal spirits in its anterior cavities have communication with those in the posterior, that the slightest movements which take place may alter very greatly the course of these spirits; and reciprocally that the smallest changes which occur in the course of the spirits may do much to change the movements of this gland.[21]

Descartes then goes on to propose in Article XXXII that the pineal gland acts to co-ordinate the various sense impressions received by the brain before they enter the realm of the mind/soul and pure understanding. So my previous account of sense impressions now needs to be reformulated. Sense data now enter the body through the senses and are passed on to the brain through the nerves. From there they proceed to the pineal gland where they are collated and organised and then are passed to the soul/mind where they enter the understanding. If this is an acceptable interpretation of Descartes' account it is extremely difficult to make this into a consistent dualist account in the modern epistemological sense. The fundamental division remains a profoundly medieval one, mind/soul on the one hand, brain/body/ flesh on the other. To suggest that the mind/soul can exist as a think- ing thing independent of the brain/body/flesh is to add something to medieval theology but it is not particularly radical. As this is in Descartes' hands a theologically based epistemology at the outset, it is not so surprising that in order to support his view he frequently adopts theological arguments – that ultimately become a theogony at crucial points in his theory. I previously showed in relation to Abelard how he allows for the experience of understanding without receiving sense data. Indeed the passage in which he discusses this concerns a 'tower argument' with a seemingly Cartesian emphasis. Yet for Abelard there is not the same dependence on theology and theogony.[22]

If Descartes' dualism is either a repetition of the medieval distinction between soul and flesh, or in fact is rather a more tri-istic view, then it becomes clear that his theogony is even more deeply medievally orientated. The dependence of Descartes' epistemology on his theogony is emphasised by the fact that immediately after he asserts his epistemological maxim, *Cogito ergo sum*, he immediately launches into his first attempt to prove the existence of God. His argument here is deeply Neoplatonic:

> Following upon this, and reflecting on the fact that I doubted, and that consequently my existence was not quite perfect (for I saw clearly that it was a greater perfection to know than to doubt), I resolved to inquire whence I have learnt to think of anything more perfect than myself was; and I recognized very clearly that this conception must proceed from some nature which was really more perfect. . . . In this way it could but follow that it had been placed in me by a Nature which was really more perfect than mine could be, and which even had within itself all the perfections of which I could form any idea – that is to say, to put it in a word, which was God.[23]

In the *Synopsis* to the *Meditations on First Philosophy*, he adds another element:

> Amongst others there is, for example, this one, 'How the idea in us of a being supremely perfect possesses so much objective reality [that is to say participates by representation in so many degrees of being and perfection] that it necessarily proceeds from a cause which is absolutely perfect. This is illustrated in these Replies by the comparison of a very perfect machine, the idea of which is found in the mind of some workman. For as the objective contrivance of this idea must have some cause, i.e. either the science of the workman or that of some other from whom he has received the idea, it is similarly impossible that the idea of God which is in us should not have God himself as its cause.[24]

This argument is very similar to that of Anselm in his reply to the fool which I reconstructed earlier. It is essentially Neoplatonic, and bearing in mind its crucial place in both texts, it turns the intellectual clock back well before Abelard. Using my account of Abelard's work one could argue against Descartes along the following lines. He has made the fundamental 'realist' mistake of the twelfth century in confusing words and things. This is caused initially by his mistaken view of language and universals and their combination with a naïve Neoplatonism that fails to consider the circularity of the argument. That Descartes relies on a realist account of universals and a realist account of the philosophy of language can be shown by his reference to universals as substances, and ideas as 'pictures' of objects that can never be greater than the substance or essence underlying or constituting the object:

> Thus the light of nature causes me to know clearly that the ideas in me are like [pictures] or images which can, in truth, easily fall short of the perfection of the objects from which they have been derived, but can never contain anything greater or more perfect.[25]

Words as mental images of objects were part of Anselm's account, and so Descartes' re-presentation of this view is, philosophically, a retrograde step from Abelard's Conceptualism which I described previously. Here the processes of language, and in particular, abstraction, constituted universal categories not by being real objective existences but as effects of language itself. Descartes does allow that the ideas that we have of objects cannot proceed from the individual mind, but of course this mind is not the brain but is that infinite universal substance whose integrity is guaranteed by God. This guarantee is essential to Descartes since without its existence his project is doomed to undermine the certainty that it seeks. Thus for Descartes the theology and the theogony are the preconditions for the success of his whole project:

> And when I consider that I doubt, that is to say, that I am an incomplete and dependent being, the idea of a being that is complete and independent, that is of God, presents itself to my mind with so much distinctness and clearness – and from the fact alone that this idea is found in me, or that I who possess this idea exist, I conclude so certainly that God exists, and that my existence depends entirely on Him in every moment of my life – that I do not think that the human mind is capable of knowing anything with more evidence and certitude. And it seems to me that I now have before me a road which will lead us from the contemplation of the true God (in whom all the treasures of sciences and wisdom are contained) to the knowledge of the other objects of the universe.[26]

Here Descartes presents us with a clear elaboration of the implicit connection between his version of methodological scepticism and its dependence on a Neoplatonic theology. It is this dependence that will lead him to work through the 'evil demon' argument and those aspects of his work that are least satisfactory. Ultimately, like many earlier medieval philosophers, Descartes falls victim to the view of, as Lovejoy would say, a necessary optimism: the world must be as it is because God could not have made it otherwise. As we saw in the last chapter, Abelard has an effective response to this, but in Descartes' hands it becomes epistemologically over-determining and serves to confirm his Neoplatonic heritage. His use of the 'perfect triangle' argument in the *Meditations on First Philosophy, Meditation V* is a good example of this.[27] All knowledge for Descartes is fundamentally dependent on the existence and knowledge of God. The essential precondition for his epistemology is a profoundly medieval theology and theogony, and whenever he finds his arguments wanting he can and does resort to the ultimate defence: 'For because God is in no wise a deceiver, it follows that I am not deceived in this.'[28]

This ultimately is nothing other than a reasserting of the Augustinian principle *Credo ut intelligam*, that privileges faith as prior to understanding and would seem to regress the work of Abelard as I analysed it previously. Perhaps of more long-term importance for my general interpretation is to outline Descartes' failure to provide an 'ethics' to support his methodological scepticism. It can be suggested that for Descartes this was not necessary as he was so steeped in Church ethics that the question of a personal 'ethics' simply did not arise. While there could be something to be said for this view, it would none the less seem, as was shown in relation to Abelard, that there is an integral relation between methodological scepticism as a methodology based on certainty of self and the need for an accompanying ethics.

Finally, there is a contradiction in Descartes' work. His refusal to acknowledge his philosophical heritage and his insistence on knowledge being located in an 'a-historical subject' contradicts those places in his writing when he refers to a progression of knowledge and to the possibility of knowledge being accumulated culturally: 'As a matter of fact I am already sensible that my knowledge increases [and perfects itself] little by little, and I see nothing which can prevent it from increasing more and more into infinitude.'[29] It is simply not clear how this is possible. Either knowledge begins anew in each subject (*subject*), which would condemn us to having to make all the same experiments and same arguments over and over again, ensuring a complete stasis and lack of cultural development; or one must agree that knowledge can be accepted at some general level, without having to repeat all the processes by which it was acquired. There is little doubt that for the most part – despite a few references to Socrates, Plato and scholasticism – Descartes adopts the first view, and occasionally bemoans not having enough time to complete all the necessary experiments himself. These references are crucial in that they become the condition of culturally accumulated knowledge and are either a strong or weak contradiction in Descartes' work depending on the kind of reading that is undertaken. But we must be careful here; it is not a case of suggesting that we abandon Descartes and start to consider Abelard the founder of the 'modern', since we would then not escape Blumenberg's earlier criticisms but only re-locate them.[30] However, it is important to recognise that Descartes' significance is not that of the innovator but as the bearer of a technology of the subject that had already found expression in texts attributed to Abelard:

> But in this Discourse I shall be very happy to show the paths I have followed, and to set forth my life as a picture, so that everyone may judge for himself; and thus in learning from the common talk what are the opinions which are held of it, a new means of obtaining self-instruction will be reached, which I shall add to those which I have been in the habit of using. . . . But regarding this Treatise simply as a history, or, if you prefer it, a fable in which, amongst certain things which may be imitated, there are possibly others also which it would not be right to follow, I hope that it will be of use to some without being hurtful to any, and that all will thank me for my frankness.[31]

Descartes inaugurates his philosophy by basing it on a fictional or fabulous technology of the subject (*subject*), composed out of the relation between the reflexive self and the text:

> But after I had employed several years in thus studying the book of the world and trying to acquire some experience, I one day formed the resolution of also making myself an object of study and of employing the strength of my mind in choosing the road I should follow. This succeeded much better, it appeared to me, than if I had never departed either from my country or my books.[32]

Here Descartes transforms the technique of the *Historia Calamitatum*, by reconstituting the autobiographical mode as the mode of contemporary philosophy. It is this mode and its supporting subject (*subject*) that has been maintained in 'modern philosophy' and is both an index of its 'modernity' and the pre-condition for a dangerous trap it opens up for us.

For Descartes the subject has become both the subject and object of philosophical work. Philosophy has become the work of one's life. Descartes in adopting the autobiographical tone, the textual manifestation of the transparent self as the subject (*subject*), for and of philosophical discussion, allows us to recognise a familiar air. In re-articulating the self-reflexive autobiographical subject (*subject*) he draws out a philosophical technology of self that is fundamental to the practice of contemporary philosophy and is inseparable from modernity. However, this subject (*subject*) still exhibits that fundamental tension that was noted in Abelard, the tendency towards self-disintegration.[33]

It is here that the Cartesian trap lies in wait. On the one hand, Descartes' project announces the possibility of a science of the subject (*subject*) as he dislocates it from the specific conditions of its emergence. On the other, in the face of the impossibility of a theogonical or theological defence in contemporary culture, this subject cannot have stability restored to it. It vacillates between doubt and certainty, producing in us the fault line that constitutes us as subjects (*subjects*) – a fault line that runs from Abelard to Descartes, Kant, Hegel, Nietzsche and Freud, and simultaneously constitutes the possibility of disintegration and multiplicity as well as an impossible need for stability, rationality, metaphysics, essentialism and transcendentalism. But this line does not have a uniform or progressive trajectory, nor is it a bar or a hyphen. It is a curve as the subject doubles back towards itself – it is the question mark that must now inevitably follow the subject (*subject*) wherever it goes.

Une façon de parler

At the outset of this inquiry I gave both an account and a critical exegesis of some of Freud's anthropological texts, and argued that it appeared as if his work in this domain, and the role of the Oedipus complex as derived from it, suffered from many of the problems I had initially attributed to Lovejoy and Collingwood. I noted Freud's use of the themes of continuity, objective reality, objective history, the contradictory tendencies in his work of progress and stasis, and the universal subject that underwrites his theory. I then suggested that if one wanted to use Freud's theories, and, in particular, the notion of the 'unconscious' as the basis of a critical approach to the subject, then Freud's theory needed to be treated cautiously.

Since then, this inquiry has taken two directions: an archaeological and a genealogical one. I have shown how inheritance patterns and subsequent changes in sexual practices began to constitute the pre-conditions for what one might call the 'Oedipal subject'. The transition from a wide range of practices and the forms of social organisation that paralleled them, to a hierarchically ordered, patriarchally based, nuclear family, became the foundation of a specific sexual and subjective life. The instances that I gave both from documentary and literary sources of father/son rivalry, and mother/son relations, lend themselves to a psychoanalytic interpretation. That there is a parallel between the development of the romance cycle and instances of familial conflict, with the constitution of an Oedipally based and orientated subjectivity, becomes a confirmatory instance of the emergence of a particular technology of the subject (*subject*), and its expression both in texts and in the social life of the period.

This enables one to specify the emergence of the 'Oedipus complex' in such a way that it allows all the universal aspects of the foundations of psychoanalysis which I have previously criticised to be dispensed with, along with the vague, general Freudian account of 'primal hordes' and their associated metaphysics and essentialism. But it does more than this, because what I am suggesting is that the 'Oedipalising' of Western culture is constituted not only in relation to primogeniture and the politics of truth, but also to the emergence of the self-reflexive autobiographical subject (*subject*).

To elaborate and develop this point it is necessary to reflect on the interpretation of the work of Stock which was analysed in some detail previously. Stock argued that the emergence of literacy from the eleventh to the twelfth century reorganised and reorientated medieval consciousness. It is the case that prior to the eleventh century, texts played an important part in every aspect of early medieval life. There was already, in the time of Charlemagne, a limited use of written records in the organising and management of estates, and furthermore, I have previously examined the significance of the early work of Gregory of Tours. In addition to this there was the inestimable value of the Bible and patristic writings. None the less, Stock's account of the implications of literacy and Clanchy's account of the spread and impact of literacy occurring in the period under study add an important and fundamentally new motif to cultural life. This motif depends on the introjection of the textual consciousness into the very conception of self, and this I referred to as 'autobiography'. This represents a very fundamental change in intellectual orientation and the power/knowledge network, as the text as an external referent, the Bible or patristic writings, became the text as the pre-condition of 'philosophical' consciousness, the *Historia Calamitatum*. The clearest expressions of this can perhaps be found later in the work of Descartes and Hegel, and the most coherent account of its preconditions is that by Kant.

At the end of the twelfth century, therefore, the Bible, the book of nature and the patristic writings have already become the philosophical auto-biography that internalises the text into subjective consciousness and becomes the basis of the textual consciousness that claims to know itself – the transparent subject (*subject*) – a *Cogito*. On the one hand, we have a sociology of Oedipus, and on the other, an account of the textualising of philosophical consciousness in the 'autobiography'. What is the connection between the two? The 'analysed' subject as Foucault suggests is the transparent subject par excellence! Moreover the analysis is undertaken by restoring to the analysand their true biographical history. Let me now expand on this.[34]

One of the interesting things about psychoanalysis is that it is essentially based on interpretative textual strategies. This occurs at three levels: firstly, at the level of its central metaphors; secondly, at the level of its clinical practice; and thirdly, at the level of its history as a 'science' according to Freud. Let us take these issues one at a time.

On the first point, it is evident even from a superficial reading of psychoanalytic theory that its central metaphor 'the Oedipus complex' is a textual one. The allusions to the play *Oedipus Rex* by Sophocles are so much of a commonplace that they pass almost unnoticed, and the implications of this are rarely considered:

> Later, but still in the first years of infancy, the relation known as the Oedipus complex becomes established: boys concentrate their sexual wishes upon their mother and develop hostile impulses against their father as being a rival, while girls adopt an analogous attitude. All of the different variations and consequences of the Oedipus complex are important; and the innately bisexual constitution of human beings makes itself felt and increases the number of simultaneously active tendencies. Children do not become clear for quite a long time about the difference between the sexes; and during this period of *sexual researches* they produce typical *sexual theories* which, being circumscribed by the incompleteness of their authors' own physical development, are a mixture of truth and error and fail to solve the problems of sexual life (the riddle of the Sphinx – that is the question of where babies come from).[35]

Here we find a good an example of the way Freud uses the textual power of myths, in this case both Oedipus and the riddle of the Sphinx, without detailing its consequences. The transition from myth to science (Sophocles to Freud), and the role of the child as author is unclear. Indeed, wherever we find Freud referring to the Oedipus complex, its relation to the text of Sophocles is simultaneously affirmed and denied. It is affirmed because to quote Oedipus is to invoke Sophocles by cultural association; it is denied because Freud's account of the actions of Oedipus is significantly different from those of the Oedipus of Sophocles, who does not know that he has killed his father until much later. There is no hostility between father and son in Sophocles' *Oedipus Rex* that involves Oedipus' relation to his mother in any way. Similarly, Oedipus does not know that he has married his mother, and it is his innocence in these two respects that becomes the condition of his tragic status – which is almost the opposite of the Freudian account of Oedipus.[36] For Freud the construction of psychoanalysis as a body of theory is dependent on textual and literary metaphors.

This brings us to our second point, the use of literary and textual strategies in the clinical practice of psychoanalysis. Freud bases the structure of psychoanalytic practice on the model of the confessional: 'So I abandoned hypnotism, only retaining my practice of requiring the patient to lie upon a sofa while I sat behind him, seeing him, but not seen myself.'[37] In a curious way this turns this inquiry back on itself as it returns by implication to the role of private confession and the Lateran Council of 1215 which I have already discussed.[38] Freud continues: 'Thus the work of analysis involves the art of interpretation, the successful handling of which may require tact and practice but which is not hard to acquire.'[39] Psychoanalysis acts as an interpretative system that treats 'speech' like a text, to be commented upon and interpreted. The speech that emerges from the object (*subject*) of the analysis, must in the first instance engage with the fundamental literary process of censorship. It is at this level that the analyst must encounter the effects of dream-work by using a textual strategy to interlock with a textually based phenomenon:

> I have given the name of *dream-work* to the process which, with the co-operation of the censorship, converts the latent thoughts into the manifest content of the dream. It consists of a peculiar way of treating the preconscious material of thought, so that its component parts become *condensed*, its psychical emphasis becomes *displaced*, and the whole of it is translated into visual images or *dramatized*, and completed by deceptive *secondary revision*. The dream-work is an excellent example of the processes occurring in the deeper, unconscious layers of the mind, which differ considerably from the familiar normal processes of thought. It also displays a number of archaic characteristics, such as the use of *symbolism* (in this case of a predominantly sexual kind) which it has since also been possible to discover in other spheres of mental activity.[40]

The reference here to translation and dramatising confirms that psycho-analysis considers its object to be a textual phenomenon and organises its clinical practice in response to this.[41] What appears as a general theoretical and clinical tendency in psychoanalysis emerges explicitly in Freud's writings as he analyses and interprets texts utilising psychoanalytic theory. This is precisely the place of his forays into biblical, anthropological and literary studies. For Freud, Sophocles' *Oedipus Rex*, the works of Shakespeare, J. G. Frazer's *The Golden Bough*, the Bible and so on, all play a crucial role in both the theoretical development and clinical practice of psychoanalysis. Psychoanalysis as a theory is dependent on the notion of both consciousness and the unconscious being structured 'like' a text, and its clinical practice appears to be organised on fundamentally textually based interpretative techniques.[42]

Now to the third point, Freud's own account of the history and development of psychoanalysis. Freud begins his account of the relation between the development of psychoanalysis and his personal life by referring to his previous versions of this in other papers, and makes the following comment: 'Since I must not contradict myself and since I have no wish to repeat myself exactly, I must endeavour to construct a narrative in which subjective and objective attitudes, biographical and historical interests, are combined in a new proportion.'[43] Freud's reference to himself as both the subject and the object of the text confirms the previous comments made in relation to Abelard and Descartes on the significance of the self-reflexive subject (*subject*). After providing us with the details of his early life Freud gives us an account of his relation with an older boy: 'Under the powerful influence of a school friendship with a boy rather my senior who grew up to be a well-known politician, I developed a wish to study law like him and to engage in social activities.[44] This is to become the model of his initiation into knowledge throughout his early life which is to be repeated with Brücke, Exner, Fleischl von Marxow, Charcot and Breuer:

> He [Breuer] was a man of striking intelligence and fourteen years older than myself. Our relations soon became more intimate and he became my friend and helper in my difficult circumstances. We grew accustomed to share all our scientific interests with each other. In this relationship the gain was naturally mine. The development of psycho-analysis afterwards would cost me his friendship. It was not easy for me to pay such a price, but I could not escape it.[45]

In some ways Freud's early intellectual life in part is dependent upon close early relations with a 'master' that reaches a crisis and comes to an end as he attempts to break free from this influence. Later on, Freud himself will become the 'master' and will reproduce similar relations with his students, his pupils.

Freud continues his account and then comes to his theory of repression which is followed by a critical account of Janet's contribution to psychoanalysis that concludes with Freud's reference to the phrase *une façon de parler*, which is immediately followed by Freud's defence of the concept of the unconscious:

> And finally he [Janet] revealed himself to my eyes and destroyed the value of his own work by declaring that when he had spoken of 'unconscious' mental acts he had meant nothing by the phrase – it had been no more than a *façon de parler*.[46]

Given the crucial textual place of this reference to Janet and a *façon de parler*, as they are situated between Freud's development of the theory of repression and his theory of the unconscious, the two fundamental bases of psychoanalysis, these pages in his autobiography need some deeper consideration.

Janet's place in this context is an interesting one, as it was Janet who according to Freud himself first published (as a result of cases in which hysterics were relieved of their neuroses) a theoretical elaboration of the unconscious:

> It is true that Pierre Janet brought forward the same evidence independently; indeed, the French worker can claim priority of publication, for it was only a decade later (in 1883 and 1885), while he was collaborating with me, that Breuer published his observation. . . . I must admit that for a long time I was prepared to give Janet very great credit for throwing light on neurotic

symptoms, because he regarded them as expressions of *idées inconscientes* which dominated the patients. But since then he has expressed himself with exaggerated reserve, as if he wanted to admit that the unconscious had been nothing more to him than a form of words, a makeshift, *une façon de parler* – that he had meant nothing real by it [1913].⁴⁷

Freud credits Janet (and Binet to some extent) with being the first discoverer of the theory of the unconscious. Yet he also resolutely criticises Janet's physiological account of hysteria and Janet's apparent insistence on claiming that all his talk of unconscious ideas was merely *une façon de parler*, and by implication that Freud's theory was the same. Freud is in effect accusing Janet of claiming that psychoanalysis was merely a way of talking, and this he rejects. Why should such an apparently trivial point be given such importance? The first of the two references to *une façon de parler* which I have just cited was altered by Freud in the 1928 edition of *An Autobiographical Study*, whereby *une façon de parler* became *manière de parler*. So what is the distinction between the two? *Une façon de parler* translates as 'a way of speaking', however *manière de parler*, translates to 'a manner of speaking' that carries with it the notion of an affected air, an affected reluctance, even to mince.⁴⁸ Given that this occurs in *An Autobiographical Study* immediately before Freud begins to defend his account of the unconscious, I will consider what follows very closely:

> But the study of pathogenic repressions and of other phenomena which have still to be mentioned compelled psycho-analysis to take the concept of the unconscious seriously. Psycho-analysis regarded everything mental as being in the first instance unconscious; the further quality of 'consciousness' might also be present, or again it might be absent. This of course provoked a denial from the philosophers, for whom 'consciousness' and 'mental' were identical, and who protested that they could not conceive of such an absurdity as the 'unconscious mental'. There was no help for it, however, and this idiosyncrasy of the philosophers could only be disregarded with a shrug. Experience (gained from pathological material, of which the philosophers were ignorant) of the frequency and power of impulses of which one knew nothing directly and whose existence had to be inferred like some fact in the external world, left no alternative open. It could be pointed out incidentally, that this was the treating of one's own mental life as one had always treated other people's. One did not hesitate to ascribe mental processes to other people, although one had no immediate consciousness of them and could only infer them from their words and action. But what held good for other people must be applicable to oneself. Anyone who tried to push the argument further and to conclude from it that one's own hidden processes belonged actually to a second *consciousness* would be faced with the concept of a consciousness of which one knew nothing, of an 'unconscious consciousness' – and this would scarcely be preferable to the assumption of an 'unconscious mental'. If on the other hand

one declared, like some other philosophers, that one was prepared to take pathological phenomena into account, but that the processes underlying them ought not to be described as mental but as 'psychoid', the difference of opinion would degenerate into an unfruitful dispute about words, though even so expediency would decide in favour of keeping the expression 'unconscious mental'. The further question as to the ultimate of this unconscious is no more sensible or profitable than the older one as to the nature of the conscious.

It would be more difficult to explain concisely how it came about that psycho-analysis made a further distinction in the unconscious, and separated it into a *preconscious* and an unconscious proper. It will be sufficient to say that it appeared a legitimate course to supplement the theories that were a direct expression of experience with hypotheses that were designed to facilitate the handling of the material and related to matters which could not be a subject of immediate observation. The very same procedure is adopted by the older sciences. The subdivision of the unconscious is part of an attempt to picture the apparatus of the mind as being built up of a number of *agencies* or *systems* whose relations to one another are expressed in spatial terms, without, however, implying any connection with the actual anatomy of the brain. (I have described this elsewhere as the topographical approach.) Such ideas are part of the speculative superstructure of psychoanalysis, any portion of which can be abandoned or changed without loss or regret the moment its inadequacy has been proved. But there is still plenty to be described that lies closer to actual experience.[49]

Freud's account of the unconscious is organised as a defence from philosophical objections. It is not at all clear why such objections should be disturbing for Freud, as in another place in his autobiography he explicitly denies the relevance of philosophy for his project:

I have carefully avoided any contact with philosophy proper. This avoidance has been greatly facilitated by constitutional incapacity. I was always open to the ideas of G. T. Fechner and have followed that thinker upon many important points. The large extent to which psycho-analysis coincides with the philosophy of Schopenhauer – not only did he see the dominance of the emotions and the supreme importance of sexuality but he was even aware of the mechanism of repression – is not to be traced to my acquaintance with his teaching. I read Schopenhauer very late in my life. Nietzsche, another philosopher whose guesses and intuitions often agree in the most astonishing way with the laborious findings of psycho-analysis, was for a long time avoided by me on that very account; I was less concerned with the question of priority than with keeping my mind unembarrassed.[50]

Not only does Freud claim that he had not read philosophy at the time that he developed psychoanalysis but that he chose not to do so for fear of his mind becoming 'embarrassed' and because of a 'constitutional incapacity', whatever that might mean. But by the time he comes to write the text of *An Autobiographical Study*, from which I previously quoted, he has read some philosophy – Schopenhauer, Nietzsche and Fechner, and presumably those other philosophers to whom he addresses his defence of the 'unconscious'. So let me now consider this argument in some detail and break it up into some smaller elements:

1. Freud begins his account by claiming his study of pathogenic repression and other unspecified phenomena have compelled him to 'take the concept of the unconscious seriously'.
2. Psychoanalysis assumes everything mental to be initially unconscious; some aspects of the mental may be conscious, some are not.
3. Philosophers who reject this notion say the mental and consciousness are identical. This is simply a question of the idiosyncrasy of the philosophers because of: a) the pathological material mentioned in item 1 above [but not specified]; and b) because science shows that there are things that exist in the world whose existence can only be inferred and this compels one to accept the unconscious as there is no other 'alternative open'. Freud does not give an example but we might provide one for him, magnetic fields or atoms, for example.
4. In one's mental life we attribute consciousness to other people without having any immediate consciousness of it, and we can only infer this from their 'words and actions'. What applies to them must apply to oneself, that is to say we must have a level of consciousness which we can only infer but is not immediately experienced.
5. If we accept item 4, then this consciousness of which we have no immediate experience becomes purely tautological unless we refer to it as an unconscious. Related to this it can be said that those philosophers who accept that the pathological phenomena (which Freud still has not described) exist, but call this 'psychoid', are really agreeing with Freud; the problem is one of 'words' and the 'unconscious mental' would in any case be a better description than the psychoid mental.
6. It is as pointless to attempt to say what the unconscious is as it is to say what the conscious is.
7. It is more difficult to say how the concept of the preconscious came about, except that it facilitated of the 'handling' of non-empirically observable phenomena. This is appropriate because the older sciences do something similar.
8. This procedure attempts to construct 'agencies' or 'systems' in a spatial relation to each other without being connected anatomically to the brain. This is the topographical method.
9. Such ideas (i.e. the preconscious/unconscious split) are part of the 'speculative superstructure' of psychoanalysis, which can be altered without 'loss or regret the moment its inadequacy has been proved'.

In fact, in this particular instance Freud does not offer much of an argument against 'the philosophers'. His assertion that pathological evidence and other data which he does not disclose compels him is just an assertion, it is not an argument. Furthermore his use of the word 'compulsion' in this context is perhaps the index of his failure to present much argument at all. There is also a curious change of tone here, where, by a metaphorical slip, the account of Freud's response to these criticisms has become the response of psychoanalysis to them. Freud and psychoanalysis have become interchangeable, an interchange that presupposes a movement of the shifting signifier 'I'.[51] As a result of this 'compulsion', psychoanalysis/ Freud assumes that all mental activity is initially unconscious. This again is an unsupported assertion. Freud has a response to this criticism that removes the onus upon him to provide an argument, suggesting that there are things in the world the existence of which can only be inferred, but that have effects in and upon the world. According to Freud this leaves no other 'alternative open' than to accept the veracity of psychoanalysis and the theory of the unconscious.

However, a reply to this is that while this argument defends and allows for the existence of inference in itself, it says nothing about psychoanalysis at all. One may be able to infer magnetic forces, atoms, but even the most naïve empiricist will support this with an account in terms of the effect of what is inferred from observable phenomena, whereas in this case Freud only refers to pathological experience and other unspecified phenomena which he fails to disclose. So far he has only argued that inference is allowable, not that the existence of the unconscious can be inferred. Freud then proceeds to 'infer' the existence of consciousness in other beings, and even if we ignore Descartes' *automata* argument and the question of how this could be known from their words and actions, and allow Freud that the existence of a consciousness can be inferred in other human beings, difficulties remain.[52] For example, a problem with his view is that it is based on his own experience of being human, which does not help him in his argument; and since there is no immediate experience of the unconscious, how can we infer its existence for either ourself or for others? We could only make such an inference from the experience of our own consciousness, unconsciousness, words and actions, and Freud has not yet shown how this could be done. Having failed to accept that Freud has shown that we have a consciousness of which we have no immediate experience, item 5 becomes irrelevant and can be rejected and item 6 has no interest.

When Freud then goes on to detail the development of the preconscious as a concept, the criteria that he uses are no different from those he has used for the concept of the unconscious, and as he failed to provide any empirical evidence or argument for its existence it offers no support for the existence of the preconscious either. Both the unconscious and the preconscious become 'agencies' or 'systems' 'in a spatial relation to each other without being connected anatomically to the brain'. Ideas such as unconscious/preconscious are systems and agencies that are part of the speculative superstructure of psychoanalysis that can be altered without loss or regret when shown to be inadequate. Far from showing the philosophers to be in error Freud has only reduced the concept of the unconscious to part of the speculative system of psychoanalysis. This would then suggest that the structural account of the conscious–preconscious–unconscious topograraphy is, as Freud suggests, not to be discovered anatomically but is part of the metaphorical, speculative superstructure of psychoanalysis. Indeed perhaps psychoanalysis is entirely such a speculative structure. It is no wonder, then, that Freud transformed Janet's phrase, *une façon de parler*, as it brilliantly captures what is fundamental to psychoanalysis as a speculative philosophy, which is neither to deny its usefulness or even its clinical efficacy. The transformation of the shifter 'I' of Freud to the 'I' of psychoanalysis becomes mirrored by that of *façon* to *manière* as Freud takes over Janet's theory, and for him *une façon de parler* now becomes capable of representing reality: 'psycho-analysis was no longer the product of delusion, it had become a valuable part of reality.'[53]

This parallels to the 'psychotic solution' of Abelard and Descartes, as pyschoanalysis becomes a speculative system based on a self-reflexive autobiographical subject (*subject*) capable of explaining 'objective' reality. Freud's elaboration of psychoanalysis has at this time taken him along a similar philosophical journey to that of Abelard and Descartes, and even within terms appropriate to the theory of psychoanalysis itself his relation to this philosophical process can now be referred to as the 'psychotic solution'.

This relation between Freud's own account of the history of psychoanalysis and his autobiography is not only to be found in *An Autobiographical Study*. The entire project of psychoanalysis as revealed in the works of Freud is punctuated with autobiographical details; he continually composes a relation to himself as a subject (*subject*) as the theory of psychoanalysis is developed. The point to be made here is more than one of passing interest. I am arguing that the development of the autobiographical subject and psychoanalysis are inseparable. Freud's own account of the interrelation between psychoanalysis and his autobiography supports this view:

Two themes run through these pages: the story of my life and the history of psycho-analysis. They are intimately interwoven. This Autobiographical Study shows how psycho-analysis came to be the whole content of my life and rightly assumes that no personal experiences of mine are of any interest in comparison to my relations with that science.[54]

We can of course refuse the dichotomy that Freud is attempting to establish here, and suggest that no distinction can be made between psychoanalysis and Freud's personal life, not simply because they are connected in the body of Freud but because they are both constituted by the same textual moment that is structured autobiographically – a moment that sustains a specific technology of self.

This brings me to one last point that relates both to the construction of psychoanalysis and its clinical practice. This is the point at which the intersection between these two aspects of psychoanalysis is so fundamental that it is almost too obvious to mention. Through the intervention of psychoanalysis the patient constructs their own autobiography and then, through the interpretative practice of the analyst, enters into a relation with this autobiography. The case study of Dora indicates the unfolding of this process very clearly. Freud begins with a general biographical account of Dora from sources other than Dora, and then through the process of analysis enables Dora to construct an autobiographical relation to this. As the 'meaning' of the content of the unconscious is returned to Dora, an autobiographical self-reflexive subject (*subject*) emerges, or at least it would at the end of the analysis.[55] A similar pattern emerges in the case of Little Hans where Freud's first contact with his patient is through a letter from Little Hans's father. From that moment a biography is to be reconstituted as Hans's autobiography. Psychoanalysis not only presupposes the composing of the subject in relation to a textual strategy, it is part of its clinical practice to make this the object of analysis, reconstituting and stabilising the relation between the subject (*subject*) and text. So if modern subjectivity has inherited the self-reflexive tradition of Abelard and Descartes as I have been suggesting, then Freud and psychoanalysis are the modern interpreters of it *par excellence*, as psychoanalysis draws out autobiographical transparency from the subject (*subject*) as the unconscious and consciousness collapse into each other.

Let me briefly summarise the significant aspects of my argument. I have shown how on three critical points we can see a specific relation between psychoanalysis and that kind of textual autobiographical subjectivity, the 'emergence' of which I described in my account of Abelard and which was consolidated and analysed in the work of Descartes. These three points are: the use of textual metaphors to constitute psychoanalytic theory; the clinical practice of psychoanalysis; and Freud's own account of the relation between the development of psychoanalysis as a theory and the biographical details of his own life. If my thesis concerning the relation between the development of an autobiographical and a textually composed subject (*subject*) is accepted, then it can be argued that the three fundamentally textually based orientations of psychoanalysis make it speak from a particularly dense space within our cultural milieu. But this place cannot be occupied or claimed in terms of its value as a science, or as a radical critique of other contemporary theories of the subject (*subject*). It is adopted precisely because psychoanalysis is particularly adept at restoring to one that sense of self as a subject (*subject*) – caught within the Cartesian trap and in danger of disintegrating and proliferating – promising reconstitution through the self-reflexive autobiographical technology of self known as – *une façon de parler*. But it is no more than this.

Philosophy with a tuning fork

I began this inquiry with a discussion of intellectual history, the history of philosophy and the history of ideas. I argued that in today's debate there is a blind spot in relation to the subject (*subject*) that does not allow the subject to be put into question. I then traced this back to the emergence of the history of ideas in the work of Collingwood, Lovejoy and Freud. These approaches were then contrasted with the method that I developed from my diagram of the work of Foucault in terms of archaeology, genealogy and power/knowledge and I proposed that, keeping Foucault's work in mind, we would be able to undertake an inquiry that would bring the subject (*subject*) into question.

I suggested that today's intellectual historians and historians of philosophy share a similar theoretical terrain, as both are dependent upon a concept of the transparent self-reflexive subject (*Cogito*) which in one way or another they accord universal status, but which they fail to specify or argue for. Furthermore their very method precludes the possibility of raising any significant questions about the status of this subject, its specific history and how it came to be accorded universality.

In this inquiry I have presented a diagram of the emergence of the *Cogito* as a specific and particular event within the history of Western culture and discovered that a hitherto unrecognised aspect of this was the developing of the self-reflexive autobiographical subject (*subject*). I then committed myself to a continuing inquiry of the implications of this subject as it is presented in the work of Abelard, Descartes and Freud. But this inquiry was undertaken less in terms of the categories and specific arguments that they utilised but rather in terms of a strategy whereby they produced the fundamental relation with themselves – in other words, as a technology of self – of subjection. So the continuities and differences between them are not to be discovered in essentialism, metaphysics, transcendentalism or any other specific categories, but are drawn out from the place from where they compose themselves, which in turn both problematises and produces their relation with themselves.

And yet, is there not just a touch of metaphysics and a whiff of essentialism in this category of the self-reflexive autobiographical subject (*subject*) as I have characterised it? Have I not by a devious historical sleight of hand produced a certain congealing, a certain solidifying of the subject (*subject*) by first putting it into question and then reducing it to yet another transversal category? And what is the relationship between autobiography and biography? In his classic study *A History of Autobiography in Antiquity*.[56] Misch suggests that the term 'autobiography' was not known before the end of the eighteenth century when it first appeared in German literature and then passed into English. The word 'autobiography' can be broken up into its component parts *graphia*, *bios*, and *auto*, which mean writing, human life, and self, respectively.[57] On the basis of Misch's definition we can contrast autobiography to biography where the element of self-reflection is absent. Misch himself takes up this point:

> He himself knows the significance of his experiences, whether he mentions it or not; he only understands his life through the significance he attaches to them. This knowledge, which enables the writer to conceive his life as a single whole, has grown in the course of his life out of his actual experience, whereas we have the life of any other person before us as a whole only *ex post facto*: the man is dead, or at all events it is all past history.[58]

There is an important point to be drawn out here, that both the modes of biography and autobiography have a relation to the concepts of death and history, and yet in each case the structure of this relation is substantially different. In the case of biography, as Misch suggests, the object of the biographical study is often dead and so the biographical text is constituted in relation to a death or certainly a history that it completes. In contrast to this, the mode of autobiography presupposes the impending death of the subject (*subject*) that it draws out. In this case the history that the autobiography reveals is constituted by a death as a future historical event that acts as an absent presence, a death that has not yet occurred but which structures the relation between self and text.

We have examples of both these kinds of relation from the history of philosophy. Plato compiles his philosophy on the basis of dialogues that disclose the life and death of Socrates, and suggests the function of philosophy: 'Ordinary people seem not to realise that those who really apply themselves in the right way to philosophy are directly and of their own accord preparing themselves for dying and death.'[59] In this case the 'preparation' involves the death of a consciousness other than the one that constructs the biographical text. Whether this death has occurred or not, it takes place outside the relation of the biographer to their text. In contrast to this an autobiography is constituted in relation to the subject (*subject*) that constructs it, and in so doing constructs a relation to their own impending death. It is this impending death that becomes the foundation on which both the psychotic solution and transparency is based. The self-reflexive subject that underlies the work of Abelard, Descartes and Freud presupposes that moment at which all that will be left of their consciousness will be their *werke*, their textuality, the material traces of their own material existence.[60] But do these comments undermine the distinction made previously between hagiography, chronicle and autobiography? In the case of hagiography and chronicle the details of the life of another are expounded and so they would clearly fall into the category of biography. This is even the case with Augustine, whose experiences of himself within the text are mediated in the first case by God and then are shaped to fit a predetermined pattern of what ought to be the case:

> His [Augustine's] conscious purpose lay not in the narration of his individual experiences, but in the arousing of religious emotions and thoughts, and he himself bore witness to this lasting effect of his work, which he experienced ever anew, alike in the writing and the reading of it.[61]

In the *Confessions* by Augustine there is no attempt to make his consciousness transparent either to himself or to the would-be reader. On the contrary he makes every effort to avoid this on the basis that he could not know himself as well as God! This reinforces previous arguments that for my purposes Augustine's work would not be classified as an autobiography. So in autobiography and biography we find two fundamentally different relations to the structuring moment of death. For the biographer it is the death of the other, it is a writing of death from an absent other to a distant death. For the autobiographer it is the death of their own consciousness that they are presupposing, and as they textualise themselves as a subject (*subject*), and their relation to this absent but impending eventuality, they constitute a 'psychotic solution' that becomes the basis of their transparency and self-reflexivity. To found one's consciousness on *Cogito ergo sum*, is to be committed to endlessly stating the 'I' in order to confirm one's own existence, as this kind of autobiographical existence can only be confirmed in the endless textualising of the utterance. To construct oneself in relation to the biography of a Jew who lived two thousand years ago is to maintain a mediated distance to the complete annihilation of one's own consciousness in death, and is consistent with our description of biography where the 'death' that mediates it is the death of an absent other. It is this pattern that is transposed in philosophy in the work of Abelard, a process I have already detailed, but in this act of transposition a number of other fundamental relations are also transformed. Two of these are the relation to self and the mechanism for the transfer of power/knowledge.

To take up the second of these issues first. The transfer of power/ knowledge appropriate to the Greeks was that of a homosexual seduction and initiation.[62] The interchange and transfer of knowledge, power, desire and pleasure occurs at the same instance and the specificity of each becomes indistinguishable.[63] The early Christian church faced a problem unknown to the Greeks: how could the principles of an emerging religion, controlled and organised by men, be taught to women, given that the religion preached sexual restraint and that the very act of transferring knowledge raised the issue of the relation between knowledge, desire and pleasure in an intellectual atmosphere in which these issues could not be discussed? Up until this moment I am still describing the mode of biography. But now new questions emerge. With the inauguration of the transparent self-reflexive subject (*subject*) based on the autobiographical mode, does this fundamental transference of knowledge change in any way? Do the instruments of analysis that I am developing allow me to specify the structure and content of this transfer and analyse its possible effects on the subject (*subject*)?

John Boswell makes a plausible case about the existence of homosexual relations in the medieval teaching institutions, the monastic schools of the early to middle medieval period.[64] Even allowing that the development of the cathedral schools may well have altered this in that they were not based on the closed life of the cloister, let me consider the implications of Boswell's suggestion in terms of its philosophical possibilities. Let me then speculate that the model for the exchange of power/knowledge in the late eleventh and early twelfth centuries is something like the following: it involves a transfer of desire and pleasure, between the master and the student. This may not involve homosexual practices but necessarily does involve the element of seduction.[65] There is a curious tension in this process from the outset.

In this relation there is a propulsion to sameness, even though in concrete terms the overall relationship is one of a fundamental imbalance between master and student – and now I consciously retain the full signifying force of the 'and'. This propulsion to sameness emerges at the point at which the questing, questioning pupil transfers their will and desire of, for and to that of the master. In exchange for a certain complicity in this play of seduction they receive power/knowledge, and with that the insight that they will one day be in the position of the master. But it is precisely here that the problem of sameness emerges, a sameness that undermines the power/knowledge – seduction structure and threatens both master and pupil with annihilation. The more they become the same, the more each threatens to obliterate and cover over the existence of the other. The process then can be redrawn along the following lines. In order to adopt the position of the intellectual or philosophical self one adopts a position to one, a master, that has access to the capital 'T' truth as it is socially constructed, regulated and validated. This becomes the occupying of a textual place in the master/pupil structure. But the difficulty is that the position that one must as a pupil define oneself in relation to, is already an effect of the reciprocal relativity of another previous master/pupil relation, that has this inherent structure of a trajectory to sameness. Both master and pupil must transform each other's desire and will to their own, but to do so would be to occupy exactly the same space, they would be the same 'I'. Not only is this an impossibility, but even if we allow that two consciousnesses could have exactly the same will, desire, knowledge and so on, then it would be the end of the whole trajectory. Power/knowledge would cease to be transferred as each consciousness annihilated the separate existence of the other.

If our epistemology tells us that we cannot discover the Truth in the realist sense, with a capital 'T', then we can only textualise the truth or speak true at the expense of the other in the master/pupil relation, a textualising and trueness that becomes a life and death struggle that is not solely a question of differences or difference, but similarity. Another element needs to be added. As was suggested at the outset of this discussion, while the pupil is to some extent complicit in this seduction, there is a fundamental imbalance at the outset as the master already has social access to textualise Truth whilst the pupil does not. So we need to account for the essential hierarchical component of this structure. Here with the help of a misreading of Derrida I shall introduce the concept of deference.[66] Deference can be used in two ways, in the sense of putting off, and in the sense of noting the hierarchical relation implicit in this trajectory of sameness. This allows me then to consider this movement in terms not of the incorporation of differences but as the production of sameness. This trajectory operates by inclusions, not solely by synthesising opposites, but by specifying exclusions and constituting similarities.

In the figure below we have an example of two models. On the left we have the kind of model that can be derived from the *Phenomenology of Spirit*.[67] Here

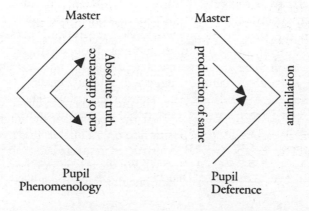

Master   Master

end of difference   Absolute truth   production of same   annihilation

Pupil   Pupil
Phenomenology   Deference

the master/pupil relation would follow the thesis, antithesis, synthesis model which would be approaching a state where all contradictions will be incorporated into the final stage of Absolute spirit, or academic Truth in the case of this analogy. Difference here is assimilated, and the end of difference is the completion of the acquisition of power/knowledge whereby the consciousness of master and pupil would include and incorporate all the differences to which they had ever ascribed. In contrast to this, on the right in the model of deference, the master already possesses the right to textualise 'true', and through the transfer of power/knowledge, and the necessary transmission of desire, pleasure and so on, the pupil is constituted in a production of the 'same' that inevitably threatens both the master and the pupil with the future point of annihilation. In this case, deference both maintains the hierarchy that prevents this annihilation and sets up an oscillation between master and pupil that while guaranteeing the production of 'sameness', allows this to operate at different intensities and different levels of agreement at different times. Deference parallels the lines of the production of the same.[68]

This is a movement whereby the master demands that the pupil defers to his truth, to his meaning, to his textuality, to his need for similarity, which confirms his position as master. But one can be a little Lacanian here and suggest that this demand cannot be met, and its consequences of the death of the one at the hands of the other are deferred.[69] However, the very movement of this deference fixes a place from which it will be possible to continue to textualise the discourse of the master. Let me return to Socrates' quotation on the function of philosophy as the preparation for death and Plato's place as Socrates' biographer. The accession of Plato to the place of Socrates is dependent on the actual death of Socrates, a death which guarantees Socrates an immortal textual place in all future philosophy and allows Plato, in the compiling and specifying of this place of immortality as the biographer, to occupy and colonise Socrates' place as master in a series of pupil relations that will follow.

What remains is to begin the analysis of the way in which Abelard's reconstruction of the autobiographical transparent textual subject alters my account of the transfer of power/knowledge, and improves upon the theoretical instruments that I am developing. From my previous account of Abelard I can make a number of suggestions that have a bearing upon the issues at hand. As already suggested, Abelard challenged the then existing modes of regulating and transferring power/knowledge in a profound way. There is an overt resistance to the transmission of knowledge from a master to a pupil within the traditional model previously outlined and he replaced it with a structure whereby knowledge could be acquired from a relation of self to text. Initially the instrument used to bring this about was sceptical dialectics. Dialectics became in his hands not simply a method of explicating the 'faith' in accordance with the then existing systems of regulation, but of uncovering the truth which ought to agree and rationally coincide with Church dogma. As we have seen his manual for knowledge *Sic et Non* was explicitly underpinned with a scepticism that was directed towards truth: 'For by doubting we come to enquiry, and by enquiring we grasp the truth.'[70]

The rigorous nature of Abelard's application of his sceptical dialectics opened up a textual space between affirmation and negation, between the yes and the no, which is occupied and realised by the self-knowing transparent subject that displaces God at the centre of its being. This possibility had emerged as the result of a shift in the traditional direction of the philosophical theology which I previously examined. Originally the intersection between philosophy and theology had provided the early church fathers with a means of defending church doctrines against the philosophical attacks of heathens and pagans (see for example Origen's work *Contra Celsus*), but by Abelard's day there had developed an internal philosophical and theological debate centred on the philosophical problem of universals and the theological question of the nature of the Trinity. Abelard's response to this in terms of the textual position that he occupies is a surprising one:

> For by doubting we come to enquiry, and by enquiring we grasp the truth, according to what even Truth himself said, 'Seek and you will find, knock and it will be opened to you'. Truth furnished us moral instruction by his own example when he chose to be found at the age of 12, sitting and questioning in the midst of doctors. By his questioning he appears to us as a pupil rather than, by preaching, as a master, although there is in him, nevertheless, the full and perfect wisdom of God.[71]

This supports a point made by Duby. The new intellectuals, the *Magistri*, attempted to base their philosophical enquiries on the construction of the persona Jesus as the 'subject' that undergoes the transition from pupil to the God *Magister*.[72] This example will allow me to make an important philosophical point. While Jesus is pupil he also incorporates in himself as pupil the complete and unlimited knowledge of God. His consciousness already incorporates the fullness of its own complete autobiographical outcome. It is transparent to itself. It is this that underpins a subtle movement in the text by which means truth with a small t, as the object of dialectics, becomes truth with a capital T, as the persona of Jesus, Christ, Magister. It must be remembered that this movement occurs in a text which goes on to doubt 158 important Church doctrines in an application of dialectics and which refuses to articulate a final Truthful, dogmatic position. Abelard has overcome the previous master/pupil trajectory and one aspect of this overcoming is the transformation of the structure of the transfer of power/knowledge from that of pupils who are dependent on this transfer as coming from an outside consciousness, to that of pupils who construct their own power/knowledge on the basis of an autobiographical textual self that is unmediated by an outside other. It is from here that one textualises as God/Magister/Father/philosopher/psychoanalyst and so on.

This tendency is reinforced by a further movement. If the relation to a master as an outside though related consciousness is refused and the action of dialectical methodological scepticism is internalised, one risks fragmenting and splitting the conception of self infinitely. As previously suggested, if all we can know of ourselves is *Cogito ergo sum*, there is a sense in which in order to confirm it as the fundamental condition of our existence we are committed to articulate it continuously. This is why in the end Descartes must support his system with the beneficence of God, for without God as the final arbiter of meaning and guarantor of the structural integrity of the *Cogito*, the application of methodological scepticism makes meaning impossible, and the dialectical subject (*subject*) itself is potentially threatened with madness.[73] Abelard's book on ethics is entitled *Scito Te Ipsum*, which is usually translated into English as *Know Thyself*. In French it carries a more reflexive meaning, *Connais-toi, toi-même*. Here the reflexive nature of knowledge is made clear. One can self-identify the 'I' by positioning oneself in relation to the capital 'T' truth of the same (a capital 'T' that becomes the autobiographical transparent subject), by occupying that space opened up by the ontological implications of the sceptical dialectic – a space from which God is banished as the 'I' takes up residence and almost simultaneously poses God's non-being. What has intervened is the self-reflexive autobiographical subject (*subject*), and the culmination of this trajectory is not to re-transcribe the life of some medieval saint, or even a heathen philosopher, it is to retranscribe one's own life and death. In response to this Abelard textualises his own life and, at the same time, the performance of his own death, in his autobiography, the *Historia Calamitatum*.

Both Abelard and Plato construct their conception of self in terms of a relation to death. For Plato it is the death of the master that allows him to occupy that same place as he textualises the biographical Socratic death. For Abelard it is his own death, as through the vehicle of his autobiography the 'certainty' of his own death becomes the condition and index of the 'certainty' that we recognise as transparency. This autobiographical moment is graphic – in that its object is to leave material traces and remains of a life that will soon cease to exist – and autoerotic in its excess. Furthermore, for Plato this death will take place in an absent scene, while for Abelard this death is one of impending presence, as his autobiography marks and constitutes a textual death that precedes yet presupposes his actual death. Abelard's autobiography is the accumulation of a life not quite dead, undead, zombied, that is structured around a transparency that refuses to recognise a position outside this autobiographical mode – this peculiar technology. A refusal, or should we write disavowal, that is the index of its psychotic structure. Psychotic because it binds itself in the constitution of self totally in terms of similarity or sameness, that in refusing to acknowledge any other than what it recognises as of the same, is engaging in a fundamental flight from the 'real', the possibility of another independently existing consciousness, life and death. It is this self-reflexive, autobiographical textual consciousness that finds expression in the system-building philosophies of Descartes, Kant, Hegel or Schreber, where the unwritten text is always *La réalité c'est moi*.

The *Cogito* owes its historical force to its psychotic and paranoid structure and far from being just an argument in a few pages of Descartes' work, is in fact a position from which to inscribe a self-reflexive consciousness – a technology of self. It allows no absences, only fullness, and presupposes that there is no remainder. Everything known to the reflexive subject (*subject*) will be lost in its own textual excess, as in the future it will be the last word on the meaning and purpose of the consciousness and death that it reveals.

This is what produces the laughter of the nominalist. The apologists for the universal subject (*subject*), in its many forms, not only ignore its particular and specific history but defend and promote a technology of the subject that produces a subject which is liable to disintegration and multiplicity. It is no more than a fault line made up of discontinuous segments. It is paranoid in its very structure and wholly determined in relation to its death. This limiting and self-defeating technology of self has inscribed on it a violence determined by an imaginary metaphysics, while its defenders live in constant fear of an untimely dawn when it will be shattered. But this is the very condition of its existence.

Afterword

This inquiry was ambitious and not without its dangers from the outset. I have brought Foucault's work into conjunction with intellectual history, the history of philosophy, and the history of ideas in the context of bypassing the dichotomy between realism and idealism which I have argued is still endemic to these disciplines. At the same time I have set out to provide an alternative to the history, structure and function of the self-reflexive transparent subject (*subject*) as proposed within these domains. What emerges from this work is that what passes for the history of the contemporary subject misrecognises its claimed origins both as a historical event and at the level of its epistemology. Philosophy today is predicated on the autobiographical voice and its supporting subject (*subject*) and is recognisable only in relation to the autobiographical *I*.

Historians tell us that in both the twelfth century and the seventeenth century the social structure was undergoing fundamental material, technical and social change. I have suggested that this involved among other things the reorganisation of the distribution and circulation of power/knowledge against a background of methodological scepticism and the construction of a reconstituted self-reflexive subject (*subject*) . Perhaps a more general claim can be made that there are times when the question of language and the position and structure of the subject (*subject*) come into the foreground of cultural life. Of the possible responses, idealism, realism, rationalism and various combinations of these, methodological scepticism can be particularly productive.

Power/knowledge is at this moment being reorganised, transferred and distributed along different lines.[1] New systems of regulation are emerging along with alternative mechanisms of authorisation. The categories used in this inquiry: primogeniture, systems of inheritance; sexual practices; power/

knowledge; the politics of truth; modifications to the transfer, dissemination and regulation of knowledge; the development of indices and cross-referencing; and the transformation of sexual practices, are all both part of this process and at the same time among its effects as what has previously counted as knowledge, and the anchoring of that knowledge in self is being fundamentally redrawn. This has shattered the universal or essential subject (*subject*).

If we consider those epochs I have analysed in this inquiry, an argument can be made that a most productive response to the crisis in knowledge of the twelfth century and the seventeenth century, as represented, in part, by Abelard and Descartes, was methodological scepticism and nominalism. This may also be the most philosophically productive response available to us at the present juncture. As we attempt to analyse the appearance, and now the disappearance of the rational subject (*subject*), the *Cogito*, that has dominated the recent history of our culture, we may well find that methodological scepticism based on a materialist nominalism and transformed to meet contemporary conditions may be a most productive approach. Certainly the work of Rorty, Skinner, Hacking, Derrida, Baudrillard, Lyotard, Habermas and others would have to be taken into account, but if we base our method on a Foucauldian rereading of Nietzsche, the historical preconditions of our own consciousness of ourselves as subjects (*subjects*) are transformed. However, methodological scepticism as the basis of a critical epistemology cannot avoid the question of ethics. Foucault recognised this pressing need at the end of his career and it is our loss that at the time of his death this work was either incomplete, or unpublished. It is the responsibility of the would-be Foucauldian to address this need. This is important because while my inquiry has decomposed the continuous history of the subject (*subject*) there is more that needs to be said. If we review the category 'history and systems of thought' the self-reflexive transparent subject occupies the place of the original 'and', and in its role of over-determining the relation between the other two elements it leaves the relation between history (and) systems of thought unchallengeable. This is precisely the problem of historicity.

This inquiry, in specifying the conditions of the emergence of the self-reflexive transparent autobiographical subject, leaves all three elements disassociated from each other. If one does not want to take recourse to universal, essential or natural values what is demanded is a nominalist ethics of self. This remains to be accomplished, but this ethical work can only be productively undertaken if we abandon the congealed, petrified and putrefied categories of modernity, modernism, and post-modernism which belong to an already disappeared epoch, and compose ourselves in the realisation that we already exist in the future time of rigorous nominalism. It is only with a thoroughgoing nominalism and its methodological counterpart, scepticism, that we can confront realism, materialism and idealism on their proper terrain and draw out both the need for and the conditions under which such an ethics can emerge.

The remnants of the already drawn out rational self-reflexive subject and its supporting body are but lines, drawings and fragmented diagrams. They constitute caricatures of the failed experiment of the Enlightenment which always was a most inappropriate response to the Philosophy of the Cave – an experiment that perhaps reached it climactic apogee in MacPherson's profound comment 'I never read anything I haven't written myself'. The manufactured body of *The Body* meets the writing of it(S)elf and finds (T)ruth in the interchange. This is not simply a matter of a technology of self whereby we manufacture ourselves according to some entirely self-determined programme that anchors itself in either universal essences or universal history or nature. Nor is it a question of a technology of self of a spontaneous machined combustion. Both these technologies inhabit the same geography of the universal dream/wish of liberal capitalism from Oxbridge to UCLA. Their time has passed away and soon their resonances will have entirely disappeared along with the nostalgia for the certainty of past and self. They should be aware that *The Body* has already disappeared and is being reconfigured through a Second, Third, Fourth and n^{th} Coming. Disassembled, reassembled, composed, decomposed, made up, made over, edited, sub-edited, recycled. Transfigured. Business personality of the year, marketer of the decade, sibling, child, cousin, parent, lover, philosopher. Multiple relations, series, relays. Lines joining dots. This is not just true of *The Body* but *Everybody*.

Relations between points on the power/knowledge network: lines, drawings, layerings, diagrams.[2] Indices of future possibilities that have already been Announced. Alphabet, hieroglyph, pictogram, braille. Aggregations, resonances echoes – pleasures. They are all wholly material.

Plato's lesson is out of time. For him the question was less whether one should enter the light but rather how could one resist being drawn back into the cave. Less an issue of being bathed in Enlightenment than of the ever-present danger of returning to barbarism. Of not being Greek enough. But this choice is for us entirely inappropriate.[3]

We should not enter the light but be the light. In this sense alone should there be any echoes of religiosity. We exist as the unified field – simultaneously particles/waves – ripples in the reality reference condemned to endlessly transpose ourselves.... This is what makes us what we are ... an aggregation of material practices and our reflections on them ... from the cave to the rock pool ... multiple reflections. We are much closer to Narcissus than Oedipus. We have gone a long way before we have finally heard the coda and understood that the subject (*subject*) is that point at which the aggregations and resonances that I am engage with material practices. . . .

As we lie on the beach in the hot summer sun, soaked in coconut oil reading philosophy, how can we not understand the nominalist materiality of our own existence? How can we imagine ourselves as anything other than multiple resonances and aggregations? Is not this beached *I* different from this writer *I* and different again from all the other *I*'s that *I* am? As the coconut oil is rubbed into our back, how can we not understand that this is not a meeting of two eternal universal consciousnesses but one of fingertip cells and back cells – of sub-molecular particles. Of lines, drawings and diagrams. Of aggregations and resonances. It is a nominal exchange that takes place at the very limits of material existences. In its very act it decentres, localises and distributes pleasures.

A centred self-reflexive subject (*Cogito*) locked in its own cavernous darkness and isolation can only experience itself in that particular way at any given moment because of an oppressive imaginary relation body/self produced by the universal historicity of intellectual history, history of philosophy, the history of ideas – let us say culture.

But surely there is more to life than that. These aggregations, these resonances released from this historicism have altogether many other tasks to perform; among them the endless work of inquiring into their multiplicity; of meeting the obligation to threaten themselves through change, and through reflections on these threats to leave traces, marks, lines – drawings, diagrams in the world for others to use, ignore, and transform; of sketching technologies of self that become future possibilities and which compose marks of uncertainty, questionings, future inquiries.

So let us finally leave the cave and draw ourselves to the surface, escaping from the suffocating darkness of metaphysics, not blinded and misled by the brightness of the fire, but by being both light and wave, particle and fluid. Flashing, reflecting, mingling with the rock pool and drawing ourselves with an unrepentant and guiltless nominalism.

After this inquiry is this all that remains of the *subject*?

Notes to the text

Introduction

1. Blumenberg, Hans, *The Legitimacy of the Modern Age*, trans. Robert M. Wallace, MIT Press, Cambridge, Mass., 1983, p. 145.
2. Oakley, F., *Omnipotence, Covenant and Order: An excursion in the history of ideas from Abelard to Leibniz*, Cornell University Press, Ithaca, NY, 1984, p. 23.
3. I am thinking here of Rorty, Skinner, Hacking and others and the *History and Theory* journal.
4. Throughout this inquiry from time to time I bracket off the subject and place it in italics. This is done to cause the reader to stumble and remind them that for the purposes of this work the subject (*subject*) is always both the subject and object of material practices and technologies of reflection and introspection.
5. Obviously there are many other alternatives.
6. The closest work to the project that I have in mind is Howard Bloch, R., *Etymologies and Genealogies: A literary anthropology of the French Middle Ages*, University of Chicago Press, Chicago, 1986. While Howard Bloch's interpretation of Foucault is rather more Kantian than my own, on the whole I find this a compelling work.
7. M. Shapiro (ed.), *Language and Politics*, Blackwell, Oxford, 1984, see Foucault, M., 'The order of discourse', p. 137.

1 Contemporary issues in the history of ideas

1. Rorty, R., Schneewind, J.B., and Skinner, Q. (eds), *Philosophy in History: Essays in the historiography of philosophy*, Cambridge University Press, Cambridge, 1984.
2. Oakley, op. cit., *Omnipotence, Covenant and Order*.
3. Rorty, R., *Philosophy and the Mirror of Nature*, Blackwell, Oxford, 1980.

4. White, Hayden, *Metahistory*, Johns Hopkins University Press, London, 1985. Both Collingwood and Lovejoy receive a passing mention in this text.
5. Said, E., *Orientalism*, Routledge & Kegan Paul, London, 1978.
6. Rorty *et al.*, op. cit., *Philosophy in History*, p. 1.
7. ibid., p. 3.
8. ibid., p. 8.
9. Lovejoy, A.O., *The Great Chain of Being: A study of the history of an idea*, Harvard University Press, Cambridge, Mass., 1964, p. 4.
10. ibid. , pp. 7–14.
11. There are a number of philosophical resonances here, in particular with Bacon's Idols in the *Novum Organum* and by association Nietzsche's *Twilight of the Idols*.
12. This issue is discussed in great detail in Chalmers, A.F., *What is this Thing Called Science?*, University of Queensland Press, 1976; Rorty *et al.*, op. cit., *Philosophy in History*, see Hacking, I., 'Five Parables'.
13. Lovejoy, op. cit., *Great Chain of Being*, p. 6.
14. ibid. , p. 4.
15. ibid., p. 15.
16. ibid., p. 16.
17. Within his definition of a text Lovejoy does not allow that a wider social text exists where ideas could be found in social and institutional practices.
18. Lovejoy, op. cit., *Great Chain of Being*, p. 22.
19. ibid., p. 7.
20. ibid., p. 5.
21. ibid., p. 32.
22. ibid.
23. ibid., p. 21.
24. ibid., p. 37.
25. There is something of a double movement here, on the one hand a deep structure is posited, that has certain Freudian resonances, on the other the tendency is for this deep structure to disappear within the category of intentionality. These issues will be discussed further in later chapters.
26. Lovejoy, op. cit., *Great Chain of Being*, pp. 253, 301.
27. ibid., p. 24.
28. ibid., pp. 22–3.
29. ibid., p. 23.
30. Collingwood, R.G., *The Idea of History*, Oxford University Press, Oxford, 1978.
31. Collingwood, R.G., *An Autobiography*, Oxford University Press, Oxford, 1967, p. 59.
32. Collingwood acknowledges the efforts in particular of Bertrand Russell and A.N. Whitehead.
33. Collingwood, op. cit., *Autobiography*, pp. 59–64.
34. Collingwood, op. cit., *Idea of History*, p. 325.
35. Collingwood, op. cit., *Autobiography*, pp. 63–9.
36. ibid., p. 70.
37. ibid., p. 37.
38. ibid., p. 75.

198 *Notes to the text*

39. Collingwood, op. cit., *Idea of History*, p. 1.
40. Collingwood, op. cit., *Autobiography*, p. 86.
41. ibid., p. 116.
42. Collingwood, op. cit., *Idea of History*, p. 10. There are a number of resonances here with the work of Abelard on the question of self-knowledge and at the more general level of ethics which will be discussed later in this work. It is also worth noting even at this early stage that the issue of the status of biography and autobiography is one of the major themes of this inquiry.
43. Collingwood, op. cit., *Autobiography*, p. 96.
44. In view of the direction of some of the discussion to follow in later chapters two distinctions should be clearly made here. First, that Collingwood's concept of the trace has nothing to do with Derrida's concept of the trace, as it is spelt out by Spivak in the introduction of *Of Grammatology*. See Derrida, J., *Of Grammatology*, trans. G.C. Spivak, Johns Hopkins University Press, Baltimore, 1980. However, it is more suggestive of M. Bloch's conception of the 'track'. See Bloch, M., *The Historian's Craft*, trans. Peter Putnam, Vintage Books, New York, 1953.
45. Collingwood, op. cit., *Idea of History*, p. 97.
46. ibid., p. 213. It should perhaps be noted that even in contemporary physics the issue of the inside and the outside of an event is becoming increasingly problematic. This is particularly so in particle physics; for an examination of this see, Zukav, G., *The Dancing Wu-Li Masters*, Fontana, London, 1982.
47. For an alternative account of presentism see Momigliano, A., *Studies in Historiography*, Weidenfeld & Nicolson, London, 1966, ch. 12, pp. 221–38.
48. Collingwood, op. cit., *Idea of History*, p. 108.
49. Collingwood's critique of positivism is to be found on pp. 127–33 in *The Idea of History*.
50. Collingwood, op. cit., *Autobiography*, p. 31.
51. ibid., p. 97.
52. Collingwood, op. cit., *Idea of History*, p. 215.
53. ibid.
54. Collingwood, op. cit., *Autobiography*, p. 113.
55. ibid., p. 246.
56. Rorty *et al.*, op. cit., *Philosophy in History*, see Burnyeat, M.F., 'The sceptic in his place and time', p. 226.
57. ibid., see Hylton, P., 'The nature of the proposition and the revolt against idealism', p. 392.
58. ibid., see Taylor, C., 'Philosophy and its history', p. 17.
59. ibid., see Taylor, C., 'Philosophy and its history', p. 22.
60. ibid., see Taylor, C., 'Philosophy and its history', p. 30.
61. ibid., see Rorty, R., 'The historiography of philosophy: four genres', p. 51.
62. ibid., see Rorty, R., 'The historiography of philosophy: four genres', p. 55.
63. ibid., see Hylton, P., 'The nature of the proposition and the revolt against idealism', p. 396.
64. This suggestion needs to be taken seriously even if Australian Departments of Social Services are filled to the brim with psychologists and psychiatrists, and not with psychoanalysts.

65. Freud, S., *Leonardo Da Vinci: A Memory of his childhood*, Ark, London, 1984, p. 30.
66. ibid.
67. ibid., p. 31.
68. Undoubtedly there are a number of resonances here to my earlier criticisms of the work of both Lovejoy and Collingwood.
69. Freud, S. 'Moses and Monotheism', in *The Origins of Religion, vol 13*, Pelican Freud Library, Penguin, Harmondsworth, 1985.
70. ibid., p. 276.
71. ibid., p. 281.
72. Freud's use of the concept of 'tracks' is not unlike that of the Annales school; see Bloch, *The Historian's Craft*, and also Collingwood's use of a similar conception.
73. Freud, op. cit., 'Moses and Monotheism', p. 310.
74. Freud, S., *Civilisation And Its Discontents*, trans. Joan Riviere, Hogarth Press, London, 1979.
75. ibid., p. 5.
76. ibid., p. 34.
77. Freud, S., *Totem and Taboo*, trans. A.A. Brill, Vintage, New York, 1946.
78. Freud, op. cit., 'Moses and Monotheism', p. 299.
79. Freud, op. cit., *Totem and Taboo*, p. 171.
80. ibid., p. 183.
81. ibid., p. 185.
82. Freud, op. cit., 'Moses and Monotheism', p. 324.
83. ibid., p. 344.
84. Freud, op. cit., *Civilisation and Its Discontents*, p. 69.
85. Foucault, M., *The Order of Things*, Tavistock, London, 1980, p. 375.
86. Foucault, M., *The History of Sexuality, vol 1: An introduction*, trans. Robert Hurley, Allan Lane, London, 1978, p. 109.
87. Foucault, M., *The Archaeology of Knowledge*, trans. A.M. Sheridan Smith, Tavistock, London, 1974, p. 204.
88. Rabinow, P. (ed.) *The Foucault Reader*, Pantheon, New York, 1984, see Foucault, M., 'What is enlightenment', p. 43.

2 History and systems of thought

1. Misquoted in Goldstein, Jan. 'Foucault among the sociologists: the disciplines and the history of the professions', *History and Theory*, 23, 1984, p. 178. This illustrates the role of the dice throw and chance in the production of any work.
2. For an additional account of how the conjunction 'and' functions see Gallop, J., *Feminism and Psychoanalysis: The daughter's seduction*, Macmillan, London, 1982, p. 1.
3. Deleuze, G., *Foucault*, trans. Seán Hand, University of Minnesota Press, Minneapolis, 1988, p. 36.
4. I must confess that Lovejoy, Collingwood and Freud as presented in the

previous pages are also no more than drawings that compose a diagram of intellectual history, the history of philosophy and the history of ideas. It was devious of me not to have mentioned this before!

5. There would be an opportunity for a very long footnote here; however, it seems more appropriate to refer the reader to the Oxford English Dictionary.

6. Nietzsche, F., *The Portable Nietzsche*, trans. Walter Kaufmann, Penguin, Harmondsworth, 1977, p. 466, see 'Twilight of the idols'.

7. At what cost could such an act of violent aggression be undertaken?

8. Gordon, C. (ed.), *Power/Knowledge. Selected interviews and other writings by Michel Foucault 1972–1977*, Pantheon, New York, 1980, see Foucault, M., 'Prison Talk', pp. 53–4.

9. Couzens Hoy, D., *Foucault A Critical Reader*, Blackwell, Oxford, 1986. Merquior, J.G., *Foucault*, Fontana, London, 1985.

10. Foucault, M., *The Use of Pleasure: History of sexuality, vol. 2*, trans. Robert Hurley, Pantheon, New York, 1985, p. 9.

11. ibid., p. 29.

12. Dreyfus, H.L., and Rabinow, P., *Michel Foucault: Beyond structuralism and hermeneutics*, Harvester, Brighton, 1982, p. 208, see Foucault, M., 'Afterword'.

13. See also Oakshott, M., *Experience and Its Modes*, Cambridge University Press, Cambridge, 1966.

14. There is also something of the notion of the Lacanian 'real' here. For Lacan the 'real' exists as an a priori substratum existing under the world of experience but it can never be apprehended directly. See Lacan, J., *Écrits*, Tavistock, London, 1972. In this context Foucault writes of the reality-reference.

15. Foucault, op. cit., *Use of Pleasure*, p. 28.

16. Cousins, M., and Hussain, A., *Michel Foucault*, Macmillan, London, 1984, p. 68.

17. Foucault, M., *The Birth of the Clinic*, trans. A.M. Sheridan, Tavistock, London, 1976; Foucault, M., *Mental Illness and Psychology*, trans. Alan Sheridan, Harper, New York, 1976; Foucault, M., *Madness and Civilisation*, trans. Richard Howard, Tavistock, London, 1979.

18. Foucault, op. cit., *Madness and Civilisation*, p. ix.

19. ibid., p. xi.

20. ibid., p. xii.

21. Gordon, op. cit., *Power/Knowledge*, Foucault, M. , 'Truth and Power', p. 109.

22. Foucault, op. cit., *Use of Pleasure*, p. 8. For an interesting critique of the Dreyfus and Rabinow interpretation of Foucault see, Minson, J.P., 'Foucault and the mill of philosophy', *Critical Philosphy*, 2(1), pp. 40–62.

23. Derrida's critique of Foucault's use of this opposition is to be found in Derrida, J., *Writing and Difference*, trans. A. Bass, University of Chicago Press, Chicago, 1978, see 'Cogito and the history of madness'. Foucault's reply is to be found the article 'My body, this paper, this fire'. *Oxford Literary Review*. 4(1), 1979. *The Birth of the Clinic* if anything is rather more phenomenological than *Madness and Civilisation*, as it locates as the object of its intervention the history of medicine, a history which in its traditional form presents itself in similar terms to the history of psychiatry.

24. Foucault, op. cit., *Madness and Civilisation*, p. xii.

25. Lévi-Strauss, C., *The Raw and the Cooked*, Cape, London, 1970.
26. Foucault, op. cit., *Madness and Civilisation*, p. xii.
27. Foucault, op. cit., *Birth of the Clinic*, p. xvi.
28. ibid., p. xvii.
29. Foucault, op. cit., *Order of Things*, p. x.
30. ibid., p. xiv.
31. ibid.
32. Dreyfus and Rabinow, op. cit., *Michel Foucault*, pp. vii–viii.
33. Foucault, op. cit., *Order of Things*, p. xxi.
34. ibid., p. 50.
35. Foucault, M., and Blanchot, M., *Foucault–Blanchot*, trans. Brian Massumi and Jeffrey Mehlman. Zone, New York, 1987, p. 73.
36. Foucault, op. cit., *Order of Things*, p. 168.
37. ibid., p. 219.
38. ibid., p. 329.
39. ibid., p. 371.
40. Foucault, op. cit., *Archaeology of Knowledge*, p. 3.
41. ibid., p. 4.
42. ibid.
43. ibid., p. 6.
44. The question of the document is a central one to the history of philosophy, and particularly both to those studies derived from Nietzsche, and those that are placed more directly within the Annales school of history; in this respect see Bloch, op. cit., *The Historian's Craft*.
45. Foucault, op. cit., *Archaeology of Knowledge*, p. 6.
46. ibid., p. 7.
47. ibid., p. 12.
48. ibid., p. 14.
49. The metaphor that relates the birth of the *Cogito* to a tranquillised sleep is, of course, well chosen by Foucault in view of the many references in Descartes' work to the distinction between sleeping and waking states. Descartes, R., *The Philosophical Works of Descartes, vols 1 and 2*, trans. Elizabeth S. Haldane and G.T.R. Ross, Cambridge University Press, New York, 1967. See in particular 'Discourse on method of rightly conducted reason', and 'Meditations on first philosophy'.
50. Foucault, op. cit., *Archaeology of Knowledge*, p. 16.
51. ibid., p. 25.
52. ibid., p. 24.
53. For a highly critical view of Foucault's account of the history of ideas and his use of the archive see Merquior, op. cit., *Foucault*, chs 5 and 6.
54. Foucault, op. cit., *Archaeology of Knowledge*, p. 25.
55. ibid., p. 27.
56. ibid., p. 28.
57. ibid.
58. ibid., p. 52.
59. ibid., p. 117.
60. ibid., p. 130. The archive '*is the general system of the formation and the*

transformation of statements. The analysis of the archive, then, involves a privileged region: at once close to us, and different from our present existence, it is the border of time that surrounds our presence, which overhangs it, and which indicates it in its otherness: it is that which, outside ourselves, delimits us. The description of the archive deploys its possibilities (and the mastery of its possibilities) on the basis of the very discourses that have just ceased to be ours; its threshold of existence is established by the discontinuity that separates us from what we can no longer say, and from that which falls outside our discursive practice; it begins with the outside of our own language (*langage*); its locus is the gap between our own discursive practices.'

61. See Deleuze, G., and Guattari, F., *Anti-Oedipus*, trans. Robert Hurley, Mark Seem and Helen R. Lane, Viking, New York, 1977.

62. Foucault, op. cit., *Archaeology of Knowledge*, p. 138. All the previous small quotations not indented are taken from pages 136–8.

63. ibid., p. 142.

64. Patton, P., 'Of power and prisons', in Morris M., and Patton, P. (eds), *Michel Foucault: Power, truth and strategy*, Feral, Sydney, 1979, p. 111. 'The point of inflexion is marked by the entry in force of the theme of power in Foucault's discourse. This involves a shift of emphasis from the discursive to the non-discursive, which is inseparable from a change in the conception of power itself.'

65. Foucault, M., 'Discourse on Language', appendix to the American edition to *The Archaeology of Knowledge*, Pantheon Books, New York, 1972. All references to this work are taken from this translation.

66. ibid. , p. 219.

67. Bouchard, D., (ed.) *Language, Counter-memory, Practice: Selected essays and interviews by Michel Foucault*, trans. Donald F. Bouchard and Sherry Simon, Cornell University Press, New York, 1980, see Foucault, M., 'Nietzsche, genealogy, and history', p. 140.

68. Bouchard, op. cit., *Language*, see Foucault, M., 'Nietzsche'. p. 139.

69. ibid.

70. Gordon, op. cit., *Power/Knowledge*, see Foucault, M., 'Truth and Power', p. 114.

71. Bouchard, op. cit., *Language*, see Foucault, M., 'Intellectuals and power' and 'What is an author?' See also E. Gross, 'On speaking about pornography', in *Scarlet Women*, 13, Spring 1981.

72. Bouchard, op. cit., *Language*, see Foucault, M., 'Nietzsche', p. 164.

73. Foucault, op. cit., *Use of Pleasure*, pp. 8–9.

74. Bouchard, op. cit., *Language*, see Foucault, M., 'Nietzsche', pp. 139–64.

75. Nietzsche, F., *On the Genealogy of Morals, Ecce Homo*, trans. Walter Kaufmann, Vintage, New York, 1969.

76. Nietzsche, F., *Untimely Meditations*, trans. R.J. Hollingdale, Cambridge University Press, New York, 1983, see 'On the uses and disadvantages of history for life', pp. 57–124.

77. Bouchard, op. cit., *Language*, see Foucault, M., 'Nietzsche', p. 146.

78. ibid., p. 148.

79. ibid., p. 154.

80. Dreyfus and Rabinow, op. cit., *Michel Foucault*, p. 9.
81. Patton, P., 'Michel Foucault: the ethics of an intellectual', in *Thesis Eleven*, nos 10/11, 1984/1985, p. 78.
82. Bouchard, op. cit., *Language*, see Foucault, M., 'Revolutionary action until now', p. 221.
83. Gordon, op. cit., *Power/Knowledge*, see Foucault, M., 'Prison Talk', p. 51.
84. Foucault, M., 'Interview, the regard for truth', in Foss, P., and Taylor, P. (eds), *Art and Text, Burnout*, 16, p. 25.
85. ibid., p. 29.
86. ibid., p. 24.
87. Martin, L.H., Gutman, H., and Hutton, P.H. (eds), *Technologies of the Self*, Tavistock, London, 1988, see Foucault, M., 'Truth, power, self: an interview', p. 15.
88. Dreyfus and Rabinow, op. cit., *Michel Foucault*, see Foucault, M., 'Afterword', p. 212.
89. Gordon, op. cit., *Power/Knowledge*, see Foucault, M., 'Power and strategies', p. 142.
90. Morris and Patton, op. cit., *Power, Truth and Stategy*, see Foucault, M., 'Power and norm: notes', p. 62.
91. Gordon, op. cit., *Power/Knowledge*, Foucault, M. , 'Two lectures', p. 89.
92. Foucault, op. cit., *History of Sexuality vol. 1*, p. 93–4.
93. Foucault, op. cit., *Use of Pleasure*, p. 7.
94. Gordon, op. cit., *Power/Knowledge*, see Foucault, M., 'Prison talk', p. 52.
95. One feels an almost overwhelming desire to run off a list of popular criticisms of Foucault's work, and patiently to correct, dispute and refute them, as if somehow my drawing of Foucault had sprung to life and needed saving. This is not my project in this work and rather than undertake this task I have included in the bibliography a list of references, some critical, some laudatory, which I found helpful in coming to my appreciation of Foucault's work.
96. Armstrong, T., trans. *Michel Foucault: Philosopher*, Harvester Wheatsheaf, Hemel Hempstead, 1992, see Balibar, É., 'Foucault and Marx: The question of nominalism', pp. 38–56; Rorty *et al.*, op. cit., *Philosophy in History*, see Rorty, R., 'The historiography of philosophy: four genres', p. 73, and Hacking, 'Five parables', p. 122.
97. Foucault, M., *Death and the Labyrinth: The world of Raymond Roussel*, trans. Charles Ruas, Doubleday, New York, 1986, see 'Postscript: an interview with Michel Foucault', p. 177.
98. Rorty, *et al.*, op. cit., *Philosophy in History*, see Rorty, 'Historiography of philosophy', p. 73.
99. This was made abundantly clear in the debate between Foucault and Chomsky. Printed in Elders, Fons (eds), *Reflexive Water: The basic concerns of mankind*, Condor, 1974. 'Human nature: justice versus power', p. 135. On one occasion in an interview Foucault makes reference to death-obliteration.
100. See Habermas, J., *The Philosophical Discourse of Modernity*, Oxford, 1987; Couzens Hoy (ed.), op. cit., *Foucault: A critical reader*, see Habermas, J., 'Taking aim at the heart of the present', pp. 103–8; Diamond, I., and Quinby, L. (eds), *Feminism and Foucault*, Northeastern University Press,

Boston, 1988, see Bartky, S.L., 'Foucault, femininity and patriarchal power', pp. 61–83.

101. Kritzman, D., (ed.), *Politics, Philosophy, Culture, Interviews And Other Writing, 1977–1984*, Routledge, New York, 1988, see Foucault, M., 'Practising criticism', p. 156.

102. Couzens Hoy, op. cit., *Foucault*, see Walzer, M., 'The politics of Michel Foucault', and Taylor, M., 'Foucault on freedom and truth'; Armstrong, op. cit., *Michel Foucault*, see Rorty, R., 'Moral identity and private autonomy', pp. 328–33.

103. Dreyfus and Rabinow, op. cit., *Michel Foucault*, see Foucault, M., 'Afterword', p. 220.

104. ibid.

105. Rabinow, op. cit., *Foucault Reader*, see Foucault, 'Space, knowledge, power', p. 249.

106. ibid., see Foucault, M., 'On the genealogy of ethics: an overview of work in progress', p. 343.

107. There is a resonance here to Collingwood's analysis of 'know thyself', yet Foucault adds a profoundly material base to the possibility of this knowledge.

108. Kritzman, op. cit., *Politics, Philosophy, Culture*, see Foucault, M., 'The return of morality', p. 243.

109. In the *Reveries of The Solitary Walker* Rousseau comments on an accident that crushed two of his fingers and notes, 'This accident was even more painful for me due to the circumstances, for it was the period of the drills when the bourgeoisie was made to perform maneuvers, and we had formed a squad of three other children of my age, with whom I was supposed perform the drill in uniform with the company from my neighborhood. I had the sorrow of hearing the company drummer with my three comrades passing under my window while I was in bed.' Rousseau, J.J., *The Reveries of the Solitary Walker*, trans. Charles E. Butterworth, 1982, Harper, New York, see 'Fourth walk', p. 56.

110. Kritzman, op. cit., *Politics*, see Foucault, M., 'The minimalist self', p. 14.

111. Martin, Gutman and Hutton, op. cit., *Technologies*, see Foucault, M., 'Technologies of the Self', p. 18.

3 A diagram of the Middle Ages

1. This inquiry could not have been undertaken without the previous efforts of Georges Duby. It was conceived when already under the influence of Foucault I read the *Chivalrous Society*. See note 25, Chapter 3.

2. Eckhardt, K.A. (ed.), *Pactus Legis Salicae, 59.6*, Hanover, 1962, p. 223 (MGH Leges Nat. German IV.1); on the meaning of the term 'Salic land' see E. James, *The Origins of France*, St Martin's Press, New York, 1982, pp. 85–6.

3. Schwerin, C.F., (ed.), *Leges Saxonum und Lex Thuringorum*, Hanover and Leipzig, 1918, pp. 28–9, cc 41, 46 cited in J. O'Faolin and L. Martines (eds), *Not in God's Image*, Virago, London, 1979, p. 111.

4. Drew, K.F., *The Burgundian Code*, Philadelphia, 1972, XIV.1, p. 32.

5. Gies, F. and J., *Women in the Middle Ages*, Crowell, New York, 1978, p. 18.

6. Wemple, S.F., *Women in Frankish Society*, University of Pennsylvania Press, Philadelphia, 1981, see Part 1.
7. Herlihy, D., 'Land, family and women in continental Europe 701–1200', in *Traditio*, 18, 1962, pp. 89–120.
8. ibid., pp. 107–8.
9. Jones, Gwyn and Thomas, trans. *The Mabinogion*, Everyman's Library, London, 1975, p. 95.
10. Markale, J., *Women of the Celts*, Gordon Cremonesi, 1975, p. 38.
11. Rees, Alwyn and Brinley, *Celtic Heritage*, Thames & Hudson, London, 1961, p. 30.
12. Geoffrey of Monmouth, *History of the Kings of Britain*, trans. Lewis Thorpe, Penguin, Harmondsworth, 1979, p. 221.
13. Malory, Thomas, *Malory Works*, ed. E. Vinaver, Oxford University Press, 1977, p. 714, 'And whan sir Mordred felte that he had hys dethys wounde he threste hymselff with the myght that he had upp to the burre of kyng Arthurs speare, and ryght so he smote hys fadir, kynge Arthure, with hys swerde holdynge in both hys hondys, upon the syde of the hede, that the swerde perced the helmet and the tay of the brayne. And therewith Mordred daysshed downe starke dede to the erthe.'
14. Beroul, *Romance of Tristan*, trans. Alan S. Fedrick, Penguin, Harmondsworth, 1978, p. 39.
15. Gottfried Von Strassburg, *Tristan*, Penguin, Harmondsworth, 1978, p. 87.
16. ibid., p. 102.
17. Wemple, op. cit., *Women in Frankish Society*, p. 87.
18. ibid., p. 195.
19. It is increasingly accepted that there was a situation of yearly expeditions of pillage, etc., that in effect amounted to a redistribution of wealth. See Duby, G., *The Three Orders: Feudal society imagined*, trans. Arthur Goldhammer, The University of Chicago Press, Chicago, 1980, p. 150.
20. Bloch, M., *Feudal Society, Vol. 1*, trans. L.A. Manyon, Routledge & Kegan Paul, London, 1978, p. 29. For the impact of the invasions as a whole, see Part 1.
21. Duby, G., *The Early Growth of the European Economy*, trans. Howard B. Clarke, Weidenfeld & Nicholson, London, 1974, p. 8.
22. Gimpel, J., *The Medieval Machine*, Futura Publications, 1979; White, L. (jun.), *Medieval Technology and Social Change*, Oxford University Press, London, 1980 (see review of this in *Past and Present*, 24, 1963, pp. 90–100); Postan, M.M., *The Medieval Economy and Society*, Penguin, Harmondsworth, 1978; Bloch, M., *French Rural History*, Routledge & Kegan Paul, London, 1966; Witt, R.G., 'The landlord and the economic revival of the Middle Ages in northern Europe, 1000–1250', *American Historical Review*, 76, 1971, pp. 965–88.
23. Lewis, A.R., *The Development of Southern French and Catalan Society 718–1050*, University of Texas Press, Austin, 1965, p. 352.
24. Herlihy, D., 'Agrarian revolution in France and Italy, 801–1150', *Speculum*, 33, 1958, p. 352.
25. Duby, G., *The Chivalrous Society*, trans. Cynthia Postan, Edward Arnold, London, 1977, ch. 2.

26. Lewis, A.R., op. cit., *The Development of Southern French and Catalan Society*, see ch. 6.

27. Wood, C.T., *The French apanages and the Capetian Monarchy 1224–1328*, Harvard University Press, Cambridge, 1966, p. 3.

28. Lewis, A.W., *Royal Succession in France: Studies on the familial order and the state*, Harvard University Press, Cambridge, 1981, p. 4.

29. ibid., p. 156.

30. ibid.

31. Bloch, op. cit., *Feudal Society*, p. 189.

32. Duby, op. cit., *Chivalrous Society*, p. 74.

33. Chrétien de Troyes, *Arthurian Romances*, trans. W.W. Comfort, Everyman's Library, London, 1977.

34. Duby, G., op. cit., *Three Orders*, p. 22 'His first strategem was to weaken the Count of Flanders, who was stirring up trouble, by offering hospitality to his rebellious son (in those days, most heirs apparent did rebel against their fathers as soon as they outgrew adolescence, out of impatience to exercise unfettered control over the seigniory, in which they were egged on by companions of their own age, equally frustrated and greedy).'

35. Duby, op. cit., *Chivalrous Society*, pp. 116–17.

36. Duby, G., 'Au XIIe siècle: les "jeunes" dans le société aristocratique dans la France du nord-ouest', *Annales Economie, societe, civilisation V*, (September–October 1964). Translated and reprinted as 'Youth in aristocratic society in Northwestern France in the twelfth century', ch. 7 of *The Chivalrous Society*. Also found in F. Cheyette, *Lordship and Community in Medieval Europe*, Holt Rhinehart & Winston, 1968, pp. 198–209.

37. Duby, G., *Medieval Marriage: Two models from twelfth century France*, trans. Elborg Forster, Johns Hopkins University Press, Baltimore, 1978, pp. 96–102.

38. Chrétien de Troyes, op. cit., *Arthurian Romances*, pp. 206–207.

39. Duby, op. cit., *Medieval Marriage*, p. 79.

40. Lewis, op. cit., *Royal Succession*, p. 147.

41. Duby, op. cit., *Medieval Marriage*, p. 100.

42. Lewis, op. cit., *Royal Succession*, p. 65.

43. This is often the only point of contact with the juridical system other than when purchasing property.

44. See Duby, G., *The Knight, the Lady and the Priest*, trans. Barbara Bray, Penguin, Harmondsworth, 1985. In this indispensable work Duby analyses these tactics, strategies, tensions and alliances in great detail.

45. Cantor, N.F., *Medieval History*, Macmillan, London, 1969, p. 386.

46. Duby, op. cit., *The Knight, the Lady and the Priest*, pp. 47–8.

47. Foucault, op. cit., *History of Sexuality, vol. 1.*, p. 147. 'The blood relation long remained an important element in the mechanisms of power, its manifestations, and its rituals. For a society in which the systems of alliance, the political form of the sovereign, the differentiation into orders and castes, and the value of descent lines were predominant; for a society in which famine, epidemics, and violence made death imminent, blood constituted one of the fundamental values. It owed its high value at the same time to its instrumental role (the

ability to shed blood), to the way it functioned in the order of signs (to have a certain blood, to be of the same blood, to be prepared to risk one's blood), and also to its precariousness (easily spilled, subject to drying up, too readily mixed, capable of being quickly corrupted). A society of blood – I was tempted to say, of "sanguinity" – where power spoke *through* blood: the honor of war, the fear of famine, the triumph of death, the sovereign with his sword, executioners, and tortures; blood was *a reality with a symbolic function*. We, on the other hand, are in a society of "sex", or rather a society "with a sexuality"; the mechanisms of power are addressed to the body, to life, to what causes it to proliferate, to what reinforces the species, its stamina, its ability to dominate, or its capacity for being used.'

48. Foucault has argued in a number of places that the importance of the Fourth Lateran Council was precisely that it inaugurated the practice of yearly private confessions for all Christians. This is the first time according to Foucault that subjects are required to produce a 'true' discourse about their sexuality. Gordon, op. cit., *Power/Knowledge*, see Foucault, M., 'The confession of the flesh', pp. 215–16 and Foucault, op. cit., *History of Sexuality, vol. 1*, p. 58.

49. See Brown, P., *The Body and Society*, Faber & Faber, London, 1990.

50. For Foucault's account of this: in Rabinow, op. cit., *The Foucault Reader*, see Foucault, M., 'On the genealogy of ethics: an overview of work in progress'. This is an aspect of pastoral power as described by Foucault. See Foucault, M., op. cit., *The History of Sexuality, vol. 1*, p. 37; Dreyfus and Rabinow, op. cit., *Michel Foucault*, see Foucault, M., 'Afterword', p. 214; Rabinow, op. cit., *Foucault Reader*, see Foucault, M., 'On the Genealogy of Ethics', p. 370; Kritzman, op. cit., *Politics, Philosophy, Culture*, see Foucault, M., 'Politics and reason', pp;. 60–72.

51. Abelard, *The Letters of Abelard and Heloise*, trans. B. Radice, Penguin, Harmondsworth, 1979, p. 9.

52. Benson, R.L., and Constable, G. (eds), *Renaissance and Renewal in the 12th Century*, Harvard University Press, Cambridge, Mass., 1982.

53. Ward, J.O., 'Social dislocation, intellectual dissent and the origin of the universities in medieval Europe', presented to the August meeting of the Australian Historical Association Conference, Melbourne, 1984, p. 14, unpublished at the time of writing this chapter.

54. Benton, J.F. (ed.) *Self and Society in Medieval France: The memoirs of Abbot Guibert of Nogent, (1064?–1125)*, Harper, London, 1970.

55. Hanning, R.W., *The Individual in Twelfth Century Romance*, Yale University Press, New Haven, Conn., 1977.

56. At its worst this leads to a rather naïve kind of historical psychologism, for example see Cantor's otherwise excellent study. Cantor, op. cit., *Medieval History*, p. 361, 'Abelard was the son of a minor lord in Brittany, a wild frontier region which was accustomed to produce savage warriors but not scholars and philosophers. The tremendous social impact of the new learning may be gauged by the attractions it presented to the obscure nobleman. He made his way to the new schools of philosophy and theology at Chartres and Paris. He was recognized from the beginning as an exceptionally brilliant student, and he mastered the new dialectical methods rapidly, but he was also a difficult person,

entirely inner-directed, arrogant, disagreeable, hypercritical, and gauche.' Page 362, 'Beyond all doubt Abelard was a genius of the first rank. Everybody who met him was impressed by the force of his personality and the power of his intellect. His stormy career may reflect a psychological instability resulting from a failure to find a suitable environment in which he could fully exercise his unusual talent.'

57. cf. p. 58.
58. Ward, op. cit., 'Social Dislocation', p. 2.
59. ibid., p. 14.
60. ibid., p. 16.
61. Daiches, D., and Thorlby, A. (eds), *The Medieval World, Literature and Western Civilisation, Volume 2*, Aldus, London, 1973, see M. Parkes, 'The literacy of the laity', ch. 16.
62. Clanchy, M.T., *From Memory to Written Record, England 1066–1307*, Edward Arnold, London, 1979. See also, Clanchy, M.T., 'Remembering the past and the good old law', *History*, 55, 1970.
63. This has some important connections with Mark Poster's concerns about the possibility of analysing changes in the mode of production and communication of information. Armstrong, op. cit., *Michel Foucault*; see Poster, M., 'Foucault, the present and history', pp. 303–15; and in Poster, M. (ed.) *Humanities in Society, Foucault and Critical Theory: The uses of discourse analysis, Vol 5, Nos 3 and 4*, University of Southern California, Los Angeles, 1982, see Poster, M., 'Mode of production, mode of information: toward a critique of political economy'.
64. For an anthropological account of this see Goody, J., *Literacy in Traditional Societies*, Cambridge University Press, Cambridge, 1968, pp. 27–68; Goody, J. and Watt, I., 'The consequences of literacy', in *Comparative Studies in Society and History*, 5(3), April 1963, pp. 304–45.
65. Stock, B., *The Implications of Literacy*, Princeton University Press, Princeton, N.J., 1983, p. 63.
66. Duby, op. cit., *The Knight, the Lady and the Priest*, p. 205.
67. ibid., pp. 61–71.
68. Clanchy, op. cit., *From Memory*, p. 209.
69. ibid., p. 211.
70. ibid., pp. 237, 240.
71. Goody, J., Thirsk, J., Thompson, E.P. (eds), *Family and Inheritance: Rural society in Western Europe 1200–1800*, Cambridge University Press, Cambridge, 1976, see Goody, J., 'Inheritance, property and women: some comparative considerations', p. 15.
72. Stock, op. cit., *Implications of Literacy*, p. 327.
73. ibid., p. 333.
74. ibid., p. 528.
75. Saussure, F. de, *Course in General Linguistics*, Fontana Collins, Glasgow, 1978, pp. 7–15.
76. Stock, op. cit., *Implications of Literacy*, p. 528.
77. Duby, op. cit., *Three Orders*, chs 19 and 20, pp. 232–68.
78. Clanchy, op. cit., *From Memory*, p. 178.
79. Duby, op. cit., *Three Orders*, p. 308. There were other significant centres such as

Laon, Bec and so on but the process as a whole was one of centralisation with the object being regulation from Paris.

80. Abelard, op. cit., *Letters*, p. 10.
81. Le Goff, J., *Medieval Civilisation*, Blackwell, Oxford, 1990, p. 347.
82. Abelard, op. cit., p. 64.
83. ibid., p. 78.
84. ibid., p. 64.
85. Ward, op. cit., 'Social dislocation', pp. 12–13.
86. Duby, op. cit., *Three Orders*, p. 243.
87. Abelard, op. cit., *Letters*, p. 82.
88. Polka, B., and Zelechow, B., *Readings in Western Civilisation, Volume 1, The Intellectual Adventure of Man to 1600*, York University, Toronto, 1970, p. 121.
89. Collingwood, op. cit., *Idea of History*, p. 46.
90. Copleston, F.C., *A History of Medieval Philosophy*, Methuen, London, 1972, p. 72.
91. Wippel, J.F., and Wolter, A.B. (eds), *Medieval Philosophy: From St Augustine to Nicholas of Cusa*, Free Press, New York, 1969. See Chapter 1 St Augustine 'How great is the soul', and 'On the existence of God'.
92. It has often been pointed out that Augustine's arguments against scepticism bear a striking resemblance to those used later by Descartes.
93. Wippel and Wolter, op. cit., *Medieval Philosophy*, see 'A critique of scepticism', p. 40.
94. Carre, M.H., *Realists and Nominalists*, Oxford University Press, 1946, p. 11.
95. Wippel and Wolter, op. cit., *Medieval Philosophy*, 'A critique of scepticism', p. 42.
96. Carre, op. cit., *Realists and Nominalists*, p. 37.
97. Stock, op. cit., *Implications of Literacy*, p. 275.
98. ibid., p. 276.
99. ibid.
100. ibid., pp. 278–9.
101. ibid., pp. 313–25. A number of important figures including Allan of Lille, William of Conches and Hugh of St Victor will not be discussed; however, for the purposes of this study the relation of their work to the general project can be gained from Stock.
102. Burch, G.B., *Early Medieval Philosophy*, King's Crown Press, Columbia University, New York, 1951, p. 39.
103. Weinberg, J.R., *A Short History of Medieval Philosophy*, Princeton, NJ., 1964, p. 65.
104. Knowles, D., *The Evolution of Medieval Thought*, Longman, London, 1962, p. 105.
105. Wippel and Wolter, op. cit., *Medieval Philosophy*, 'St Anselm on the existence of God: a reply to Anselm on behalf of the Fool', and 'Anselm's reply to Gaunilon', pp. 154–76.
106. ibid., p. 155.
107. ibid., p. 156.
108. ibid., p. 159.

109. ibid., p. 160.
110. ibid.
111. ibid., p. 161.
112. ibid., p. 163.
113. Weinberg, op. cit., *Short History of Medieval Philosophy*. For a detailed account of Anselm's proof of the existence of God see pp. 59–67.
114. Stock, op. cit., *Implications of Literacy*, p. 334.
115. ibid., p. 335.
116. ibid., p. 343.

4   Drawing the subject

1. Knowles, op. cit., *Evolution of Medieval Thought*, p. 111.
2. ibid., p. 110.
3. ibid., p. 108.
4. For another account of the theory of universals debate see, Burch, op. cit., *Early Medieval Philosophy*, p. 48.
5. Cantor, op. cit., *Medieval History*, p. 366.
6. Buytaert, E.M. (ed.), *Peter Abelard*, Leuven University Press, 1974, see G. Verbeke, 'Introductory conference: Peter Abelard and the concept of subjectivity', p. 7.
7. Knowles, op. cit., *Evolution of Medieval Thought*, p. 112.
8. Hyman, A., and Walsh, J.J., *Philosophy in the Middle Ages: The Christian, Islamic and Jewish traditions*, Hackett, Indianapolis, 1973, see 'Peter Abailard: the glosses of Peter Abailard on Porphyry', p. 170. For an alternative translation of part of this see, Wippel and Wolter, op. cit., *Medieval Philosophy*, 'On universals', pp. 190–203.
9. ibid., p. 171.
10. ibid., p. 172.
11. Weinberg, op. cit., *Short History of Medieval Philosophy*, p. 82.
12. Hyman and Walsh, op. cit., *Philosophy in the Middle Ages*, p. 173.
13. Weinberg, op. cit., *Short History*, p. 80. See also in Buytaert, op. cit., *Peter Abelard*, G. Verbeke, 'Introductory conference', p. 7.
14. Hyman and Walsh, op. cit., *Philosophy*, p. 177.
15. ibid., p. 178.
16. ibid.
17. ibid., p. 179.
18. ibid.
19. ibid., p. 180.
20. ibid., p. 181.
21. ibid., p. 186.
22. ibid.
23. ibid., p. 187.
24. ibid. Weinberg, op. cit., *Short History of Medieval Philosophy*, p. 84, summarises Abelard's final position as follows, p. 87: 'Abelard answers Porphyry's

questions in terms of the foregoing doctrine. Universals *signify* things that really exist by denoting (Abelard says "nominating") singulars among which there is resemblance. Universal terms are corporeal with respect to things denoted, but incorporeal in respect to their manner of signifying, since they are words associated with concepts which signify indeterminately. Again, universals denote something existing in sensible individuals, but are understood outside the sensible things because the thing denoted in the individual can exist apart from its accidents. Finally, because the universal word signifies not only the sensible individual subject to it (i.e., those it denotes) but also the common conception, Abelard can answer his fourth question. If there are no longer any individuals of a sort normally denoted by the common universal word, there is still the common conception which continues to provide the universal word with significance. By this means, we can significantly and truly say, "There are no roses," when in fact there are no longer roses.'

25. Hyman and Walsh, op. cit., *Philosophy*, p. 188.
26. Knowles, op. cit., *Evolution of Medieval Thought*, p. 112.
27. ibid., p. 123.
28. Weinberg, op. cit., *Short History*, pp. 74–5.
29. Copleston, op. cit., *History of Medieval Philosophy*, p. 82.
30. Stock, op. cit., *Implications of Literacy*, p. 375.
31. ibid.
32. Saussure, op. cit., *Course in General Linguistics*, ch. III, 'The object of linguistics'.
33. Stock, op. cit., *Implications of Literacy*, p. 384.
34. ibid.
35. Cantor, op. cit., *Medieval History*, p. 369.
36. Polka and Zelechow, op. cit., *Readings in Western Civilisation*, p. 102.
37. ibid., p. 104.
38. ibid., p. 108.
39. ibid., p. 114.
40. Abelard, P., *A Dialogue of a Philosopher with a Jew, and a Christian*, trans. Pierre J. Payer, Pontifical Institute of Medieval Studies, Toronto, 1979, p. 86.
41. Weinberg, op. cit., *Short History of Medieval Philosophy*, p. 74; and Abelard, op. cit., *The Letters of Abelard and Heloise*, see Radice, B., 'Introduction,' p. 37: 'His famous *Sic et Non* (Yes and No) had been written with this purpose in mind, though more than anything it had given a false and damaging picture of him as a sceptic.' For his *Confession of Faith* see, Abelard, op. cit., *Letters*, pp. 270–1.
42. Luscombe, D.E., *Peter Abelard*, The Historical Association, London, 1979, p. 30.
43. Polka and Zelechow, op. cit., *Readings in Western Civilisation*, p. 117.
44. Abelard, op. cit., *A Dialogue of a Philosopher*, p. 25.
45. ibid.
46. Abelard, op. cit., *Letters*, p. 259.
47. ibid.
48. ibid., p. 260.
49. ibid., p. 264. 'In the cloister those are said to know letters who have learned to

pronounce them; but as far as understanding them is concerned, those who admit they cannot read have books given to them which is just as much sealed as for those whom they call illiterate.'
50. ibid., p. 78.
51. Abelard, P., *Peter Abelard's Ethics*, trans. D.E. Luscombe, Clarendon Press, Oxford, 1971. 'Scito te ipsum', or 'Know thyself' is translated under this title.
52. ibid., p. xxx.
53. Buytaert, op. cit., *Peter Abelard*, see Luscombe, D.E., 'The ethics of Abelard: some further considerations', p. 81.
54. Abelard, op. cit., *Peter Abelard's Ethics*, p. 21.
55. ibid., p. 23.
56. ibid., p. 27.
57. Abelard, op. cit., *A Dialogue of a Philosopher*, p. 165.
58. Lovejoy, op. cit., *Great Chain of Being*, p. 70.
59. Abelard, op. cit., *Peter Abelard's Ethics*, p. 45.
60. ibid., pp. 59–64.
61. ibid., p. 115.
62. Buytaert, op. cit., *Peter Abelard*, see Luscombe, 'The ethics of Abelard', p. 82.
63. Some care has to be taken here about how this is described, as 'private confession' had been a long-term monastic practice; however, there is little doubt that the entry of this into the public domain did have a considerable impact. It should also be noted that 'private' confession did not overturn the 'public' practice; they in fact existed side by side for a considerable time, perhaps because of the revenue-collecting function of public penances. However, the widespread use of 'private' confession certainly raised the question of individual psychology to a previously unknown importance. Abelard, op. cit., *Peter Abelard's Ethics*, see Luscombe, D.E., 'Introduction', p. xxii, 'The development in the twelfth century of the practice of private confession – a development to which Abelard himself in his Ethics gave considerable support – brought into sharper relief the importance of taking into acount the psychology of the individual sinner or penitent.'
64. Gordon, op. cit., *Power/Knowledge*, see Foucault, M., 'Confession of the flesh', p. 215.
65. Foucault, op. cit., *History of Sexuality, vol.1*, p. 59.
66. Buytaert, op. cit., *Peter Abelard*, see Verbeke, 'Introductory conference', p. 1.
67. Luscombe, op. cit., *Peter Abelard*, p. 37.
68. Carre, op. cit., *Realists and Nominalists*, p. 10.
69. Abelard, op. cit., *Letters*, see 'Letter 7 Albelard to Heloise', p. 269.
70. Stone, D., 'On the authenticity of the Abelard–Heloise letters', thesis submitted in partial fulfilment of requirements for MA qualifying, University of Sydney, 1979, p. 9.
71. ibid., p. 9.
72. ibid., pp. 20–7.
73. ibid., p. 34.
74. ibid., p. 93.
75. Luscombe, op. cit., *Peter Abelard*, p. 28. See also p. 25: 'For long the genuineness of these materials has been challenged. For this reason most of the

information provided above has been taken from other sources than the *Historia Calamitatum* and the letters of Abelard and Heloise. Had the strong, personal views found in these documents been conveyed as well, this pamphlet would doubtless be more colourful, but the letters are best read as a whole, and the purpose of the self-denying ordinance observed here is to underline the point that the events discussed in *Historia Calamitatum* and in the letters are reasonably well confirmed by other contemporary sources.... But it does mean that even if the *Historia* or the letters were concocted or forged by a third person, or were wholly invented by Abelard or by Heloise alone, that person relied on a basis of probable fact that can be extensively corroborated from other sources.'

76. Delhez-Sarlet, C., and Catani, M., *Individualisme et Autobiographie en Occident*, Editions de l'universite de Bruxelles, 1979, see de Gandillac, M., 'Abelard (et Héloise)'.
77. Abelard, op. cit., *Letters*, p. 26.
78. Cantor, op. cit., *Medieval History*, p. 363.
79. Abelard, P., trans. Muckle, J.T., *The Story of Abelard's Adversities*, The Pontifical Institute of Medieval Studies, Toronto, 1964, see Gilson, Étienne, 'Preface', p. 7.
80. Brown, P., *Augustine of Hippo*, Faber & Faber, London, 1975, p. 175.
81. Buytaert, op. cit., *Peter Abelard*, see Verbeke, 'Introductory conference', p. 8.
82. Augustine, *Confessions*, trans. and introd. by R.S. Pine-Coffin, Penguin, Harmondsworth, 1979, p. 7.
83. ibid., p. 202.
84. ibid., p. 166.
85. Benton, op. cit., *Self and Society in Medieval France*, p. 35.
86. ibid., p. 11. Benton also offers the following explanation for the details of Guibert's text, p. 26: 'Guibert's fear of mutilation requires special attention because it raises the question of whether his relationship to his mother and his fears together fit the Freudian model of a castration complex. While the evidence available is insufficient to warrant any unqualified application of psychoanalytic theory to the culture of medieval Europe, the concurrence of circumstances in this particular case is striking.'
87. Cantor, op. cit., *Medieval History*, p. 364.
88. Gregory of Tours, *The History of the Franks*, Penguin, Harmondsworth, 1979.
89. ibid., p. 63.
90. ibid., p. 601.
91. Joinville and Villehardouin, *Chronicles of the Crusades*, Penguin, Harmondsworth, 1980. This edition includes the two works, *The Conquest of Constantinople* (Villehardouin) and *The Life of St Louis* (Joinville).
92. ibid., p. 181.
93. ibid., p. 353.
94. Martin, Gutman, Hutton, op. cit., *Technologies of the Self*, see Foucault, M., 'Technologies of Self', pp. 27–30.
95. ibid., pp. 19–22.
96. This is examined in more detail in the discussion of the work of Chrétien de Troyes which begins on p. 148.

97. Abelard, op. cit., *Letters*, p. 57.

98. ibid., 'Letter 4 Abelard to Heloise', see pp. 146, 147.

99. ibid., p. 61.

100. ibid., 'Letter 7 Abelard to Heloise', pp. 196–7.

101. ibid., p. 67.

102. ibid., 'Letter 4 Abelard to Heloise', p. 147.

103. ibid., 'Letter 3 Heloise to Abelard', p. 131.

104. ibid., 'Letter 1 Heloise to Abelard', p. 115.

105. For an example of how this kind of work could be approached see, in Pateman, C., and Grosz, E., (eds) *Feminist Challenges: Essays in Social and Political Theory*, Allen & Unwin, Sydney, 1986, Gatens, M. , 'Feminism, philosophy and riddles without answers'.

106. Abelard, op. cit., *Letters*, p. 66.

107. For an alternative account of this see Le Doeuff, M., 'Women and Philosophy', in *Radical Philosophy*, 17, 1977.

108. See Boswell, J., *Christianity, Social Tolerance and Homosexuality*, The University of Chicago Press, 1980, and Foucault, op. cit., *Use of Pleasure*.

109. Abelard, op. cit., *Letters*, 'Letter 3 Heloise to Abelard', p. 133.

110. ibid., p. 69.

111. ibid.

112. ibid., pp. 71–2.

113. The manner of Heloise's entry to the convent of Argenteuil was a continued source of complaint by Heloise to Abelard which they both refer to frequently in the *Letters*.

114. ibid., p. 75.

115. Baker, D. (ed.), *Medieval Women*, Blackwell, Oxford, 1978, see Giles Constable, 'Aelred and the nun of Watton', p. 208.

116. Clanchy, op. cit., *From Memory to Written Record*, p. 212.

117. Abelard, op. cit., *Letters*, 'Letter 3 Heloise to Abelard', p. 130.

118. Abelard, op. cit., *A Dialogue of a Philosopher*, p. 101.

119. ibid., p. 104.

120. Abelard, op. cit., *Letters*, p. 104.

121. ibid., p. 102.

122. ibid., 'Letter 2 Abelard to Heloise', p. 125.

123. ibid., 'Introduction', p. 21.

124. Knowles, op. cit., *Evolution of Medieval Thought*, p. 91.

125. Stock, op. cit., *Implications of Literacy*, p. 455.

126. ibid., p. 531.

127. Chrétien de Troyes, op. cit., *Arthurian Romances*, see 'Erec and Enide', p. 1.

128. ibid., p. 1.

129. ibid., p. 3.

130. ibid., p. 4.

131. ibid., p. 9.

132. ibid., p. 14.

133. ibid., p. 18.

134. ibid., p. 32.

135. ibid., pp. 33–4.

136. ibid., p. 36.
137. ibid., p. 39.
138. ibid., p. 60.
139. ibid., p. 63.
140. ibid., p. 64.
141. ibid., p. 68.
142. ibid., p. 76.
143. ibid., p. 6.
144. Gottfried Von Strassburg, op. cit., *Tristan*, pp. 276–7.
145. Foucault, op. cit., *History of Sexuality, vol. 1*, p. 58.
146. Chrétien de Troyes, op. cit., *Arthurian Romances*, see 'Yvain', p. 269.
147. ibid., pp. 180–269.
148. ibid., pp. 202–3.
149. See R.W. Hanning, 'The Individual in Twelfth Century Romance', and 'The Social Significance of Twelfth-Century Chivalric Romance', in *Medievalia et Humanistica*, 3, 1972.
150. Hanning, op. cit., 'The Social Significance of Twelfth-Century Chivalric Romance', p. 9.
151. Chrétien de Troyes, op. cit., *Arthurian Romances*, see 'Yvain', pp. 216–17.
152. In this context two other texts not mentioned above would be of some interest, Gerald of Wales, *The Journey Through Wales/The Description of Wales*, Penguin, Harmondsworth, 1980; Gerald of Wales, trans. H.E. Butler, *The Autobiography of Giraldus Cambrensis*, Cape, London, 1937. It is interesting to note that Chrétien's works in general involve a great deal of dialogue as well as reflective formulations; more will be said about this and its relation to concepts of self in the next chapter.
153. See Boase, R. *The Origin and Meaning of Courtly Love*, Manchester University Press, 1977, and Wood, C.T., *The Age of Chivalry: Manners and Morals 1000–1450*, Weidenfeld & Nicolson, 1970.
154. Moller, H., 'The meaning of courtly love', in *Journal of American Folklore*, 73, 1960, pp. 39–52; Knight, S.K. 'Proesce and Cortoisie: Ideology in Chrétien de Troyes "Le Chevalier au Lion"', in *Studium*, 14, 1982, pp. 1–51.
155. Duby, G., op. cit., *Chivalrous Society*, ch. 7.
156. Lucas, A.M., *Women in the Middle Ages*, Harvester, Brighton, 1983, see chs 1 and 2.
157. It is interesting that Foucault accepts and supports Duby's view, see Gordon, op. cit., *Power/Knowledge*, Foucault, M., 'The confessions of the flesh', p. 202.

5 Subversions of the subject

1. Derrida's well known criticism of logocentrism would allow another series of readings here but the conflation of Derrida and Foucault is not without its own difficulties. Refer p. 70, p. 200 note 23, and p. 217 note 48.
2. Blumenberg, op. cit., *Legitimacy of the Modern Age*, p. 145.
3. ibid., p. 184.
4. ibid.

5. Kenny, A., (ed.) *Descartes' Philosophical Letters*, University of Minnesota Press, Minneapolis, 1981, p. 83.
6. ibid., p. 99.
7. Blumenberg, op. cit., *Legitimacy of the Modern Age*, p. 185.
8. ibid., p. 378. All the following quotations in this argument in the main body of the text are taken from this page.
9. Foucault takes up this issue of the level of the metaphors that distinguish the 'Dark Ages' from the Enlightenment in a number of his works but in particular in *Madness and Civilisation*.
10. Blumenberg, op. cit., *Legitimacy of the Modern Age*, p. 378.
11. As I have pointed out earlier Foucault also seems at times to fall into this position.
12. Descartes, op. cit., *Philosophical Works of Descartes, vol. 1*, 'Rules for the direction of the mind', p. 7, 'All that I take note of is the meaning of the Latin of each word, when, in cases where an appropriate term is lacking, I wish to transfer to the vocabulary that expresses my own meaning those that I deem most suitable.'
13. ibid., 'Meditations on first philosophy', p. 141.
14. ibid., 'Meditations on first philosophy, Meditation II', p. 152.
15. ibid., 'Meditations on first philosophy, Meditation VI', p. 190.
16. ibid., 'Discourse on method', p. 101.
17. ibid., 'Discourse on method', p. 107.
18. ibid., 'Discourse on method', p. 115.
19. ibid., 'Meditations on first philosophy, Meditation VI', p. 197.
20. ibid.
21. ibid., 'The passions of the soul, Article XXXI', pp. 345–6.
22. I would suggest that any reading of Descartes that claims his theology is conceptually subservient to his modern epistemology to prevent him from persecution by the Church is fundamentally misguided.
23. Descartes, op. cit., *Philosophical Works of Descartes, vol. 1*, 'Discourse on Method', p. 102.
24. ibid., 'Meditations on first philosophy: synopsis', p. 142.
25. ibid., 'Meditations on first philosophy, Meditation III', p. 163.
26. ibid., 'Meditations on first philosophy, Meditation IV', p. 172.
27. ibid., 'Meditations on first philosophy, Meditation V', p. 180–2.
28. ibid., 'Meditations on first philosophy, Meditation VI', p. 199.
29. ibid., 'Meditations on first philosophy, Meditation III', p. 167.
30. See Nelson, B., *On the Roads to Modernity*, Rowman & Littlefield, New Jersey, 1981, ch. 12, for an example of an otherwise excellent account of the place of Abelard which regrettably fails to come to terms with this issue.
31. Descartes, op. cit., *Philosophical Works, vol. 1*, 'Discourse on Method', p. 83.
32. ibid., p. 87.
33. Descartes stabilises this by resorting to a theological and theogonical defence internal to the system.
34. Foucault's most systematic account of his relation to the theory of psychoanalysis is to be found in *The History of Sexuality, Vol. 1: An introduction*.
35. Freud, S., *The Standard Edition of the Complete Psychological Works of Sigmund*

Freud Vol. XX, trans. James Strachey, London, Hogarth, see 'An autobiographical study', p. 36.
36. See Freud, S., *The Pelican Freud Library, Vol. 8, Case Studies 1*, Penguin, Harmondsworth, 1977, 'An analysis of a phobia in a five-year-old boy ("Little Hans")'. For an interesting account of this see Foss, P., and Morris M. (eds), *Language, Sexuality and Subversion*, Feral, 1978, Campioni, M., and Gross, E., 'Little Hans: the production of Oedipus'.
37. Freud, op. cit., see 'An autobiographical study', p. 28.
38. Foucault, op. cit., *History of Sexuality, Vol. 1: An introduction*, pp. 59–63.
39. Freud, op. cit., see 'An autobiographical study', p. 41.
40. ibid., p. 45.
41. See, Lacan, J., op. cit., *Écrits*, ch. 5, 'Agency of the letter in the unconscious' and Derrida, op. cit., *Writing and Difference*, ch. 7, 'Freud and scene of writing'.
42. This is precisely where the work of Lacan reinterprets Freud.
43. Freud, op. cit., 'An autobiographical study', p. 7.
44. ibid., p. 8. It is well known that Freud burnt a lot of his early papers. This might be analagous to Descartes' hiding his theoretical past.
45. ibid., p. 19.
46. ibid., p. 31.
47. Freud, S., *The Pelican Freud Library, vol I, Introductory Lectures on Psychoanalysis*, Penguin, Harmondsworth, 1978, p. 296.
48. There is now another somewhat Derridean point to be made here. What distinguishes the noun *manière* from the adjective *maniéré* are just the two accents (˝) which denote a different meaning, as the adjective *maniéré* means among other things genteel, and in relation to literature and the arts mannered, or cultured. So what Freud had initially taken for an insult to his whole project of psychoanalysis in 1913, had by 1928 become the basis of a congratulation from Janet on the worth of psychoanalysis, as it passed into the textual auto-biographical subjectivity of Freud.
49. Freud, op. cit., 'Autobiographical study', pp. 31–3.
50. ibid., p. 59.
51. See Benveniste, E., *Problems in General Linguistics*, University of Miami Press, Florida, 1971, 'Subjectivity in language', p. 223.
52. Descartes, op. cit., 'Discourse on method', p. 116.
53. Freud, op. cit., 'Autobiographical study', p. 52.
54. ibid., p. 71.
55. Freud, op. cit., *Pelican Freud Library, vol. 8, Case Studies 1*, 'Dora and Little Hans'.
56. Misch, G., *A History of Autobiography in Antiquity, vol. 1*, Greenwood, Westport, Conn., 1973.
57. ibid., p. 5.
58. ibid., p. 7.
59. Plato, *The Last Days of Socrates*, Penguin, Harmondsworth, 1982, p. 107.
60. Burchell, G., Gordon, C., Miller, P., *The Foucault Effect: Studies in governmentality*, Harvester Wheatsheaf, Hemel Hempstead, 1991, see Foucault, M., 'Politics and the study of discourse', pp. 53–72.
61. Misch, op. cit., *History of Autobiography in Antiquity*, vol. 2, p. 637.

62. See Boswell, J., op. cit., *Christianity, Social Tolerance and Homosexuality*, for an interesting account of the significance of this for Western culture.
63. See a very detailed discussion of this and associated phenomena in Foucault, op. cit., *The Use of Pleasure*.
64. Boswell, op. cit., *Christianity, Social Tolerance and Homosexuality*, see section III, chs 7, 8 and especially 9, 'The triumph of Ganymede: gay literature of the high Middle Ages'.
65. See in Botsman, P., (ed.) *Theoretical Strategies*, Local Consumption Publications, Sydney, 1982, Baudrillard, J., 'Oublier Foucault'. The question of seduction in this context takes us back to my previous comments on Abelard and Heloise.
66. Derrida, J., op. cit., *Of Grammatology*, see Gayatri Spivak, 'Translator's Preface', pp. xliii–xlv; and *Writing and Difference: Freud and the Scene of Writing*. See also Lyotard, J. F., *The Post Modern Condition: A report of knowledge*, Manchester University Press, Manchester, 1984, p. 80, for the way that Lyotard uses the concept of deference.
67. Hegel, G. W. F., *Phenomenology of Spirit*, trans. A. V. Miller, Oxford University Press, London, 1979.
68. An interesting use of this concept has been made in Patton, P., and Poole, R., (eds), *War/Masculinity*, Intervention Publications, Sydney, 1985, Farrar, A., 'War: Machining male desire', p. 69.
69. Lacan, op. cit., *Écrits*, see 'The significance of the phallus', pp. 286–7.
70. Polka and Zelechow, op. cit., *Readings in Western Civilisation, vol. 1*, see Abelard, P., 'Sic et non', p. 114.
71. ibid.
72. Duby, op. cit., *Three Orders*, p. 243.
73. This has a direct bearing on Lacan's view of the 'paranoiac' nature of knowledge and the structure of the ego. See Lacan, op. cit., *Écrits*, p. 327–31, for an indication of where he takes up these issues.

Afterword

1. This is precisely where computers play their revolutionary role.
2. Deleuze, G., and Guattari, F., *A Thousand Plateaus: Capitalism and schizophrenia*, trans. Brian Massumi, University of Minnesota Press, Minneapolis, 1987.
3. Failing to realise this was Nietzsche's mistake.

Bibliography

The bibliography has been organised in the following way: the first section contains books cited; the second section lists articles cited in the inquiry; and the third section includes supplementary material consulted in reference to Foucault but not otherwise cited.

Books

Abelard, P.,*The Story of Abelard's Adversities*, trans. J. T. Muckle, Pontifical Institute of Medieval Studies, Toronto, 1964.

Abelard, P., *Peter Abelard's Ethics*, trans. D. E. Luscombe, Clarendon Press, Oxford, 1971.

Abelard, P., *A Dialogue of a Philosopher with a Jew, and a Christian*, trans. Pierre J. Payer, Pontifical Institute of Medieval Studies, Toronto, 1979(a).

Abelard, P., *The Letters of Abelard and Heloise*, trans. B. Radice, Penguin Books, Harmondsworth, 1979(b).

Armstrong, T. trans., *Michel Foucault Philosopher*, Harvester Wheatsheaf, Hemel Hempstead, 1992.

Augustine, *Confessions*, trans. and introd. by R. S. Pine-Coffin, Penguin, Harmondsworth, 1979.

Baker, D. (ed.), *Medieval Women*, Blackwell, Oxford, 1978.

Benson, R. L., and Constable, G. (eds), *Renaissance and Renewal in the 12th Century*, Harvard University Press, Cambridge, Mass., 1982.

Benton, J. F. (ed.) *Self and Society in Medieval France: The Memoirs of Abbot Guibert of Nogent (1064?–1125)*, Harper Torchbooks, London, 1970.

Benveniste, E., *Problems in General Linguistics*, University of Miami Press, Florida, 1971.

Beroul, *Romance of Tristan*, trans. Alan S. Fedrick, Penguin, Harmondsworth, 1978.

Bloch, M., *The Historian's Craft*, trans. Peter Putnam, Vintage Books, New York, 1953.

Bloch, M., *French Rural History*, Routledge & Kegan Paul, London, 1966.

Bloch, M., *Feudal Society, Vol. 1*, trans. L. A. Manyon, Routledge & Kegan Paul, London, 1978.

Blumenberg, Hans, *The Legitimacy of the Modern Age*, trans. Robert M. Wallace, MIT Press, Cambridge, Mass., 1983.

Boase, R., *The Origin and Meaning of Courtly Love*, Manchester University Press, 1977.

Boswell, J., *Christianity, Social Tolerance and Homosexuality*, University of Chicago Press, Chicago, 1980.

Bouchard, D. (ed.) *Language, Counter-memory, Practice: Selected Essays and Interview by Michel Foucault*, trans. Donald F. Bouchard and Sherry Simon, Cornell University Press, New York, 1980.

Brown, P., *Augustine of Hippo*, Faber & Faber, London, 1975.

Brown, P., *The Body and Society*, Faber & Faber, London, 1990.

Burch, G. B., *Early Medieval Philosophy*, King's Crown Press, Columbia University, NY, 1951.

Burchell, G., Gordon, C., and Miller, P., *The Foucault Effect: Studies in Governmentality*, Harvester Wheatsheaf, Hemel Hempstead, 1991.

Buytaert, E. M. (ed.), *Peter Abelard*, Leuven University Press, 1974.

Cantor, N. F., *Medieval History*, Macmillan, London, 1969.

Carre, M. H., *Realists and Nominalists*, Oxford University Press, Oxford, 1946.

Chalmers A. F., *What is this Thing Called Science?*, University of Queensland Press, St Lucia, 1976.

Chrétien de Troyes, *Arthurian Romances*, trans. W. W. Comfort, Everyman's Library, London, 1977.

Clanchy, M. T., *From Memory to Written Record, England 1066–1307*, Edward Arnold, London, 1979.

Collingwood, R. G., *An Autobiography*, Oxford University Press, Oxford, 1967.

Collingwood, R. G., *The Idea of History*, Oxford University Press, Oxford, 1978.

Copleston, F. C., *A History of Medieval Philosophy*, Methuen, London, 1972.

Cousins, M., and Hussain, A., *Michel Foucault*, Macmillan, London, 1984.

Couzens Hoy, D. (ed.), *Foucault: A critical reader*, Blackwell, Oxford, 1986.

Daiches, D., and Thorlby, A. (eds), *The Medieval World, Literature and Western Civilisation, Volume 2*, Aldus, London, 1973.

Deleuze, G., *Foucault*, trans. Seán Hand, University of Minnesota Press, Minneapolis, 1988.

Deleuze, G., and Guattari, F., *Anti-Oedipus*, trans. Robert Hurley, Mark Seem and Helen R. Lane, Viking, New York, 1977.

Deleuze, G., and Guattari, F., *A Thousand Plateaus: Capitalism and schizophrenia*, trans. Brian Massumi, University of Minnesota Press, Minneapolis, 1987.

Delhez-Sarlet, C., and Catani, M., *Individualisme et Autobiographie en Occident*, Editions de l'Université de Bruxelles, Bruxelles, 1979.

Derrida, J., *Writing and Difference*, trans. A. Bass, University of Chicago Press, Chicago, 1978.

Derrida, J., *Of Grammatology*, trans. Gayatri Chakravorty Spivak, Johns Hopkins University Press, Baltimore, 1980.

Descartes, R., *The Philosophical Works of Descartes, vols 1 and 2*, trans. Elizabeth S. Haldane and G. T. R. Ross, Cambridge University Press, Cambridge, 1967.

Diamond, I., and Quinby, L. (eds), *Feminism and Foucault*, Northeastern University Press, Boston, 1988.

Dreyfus, H. L., and Rabinow, P., *Michel Foucault: Beyond structuralism and hermeneutics*, Harvester, Brighton, 1982.

Drew, K. F., *The Burgundian Code*, University of Pennsylvania Press, Philadelphia, 1972.

Duby, G., *The Early Growth of the European Economy*, trans. Howard B. Clarke, Weidenfeld & Nicolson, London, 1974.

Duby, G., *The Chivalrous Society*, trans. Cynthia Postan, Edward Arnold, London, 1977.

Duby, G., *Medieval Marriage: Two models from twelfth-century France*, trans. Elborg Forster, Johns Hopkins University Press, Baltimore, 1978.

Duby, G., *The Three Orders: Feudal society imagined*, trans. Arthur Goldhammer, University of Chicago Press, Chicago, 1980.

Duby, G., *The Knight, the Lady and the Priest*, trans. Barbara Bray, Penguin, Harmondswoth, 1985.

Eckhardt, K. A. (ed.), *Pactus Legis Salicae, 59.6*, Hanover (MGH Leges Nat. German iv.i), 1962.

Elders, Fons (ed.), *Reflexive Water: The basic concerns of mankind*, Condor, Souvenir Press, London, 1974.

Foucault, M., *The Archaeology of Knowledge*, trans., A. M. Sheridan Smith, Tavistock, London, 1974.

Foucault, M., *The Birth of the Clinic*, trans. A. M. Sheridan, Tavistock, London, 1976(a).

Foucault, M., *Mental Illness and Psychology*, trans. Alan Sheridan, Harper, New York, 1976(b).

Foucault, M., *The History of Sexuality, vol. 1: An introduction*, trans. Robert Hurley, Allan Lane, London, 1978.

Foucault, M., *Madness and Civilisation*, trans. Richard Howard, Tavistock, London, 1979.

Foucault, M., *The Order of Things*, Tavistock, London, 1980.

Foucault, M., *The Use of Pleasure, History of Sexuality, vol 2*, trans. Robert Hurley, Pantheon, New York, 1985.

Foucault, M., *Death and the Labyrinth: The world of Raymond Roussel*, trans. Charles Ruas, Doubleday, New York, 1986.

Foucault, M., and Blanchot, M., *Foucault–Blanchot*, trans. Brian Massumi and Jeffrey Mehlman, Zone, New York, 1987.

Freud, S., *Totem and Taboo*, trans. A. A. Brill, Vintage, New York, 1946.

Freud, S., *The Standard Edition of the Complete Psychological Works of Sigmund Freud Vol. XX*, trans. James Strachey, Hogarth, London, 1968.

Freud, S., *The Pelican Freud Library, Vol 8, Case Studies 1*, Penguin, Harmondsworth, 1977.

Freud, S., *The Pelican Freud Library, vol 1, Introductory Lectures on Psychoanalysis*, Penguin, Harmondsworth, 1978.

Freud, S., *Civilisation and Its Discontents*, trans. Joan Riviere, Hogarth, London, 1979.

Freud, S., *Leonardo Da Vinci: A memory of his childhood*, Ark, London, 1984.

Freud, S., *The Origins of Religion*, vol. *13*, Pelican Freud Library, Penguin, Harmondsworth, 1985.

Gallop, J., *Feminism and Psychoanalysis: The daughter's seduction*, Macmillan, London, 1982.

Geoffrey of Monmouth, *History of the Kings of Britain*, trans. Lewis Thorpe, Penguin, Harmondsworth, 1979.

Gerald of Wales, *The Autobiography of Giraldus Cambrensis*, trans. H. E. Butler, Cape, London, 1937.

Gerald of Wales, *The Journey Through Wales/The Description of Wales*, Penguin, Harmondsworth, 1980.

Gies, F. and J., *Women in the Middle Ages*, Crowell, New York, 1978.

Gimpel, J., *The Medieval Machine*, Futura, London, 1979.

Goody, J., *Literacy in Traditional Societies*, Cambridge University Press, Cambridge, 1968.

Goody, J., Thirsk, J., and Thompson, E. P. (eds), *Family and Inheritance: Rural society in Western Europe 1200–1800*, Cambridge University Press, Cambridge, 1976.

Gordon, C. (ed.), *Power/Knowledge: Selected interviews and other writings by Michel Foucault 1972–1977*, Pantheon, New York, 1980.

Gottfried Von Strassburg, *Tristan*, Penguin, Harmondsworth, 1978.

Gregory of Tours, *The History of the Franks*, Penguin, Harmondsworth, 1979.

Habermas, J., *The Philosophical Discourse of Modernity*, Cambridge in association with Blackwell, Oxford, 1987.

Hanning, R. W., *The Individual in Twelfth Century Romance*, Yale University Press, New Haven, Conn., 1977.

Hegel, G. W. F., *Phenomenology of Spirit*, trans. A. V. Miller, Oxford University Press, London, 1979.

Howard Bloch, R., *Etymologies and Genealogies: A literary anthropology of the French Middle Ages*, The University of Chicago Press, Chicago, 1986.

Hyman, A., and Walsh, J. J., *Philosophy in the Middle Ages: The Christian, Islamic and Jewish traditions*, Hackett, Indianapolis, 1973.

James, E., *The Origins of France: from Clovis to the Capetians, 500–1000*, St Martin's Press, New York, 1982.

Joinville and Villehardouin, *Chronicles of the Crusades*, Penguin, Harmondsworth, 1980.

Jones, G. and T., trans., *The Mabinogion*, Everyman's Library, London, 1975.

Kenny, A. (ed.), *Descartes' Philosophical Letters*, University of Minnesota Press, Minneapolis, 1981.

Knowles, D., *The Evolution of Medieval Thought*, Longman, London, 1962.

Kritzman, D. (ed.), *Michel Foucault: Politics, philosophy, culture, interviews and other writing, 1977–1984*, Routledge, New York, 1988.

Lacan, J., *Écrits*, trans. Alan Sheridan, Tavistock, London, 1972.

Le Goff, J., *Medieval Civilisation*, Blackwell, Oxford, 1990.

Lévi-Strauss, C., *The Raw and the Cooked*, Cape, London, 1970.

Lewis, A. R., *The Development of Southern French and Catalan Society, 718–1050*, University of Texas Press, Austin, 1965.

Lewis, A. W., *Royal Succession in France: Studies on the familial order and the state*, Harvard University Press, Cambridge, Mass., 1981.

Lovejoy, A. O., *The Great Chain of Being: A study of the history of an idea*, Harvard University Press, Cambridge, Mass., 1964.

Lucas, A. M., *Women in the Middle Ages*, Harvester, Brighton, 1983.

Luscombe, D. E., *Peter Abelard*, The Historical Association, London, 1979.

Lyotard, J. F., *The Postmodern Condition: A report of knowledge*, Manchester University Press, Manchester, 1984.

Malory, Thomas, *Malory Works*, ed. E. Vinaver, Oxford University Press, Oxford, 1977.

Markale, J., *Women of the Celts*, Gordon Cremonesi, London, 1975.

Martin, L. H., Gutman, H., and Hutton, P. H. (eds), *Technologies of the Self*, Tavistock, London, 1988.

Merquior, J. G., *Foucault*, Fontana, London, 1985.

Misch, G., *A History of Autobiography in Antiquity, vol 1*, Greenwood, Westport, Conn., 1973.

Momigliano, A., *Studies in Historiography*, Weidenfeld & Nicolson, London, 1966.

Nelson, B., *On the Roads to Modernity*, Rowman & Littlefield, New Jersey, 1981.

Nietzsche, F., *On the Genealogy of Morals, Ecce Homo*, trans. Walter Kaufmann, Vintage Books, New York, 1969.

Nietzsche, F., *The Portable Nietzsche*, trans. Walter Kaufmann, Penguin, Harmondsworth, 1977.

Nietzsche, F., *Untimely Meditations*, trans. R. J. Hollingdale, Cambridge University Press, Cambridge, 1983.

O'Faolin, J., and Martines L. (eds), *Not in God's Image*, Virago, London, 1979.

Oakley, F., *Omnipotence, Covenant & Order: An excursion in the history of ideas from Abelard to Leibniz*, Cornell University Press, Ithaca, NY, 1984.

Oakshott, M., *Experience and Its Modes*, Cambridge University Press, Cambridge, 1966.

Pateman, C., and Grosz, E. (eds), *Feminist Challenges: Essays in social and political theory*, Allen & Unwin, Sydney, 1986.

Plato, *The Last Days of Socrates*, Penguin, Harmondsworth, 1982.

Polka, B., and Zelechow, B., *Readings in Western Civilisation, Volume 1, The Intellectual Adventure of Man to 1600*, York University, Toronto, 1970.

Postan, M. M., *The Medieval Economy and Society*, Penguin, Harmondsworth, 1978.

Rabinow, P. (ed.), *The Foucault Reader*, Pantheon, New York, 1984.

Rees, A. and Rees, B., *Celtic Heritage*, Thames & Hudson, London, 1961.

Rorty, R., *Philosophy and the Mirror of Nature*, Blackwell, Oxford, 1980.

Rorty, R., Schneewind, J. B., and Skinner, Q. (eds), *Philosophy in History: Essays in the historiography of philosophy*, Cambridge University Press, Cambridge, 1984.

Rousseau, J. J., *The Reveries of the Solitary Walker*, trans. Charles E. Butterworth, Harper, New York, 1982.

Said, E., *Orientalism*, Routledge and Kegan Paul, London, 1978.

Saussure, F. de, *Course in General Linguistics*, Fontana, Glasgow, 1978.

Schwerin, C. F. (ed.), *Leges Saxonum und Lex Thuringorum*, Hanover and Leipzig, 1918.

Shapiro, M. (ed.), *Language and Politics*, Blackwell, Oxford, 1984.

Stock, B., *The Implications of Literacy*, Princeton University Press, Princeton, NJ, 1983.

Weinberg, J. R., *A Short History of Medieval Philosophy*, Princeton University Press, Princeton, NJ, 1964.

Wemple, S. F., *Women in Frankish Society*, University of Pennsylvania Press, Philadelphia, 1981.

White, Hayden V., *Metahistory*, Johns Hopkins University Press, London, 1985.

White, L., jun., *Medieval Technology and Social Change*, Oxford University Press, London, 1980.

Wippel, J. F., and Wolter, A. B. (eds), *Medieval Philosophy: From St Augustine to Nicholas of Cusa*, Free Press, New York, 1969.

Wood, C. T., *The French Apanages and the Capetian Monarchy 1224–1328*, Harvard University Press, Cambridge, 1966.

Wood, C. T., *The Age of Chivalry: Manners and morals 1000–1450*, Weidenfeld & Nicolson, 1970.

Zukav, G., *The Dancing Wu Li Masters*, Fontana Paperbacks, London, 1982.

Articles

Baudrillard, J., 'Oublier Foucault', in Botsman, P. (ed.), *Theoretical Strategies*, Local Consumption Publications, Sydney, 1982.

Campioni, M., and Gross, E., 'Little Hans: the production of Oedipus', in Foss, P., and Morris, M. (eds), *Language, Sexuality and Subversion*, Feral, Sydney, 1978.

Clanchy, M. T., 'Remembering the past and the good old law', in *History*, 55, 1970.

Duby, G., 'Au XIIe siècle: les "jeunes" dans le société aristocratique dans la France du nord-ouest', in *Annales Economie, societe, civilisation*, V, September–October 1964.

Farrar, A., 'War: machining male desire', in Patton, P., and Poole, R. (eds), *War/Masculinity*, Intervention Publications, Sydney, 1985.

Foucault, M., 'Interview, the regard for truth', in Foss, P., and Taylor, P. (eds), *Art and Text, Burnout*, 16, summer 1984/5.

Foucault, M., 'Discourse on language', appendix to the American edition of *The Archaeology of Knowledge*, Pantheon, New York, 1972.

Foucault, M., 'My Body, this paper, this fire', in *Oxford Literary Review*, 4(1), 1979.

Goldstein, Jan, 'Foucault among the sociologists: the disciplines and the history of the professions', in *History and Theory*, 23, 1984.

Goody, J., and Watt, I., 'The Consequences of Literacy', in *Comparative Studies in Society and History*, 5(3), April 1963.

Gross, E., 'On speaking about pornography', in *Scarlet Women*, 13, Spring 1981.

Hanning, R. W., 'The social significance of twelfth-century chivalric romance', in *Medievalia et Humanistica*, 3, 1972.

Herlihy, D., 'Agrarian revolution in France and Italy, 801–1150', in *Speculum*, 33, 1958.

Herlihy, D., 'Land, family and women in continental Europe, 701–1200', in *Traditio*, 18, 1962.

Knight, S., 'Proesce and cortoisie: ideology in Chrétien de Troyes "Le Chevalier au Lion"', in *Studium*, 14, 1982,

Le Doeuff, M., 'Women and philosophy', in *Radical Philosophy*, 17, 1977.

Minson, J. P., 'Foucault and the Mill of Philosophy', in *Critical Philosophy*, 2(1), 1985.

Moller, H., 'The meaning of courtly love', in *Journal of American Folklore*, 73, 1960.

Patton, P., 'Of power and prisons', in Morris, M., and Patton, P. (eds), *Michel Foucault: Power, truth, and strategy*, Feral, Sydney, 1979.

Patton, P., 'Michel Foucault: The ethics of an intellectual', in *Thesis Eleven*, 10/11, Melbourne, 1984/1985,

Poster, M., 'Mode of production, mode of information: toward a critique of political economy', in Poster, M. (ed.), *Humanities in Society, Foucault and Critical Theory: The uses of discourse analysis*, Vol. 5, Nos 3 and 4, University of Southern California, Los Angeles, 1982.

Stone, D., 'On the authenticity of the Abelard-Heloise letters', thesis submitted in partial fulfilment of requirements for MA qualifying, University of Sydney, 1979.

Ward, J. O., 'Social dislocation, intellectual dissent and the origin of the universities in medieval Europe', presented to the August meeting of the Australian Historical Association Conference, Melbourne, 1984.

Witt, R. G., 'The landlord and the economic revival of the Middle Ages in northern Europe, 1000–1250', in *American Historical Review*, 76, 1971.

Other works relevant to Foucault

Arac, J. (ed.), *After Foucault: Humanistic knowledge, postmodern challenges*, Rutgers University Press, New Brunswick, NJ, 1991.

Ball, S. (ed.), *Foucault and Education*, Routledge, London, 1990.

Bernauer, J., and Rasmussen, D. (eds), *The Final Foucault*, MIT Press, Cambridge, Mass., 1988.

Foucault, M., *I Pierre Rivière, having slaughtered my mother, my sister, and my brother*, Penguin, Harmondsworth, 1973.

Foucault, M., *This is not a Pipe*, trans. James Harkness, University of California Press, Berkeley, 1983.

Foucault, M., *Herculine Barbin: Being the recently discovered memoirs of a nineteenth-century French hermaphrodite*, trans. Richard McDougall, Pantheon, New York, 1980.

Foucault, M., and Binswanger, L., *Dream and Existence*, trans. Forrest Williams and Jacob Needleman, *Review of Existential Psychology and Psychiatry*, 19(1), 1986.

Gane, M. (ed.) *Towards A Critique of Foucault*, Routledge & Kegan Paul, London, 1986.

Lacapra, D., 'Rethinking intellectual history and reading texts', in *History and Theory*, 19(3), 1980.

Lemert, C., and Gillan, G., *Michel Foucault: Social theory as trangression*, Columbia University Press, New York, 1982.

Major-Poetzl, P., *Michel Foucault's Archaeology of Western Culture: Toward a new science of history*, University of North Carolina Press, Chapel Hill, 1983.

Megill, A., 'Foucault, structuralism, and the ends of history', in *Journal of Modern History*, 51, 1979.

Minson, J., *Genealogies of Morals: Nietzsche, Foucault, Donzelot and the eccentricity of ethics*, Macmillan, London, 1985.

Patton, P., 'Marxism in crisis: no difference', in Allen, J., and Patton, P. (eds), *Beyond Marxism? Interventions After Marx*, Intervention Publications, Sydney, 1983.

Poster, M., *Foucault, Marxism and History*, Polity, Cambridge, 1984.

Racevskis, K., *Michel Foucault and the Subversion of the Intellect*, Cornell University Press, Ithaca, NY, 1983.

Rajchman, J., 'The story of Foucault's history', in *Social Text*, 8, winter 1983/84.

Sheridan, A., *Michel Foucault: The will to truth*, Tavistock, London, 1980.

Shiner, L., 'Reading Foucault: anti-method and the genealogy of power-knowledge', in *History and Theory*, 21(3), 1982.

Smart, B., *Michel Foucault*, Tavistock, London, 1985.

Young, R., *White Mythologies*, Routledge, London, 1990.

White, Hayden V., 'Foucault decoded: notes from the underground', in *History and Theory*, 22(1), 1973.

Zinner, G., 'Michel Foucault: La volonte de savoir', in *Telos*, 36, Summer, 1978.

For a comprehensive biographical chronology of Michel Foucault see above: Bernauer, J., and Rasmussen, D. (eds), *The Final Foucault*.

For further information on the work of Foucault contact:
Bibliothèque du Saulchoir,
Association pour le Centre Michel Foucault,
43 *bis*, rue de la Glacière, 75013
Paris, France.

Name index

Abelard, P., 85, 97, 99, 102–106,
112–133, 137–149, 154, 157,
159, 162, 164, 168–171, 175,
181–183, 185, 188–191, 193,
198, 210–211, 213–214, 218
Aelred of Rievaulx 144
Allan of Lille 209
Ambrose 108
Anselm of Bec and Canterbury
100–101, 109–112, 126, 131,
162, 166, 168
Anselm of Laon 103–104
Aquinas, T., 1, 162
Aristotle 1, 12, 16, 26, 115–116, 120
Artaud, A., 58
Astrolabe 143
Augustine of Hippo 105–109, 127,
131–135, 138, 160–162,
164–165, 185, 209

Bachelard, G., 5, 55
Bacon, F., 197
Baldwin/Hollister 99
Baudrillard, J., 193, 218
Benton, J. F., 132, 135, 213
Berengar of Tours 108–109, 113
Bernard of Clairveaux 97, 124–125,
130
Binet, A., 177
Blanchot, M., 52
Bloch, M., 198
Blumenberg, H., 160–164, 170

Boethius 113–116
Boswell, J., 186, 214, 218
Breasted, J. H., 31
Breuer, J., 176
Brücke, E. W., von 176

Canguilhem, G., 55
Cantor, N. F., 133, 207
Cellini, B., 133–134
Charcot, J. M., 176
Charlemagne 173
Chrétien De Troyes 85, 92–93,
148–154, 156, 158–159, 215
Chomsky, N., 203
Clanchy, M. T., 144, 173
Collingwood, R. G., 2, 5–8, 15–28,
35, 42–43, 51, 53, 56, 75, 172,
183, 198–199, 204
Colvius, A., 161
Constable/Benson 104
Cook Wilson, 16
Cousins, M., 43
Couzens Hoy, D., 42
Culhwch 86

Darwin, C., 35
Deleuze, G., 40–41, 193
Derrida, J., 70, 187
Descartes, R., 1, 28, 37–38, 56–57,
76, 147, 160–173, 175,
180–183, 185, 190–191 193,
201, 209, 216

227

General index

Titles by Foucault are in italics.

Academy 7, 12
archaeology 51, 53, 56, 59–62, 66, 71, 75, 183
Archaeology of Knowledge 53–55, 57–59, 61, 63
autobiography 3, 16, 25, 132–138, 173, 178, 181–182, 190, 198

biography 12, 184–186, 198
Birth of the Clinic 45, 49, 64

Care of Self 83
chance 15, 45, 66
chronicle 135–137, 185
Cogito 1, 3, 12, 14, 19, 24, 26, 28–29, 36–38, 54, 56–57, 60, 63, 67, 70–71, 74–75, 162, 168, 173, 183, 190, 201
Conceptualism 120, 127, 169
Confessions of the Flesh 83
Council of Rome (1059) 108
Council of Sens 105, 124
Council of Soissons 144

death 25, 36–37, 184–185, 187–188, 190–191, 193
deconstruction 70
deference 187–188
desire 36–37, 64
diagram 40, 45, 76, 80, 82, 84–85, 183, 193–195
Discipline and Punish 74–75
discontinuity 9, 45, 51–52, 54, 70
Discourse on Language 64

dogmatism 13, 17–18
domination 66, 74, 77–78, 80

emergence 70
empiricism 9
Enlightenment 161–164, 216
episteme 53
epistemology 1, 9–10, 14–15, 68, 74–76, 127, 162, 168, 187, 192
essentialism 80, 83, 172, 183–184
ethics 1, 17–18, 73, 127, 170
ethics of self 82
event 20, 59–60, 63, 65

feudalism 88, 90
Fourth Crusade 137
Fourth Lateran Council (1215) 85, 95, 130, 155, 174, 207

genealogy 3, 57, 62–66, 68–76, 183

historian(s) of ideas 8, 29, 38, 45, 162
historian(s) of philosophy 2, 5–8, 25–29, 36, 38, 42, 45, 53, 63, 75, 162, 183
history and systems of thought 39–40, 44–45, 72
history of ideas 1–6, 8–9, 14–16, 18, 23–25, 27–29, 38–39, 42–45, 48, 50, 53–54, 58–59, 61–63, 79, 83, 159, 183
history of philosophy 1–2, 4, 6, 8, 15–17, 19, 26–29, 38–39,

230

Copyright acknowledgements

Acknowledgement is made to the following for permission to reprint from previously published material.

An early version of 'The Politics of Primogeniture' appeared as 'The politics of primogentiture: sex, consciousness and social organisation in North Western Europe (900–1250 AD)', in *Feudalism: Comparative Studies*, Sydney Studies in Society and Culture, No. 2, edited by E. Leach, S. N. Mukherjee and John Ward, published by Pathfinder Press, Sydney, 1985.

Part of 'Towards a Genealogy' was previously published as '"My struggle": the congealing of history', in *The Cultural Construction of Race*, Sydney Studies in Society and Culture, No. 4, edited by Marie de Lepervanche, and Gillian Bottomley, published by Meglamedia, Annandale, 1988, and as 'On Foucault and history' in *On the Beach*, double issue 7/8, Summer–Autumn 1985.

The Letters of Abelard and Heloise, translated by Betty Radice, Penguin Classics, 1974, © Betty Radice, 1974. Reproduced by permission of Penguin Books.

The Philosophical Works of Descartes, volumes 1 & 2, translated by Elizabeth S. Haldane and G. R. T. Ross, Cambridge, 1967. Reprinted with the permission of Cambridge University Press.

Selections from *Medieval Philosophers*, volume 1 edited and translated by Richard McKeon. Copyright 1929 Charles Scribner's Sons; copyright renewed © 1957 Richard McKeon. Reprinted with the permission of Charles Scribner's Sons, an imprint of Macmillan Publishing Company.

Foucault, Michel, *The Archaeology of Knowledge*, translated from the French by A. M. Sheridan Smith, Tavistock Publications, Limited, 1977. © Tavistock Publications, Limited, 1972. Reprinted with the permission of Tavistock Publications.

Foucault, Michel, *The Order of Things*, Tavistock Publications Limited, 1980. © Tavistock Publications Limited, 1970. Reprinted with the permission of Tavistock Publications.

Stock, Brian, *The Implications of Literacy*, Princeton, 1983. © 1983 by Princeton University Press. Reprinted by permission of Princeton University Press.

Freud, Sigmund, *The Standard Edition of Freud*, volume XX, translated and edited by James Strachey, The Hogarth Press, 1968. Reprinted with the permission of The Institute of Psycho-Analysis and The Hogarth Press.

Chrétien De Troyes, *Arthurian Romances*, translated by W. W. Comfort, J. M. Dent & Sons Ltd, 1977. © Introduction and notes, J. M. Dent & Sons 1975.